*The Human Elder in Nature,
Culture, and Society*

LIVES IN CONTEXT

Series Editor: Mihaly Csikszentmihalyi, *University of Chicago*

Perhaps the most important challenge for contemporary psychology is to apply its conceptual models and experimental findings to the explanation and understanding of individual lives lived in the complex world outside the laboratory. This task requires a more integrative, holistic, socially, and historically informed approach to the study of individual behavior than is usually practiced by psychologists. The *Lives in Context* series offers scholars an opportunity to take up the challenge, to publish their best work—work that combines empirical and theoretical rigor with an understanding of the whole person in natural settings.

The Human Elder in Nature, Culture, and Society, David Gutmann

Transforming School Cultures, Martin L. Maehr and Carol Midgley

Life Choices: Understanding Dilemmas and Decisions, Tod Sloan

Forthcoming

Working It Out: Implications of Parental Employment on Family Life, Ann C. Crouter and Susan McHale

Leisure Experience and Human Development, Douglas A. Kleiber

Human Being, Animal Being: Children's Interactions with Animals, Eugene O. Myers

Evolutionary Principles of Human Adolescence, Glenn Weisfeld

The Human
Elder in Nature,
Culture, and
Society

DAVID GUTMANN
Northwestern University

■ WestviewPress
A Division of HarperCollins*Publishers*

Lives in Context

Copyright © 1997 by Westview Press, A Division of HarperCollins Publishers, Inc.

Published in 1997 in the United States of America by Westview Press, 5500 Central Avenue, Boulder, Colorado 80301-2877, and in the United Kingdom by Westview Press, 12 Hid's Copse Road, Cumnor Hill, Oxford OX2 9JJ

Library of Congress Cataloging-in-Publication Data
Gutmann, David, 1925–
    The human elder in nature, culture, and society / David
Gutmann.
        p.   cm. — (Lives in context)
    Includes bibliographical references and index.
    ISBN 0-8133-2973-6 — ISBN 0-8133-2974-4 (pbk.)
    1. Aged—Psychology.   2. Aged—Cross-cultural studies.   I. Title.
II. Series.
HQ1061.G865   1997
305.26—dc21   96-39389
                                                                                                                    CIP

The paper used in this publication meets the requirements of the American National Standard for Permanence of Paper for Printed Library Materials Z39.48-1984.

10   9   8   7   6   5   4   3   2   1

To Stephanie and Ethan,
my children, who now teach me

Contents

Foreword

Harvey Peskin

This collection of major papers illuminates the ripening and converging lines of a major researcher, theorist, clinician, and critic in the study of the human lifespan. David Gutmann's core concepts belong to the anlage of adult development as a master discipline that accommodates psychology, cultural anthropology, sociology, history, and psychoanalysis. David Gutmann's well-realized thought and powerful presence in lifespan study have come to fruition, as these collected papers attest, not effortlessly or facilely but with a restless, even vehement creativity. His delivery alone—the surgent, proactive, and sculpted crafting of his prose—has helped move the second half of the lifespan well off its workaday plateau, even arrest its quiescent decline and thrust it into the developmental prominence previously reserved for the so-called formative years of youth. If Gutmann's medium is also message, life's second season is distinctively seasoned between the piquant and the pungent. Gutmann's view replaces the blander aftertaste of the later years with a foretaste of the reclaimed powers drawn from early life. Late life prepares then, if you will, for a repast.

But not only has Gutmann, like Jung, enhanced the later years with strong appetite, he has done so without Jung's counterageist condescension toward the first half of life. (However, Gutmann openly disdains, not youth, but the condescension that drives counterculture youth.) Instead, Gutmann's privileging of parenthood as being at the core of adult identity binds both halves of life with an interdependence that embraces much more of the life course than one would predict from his starting point in gerontology. In this respect, he is like Erikson (starting from the opposite side of childhood and youth), who, undaunted by the great divide of youth and adulthood, reached for a theory of human development itself. These collected papers track Gutmann's intellectual journey from its onset at the traditional gerontology of biological decline and social disengagement to a complex relational theory threading its terms through the fabric of social units from family to culture as they function in tribal insularity or in alienating modernity.

The reader can pass into Gutmann's wide conceptual net from several disciplinary openings, each entry changing somewhat one's understanding of the rest. My entry point came from my own research on the longitudinal samples of the Intergenerational Studies at the University of California. Gutmann's published papers helped me understand that parenting (before, during, and after) may be a powerful organizer of how the past is drawn upon for healthy adult functioning.

Finding Gutmann's seminal papers on what later came to be called "reclaimed powers" gave me early encouragement and direction for my own formulation of "uses of the past" in adult psychological health. As surprising as it now seems to me, a person's parental status had not usually been considered of major importance to the organization of psychological health. For so profoundly "tribal" is the parental task that it would hardly seem to be an active ingredient in discriminating such a profoundly individual state as personal adjustment or psychological health. Indeed, mainstream study of adult development has not looked to parenting to find the self's uniqueness. Gutmann himself is not primarily concerned with individual differences in parental or postparental competence or psychological health. But his pursuit of normative dispositions of personal mastery during these eras establishes the larger context that the parental dimension organizes the adult lifespan. This understanding, in turn, has organized a significant branch of adult-life-span theory and thinking. His papers track parenthood as a sleeping giant in adult development, unnoticed at first, then never slumbering again in his later theoretical and clinical work. In two stages Gutmann shifted away from the explanatory power of late-life chronological age to the advent and transformation of the parental imperative.

The first shift represents this imperative to parent as the parental emergency, whose phasing out ushers in the cultivation of more inward sensibilities and resources that have lain fallow during the emergency. Hence, the androgyny of postparenting. Here, Gutmann (like Jung, who, however, remained conceptually indifferent to parenting as such) refuses to treat aging as an enervated, spent state of diminished resolve and dimming purpose. Rather, with active parenting settled, one has more to spend again—but in a currency undervalued by the achievement motif of life's first half. Predictably, the nuanced vitality of the second half is mistaken for the impassivity and impotence of social disengagement. Indeed, these opposing but deceptively similar faces of late-life passivity (especially in the male) are arguably questions for differential diagnosis, whether within individuals or between cultures, as Gutmann addresses in his clinical papers and social commentaries. He cogently persuades us that accurate diagnosis requires assessing not only the individual's but the culture's receptivity to this potential for re-generativity or de-generativity, for construing passive and magical mastery as a life or death force.

The progressive or regressive, syntonic or dystonic impact of such force will depend essentially on the welcome or, alternatively, threat that individual and culture extend to the so-called pregenital (or ungendered) energies that become available after the male/female polarization and gender stereotypy of active parenting have lapsed. But these energies are reclaimed as a new, advanced state of Eros in late adulthood and perhaps should more properly be called postgenital (although Gutmann does so only by implication), liberated from the yoke of genital primacy to serve new inner states. Indeed, the genital primacy that serves the parental emergency is called by Gutmann a "transient deviation" from the mainstream of Eros, a brilliant conceptual reversal of the classical psychoanalytic claim that it is the pregenital that is transient or otherwise deviant. What for Freud is the end point and highest achievement of libidinal development—the genital personality—is for Gutmann only the parental midway station to the yet more advanced androgyny. Beyond the procreative function, classical Freudians typically expect a kind of genital exhaustion that regresses the older adult back to a more primitive sensuality related to somatization and emotional diffusion. Gutmann's conceptual breakthrough here is to bring fresh rapprochement to libido theory and adult development by thus proposing the continuity of psychosexual development—specifically, the confluence of masculine and feminine—beyond procreation and thus beyond midlife. (Such enriched complexity of early developmental stages in middle and late adulthood is crucial also in Kohut's treatment of narcissism and Jaques' aggression.) The new energies of the postgenital stage, of course, potentiate a range of expressions, from self-absorbed dependency to relational intimacy, all with their own culturally laden meanings of approbation or disapproval.

The second, more recent conceptual shift—less complete, yet as evocative, original, and decisive as the first—is Gutmann's proposal that the parental imperative does not end with the parental emergency, but may yet undergo another transformation: that of elders as emeritus parents. His relational model does not revert to the social detachment that Jungian self theory and William Henry's disengagement presuppose once the tribal tasks of adulthood have been settled. Rather, emeritus parenting casts a still wider net of human connectedness (much as Erikson finds spiritual expression of relational dependability in his last adult stage of Integrity), capturing the continuity of the postparental commitment to spiritual and cultural service with the erstwhile tasks of parental responsibility.

In thus not dropping out, the elder in the Third Age becomes a third force that models the alleviation of tensions between the prior family generations of adult child and grandchild. The grandchild of the third generation ideally stands to see the willing succession, rather than the willful wresting, of power from grandparent to parent. As the grandparent, in turn, moves to a new staying power of authority beyond the family, the child is reassured, his fear calmed that Oedipal conflict does not end with winners in command and losers in oblivion. The emeritus parent, then, parents intergenerationally and reassuringly, perhaps the vital core behind elders' passive mastery. That the emeritus parent might so participate in Oedipal resolution slipped between the conceptual cracks in Freud's dismissal of adult development and Jung's dismissal of Freud's child-centered vision. But again, we see Gutmann drawing psychoanalytic theory further into adulthood, not by violating but by enriching the basic terms of the theory.

Yet, as Gutmann warns, the efficacy and dignity—rather than the oblivion—of aging in modern and transitional societies are unprotected indeed. Characteristically the psychoanalytic activist for the empowerment of the older adult, Gutmann appeals not to society's gratuitous charity (for our ageist societies are themselves culturally anomic) but to elders' own capacity for vigorous self-help. On this sober, but not somber, uncertainty ends *Reclaimed Powers* (1994): "We will have to enlist the elders, who have traditionally been the wardens of culture, to help and guide us in the vital processes of reversing deculturation and of crafting new myths on which reculturation can be based. We owe this redemption not only to our aging parents. We also owe it to the oncoming generations of children" (p. 253). Gutmann's project is no less than reviving the providence of the emeritus parent over parenthood itself.

Gutmann does not similarly exhort dwellers in life's first half to reclaim powers lost to repressive society. Far from it. Here he is no longer the innovator of social change, but the skeptical, even caustic critic of human-potential experiments— from feminists to flower children—that would preempt and rearrange the early "tectonics" of the human species. For Gutmann, the ascent to human wholeness is unhurried, conservative, and unmoved by facile alternatives and fast-track solutions. Counterculture youth, making up in presumption for what they lack in living, imitate but can never achieve before their time the elders' ascension to internal states of selfhood, community, and spirituality. Such mimicry especially becomes a mockery of the elder's androgyny, for authentic gender reversal arrives only in succession to real gender differentiation earned in the crucible of species survival: the parental imperative to mother and father. New Age parents who would self-servingly bypass such species-serving by cutting to androgynous, unisex parenting impair both their own and their child's very vitality for androgyny at midlife. For males come to accept their midlife feminine component not through prior androgyny but through a secure masculine identity; correspondingly for females. This is Gutmann's proposed developmental scenario.

If the counterculture flouts boundaries between self and species, Gutmann lines them up single file—species first, self next, once childrearing is discharged. Policing these boundaries almost as battle lines, Gutmann still allows that a father's masculine identity must accommodate an androgynous capacity for the sake of parenting. Gutmann is obviously touched, as is this reader, by the subtlety of his psychodynamic intelligence, that a husband "mothers" his wife so that she can devote herself to mothering their child. In turn, husband can be vicariously mothered not only from what child receives from mother but through what his wife receives from him. Such androgynous capacity connects husband and wife intimately, otherwise stationed so far apart in their gendered charge to rear the child. Androgyny after all does not suddenly arise when the parental emergency ends, but indeed is at play in the cross-identifications of true parenting. Although Gutmann does not venture here, we know more today about the parent who, fearing such cross-over, may strike out at or withdraw from a child disposed to cross-gender behavior, like male effeminacy or homosexuality. Today, we are as likely to suppose that such dispositions have caused certain parents—those overinvested in genital primacy—to abandon the child rather than that parental abandonment causes the child's disposition.

Gutmann's silence about the clinical casualties of excessive genital primacy is interesting. His guardianship of species and culture seems to absolve genital primacy of the rigorous, even severe accountability that so-called androgynous parenting is held to. But when the parental emergency has passed and species survival is less urgent, Gutmann's clinical attention is no longer secondary, but turns as much to tyrannical as to deficient displays of mastery. Gutmann's clinical papers make invaluable contributions to understanding late-life psychopathology. I refer particularly to his observations of patients for whom the gender reversal in later life threatens with loss of mastery. The situation, for example, no longer holds that mother will stay the keeper of a father's denied passivity and intimacy, leaving the man to face the personal agony of what could so long be denied. This is the underbelly of reclaimed powers. The counterphobic motivation of the excessively genital father or feminized mother is now acknowledged and examined in the light of postparenthood rather than parenthood.

Intimacy fits uneasily under either self or species, yet is clearly tied to both. At worst, intimacy between partners threatens the parental priority for childrearing as it threatens the communal ethos of counterculture. Is then the capacity for intimacy between partners, curbed during parenting, reclaimed in the androgynous safety of postparenthood? Curiously, Gutmann does not address intimacy after the parental function has been discharged. It is to this issue that we direct our closing attention.

Intimacy as a reclaimed power of later adulthood is not self-evident in Gutmann's portrayal of androgyny. Indeed, this oversight exposes somewhat the ambiguity of the concept itself. On the one hand, if the man returns emotionally from the periphery to the home, he no longer needs to keep away from the woman who had earlier completed him. Correspondingly, neither does the woman for her man. On the other hand, this very completion might imply that now each, being complete unto himself or herself, needs little from the other. Gender reversal alone does not indicate whether males and females maintain their prior separateness by merely switching gender roles or dispositions, investing themselves yet again in opposite corners of the emeritus playing field, or whether they have instead so integrated the gender capacities of the other that the erstwhile self/other distinction is transformed to a more inclusive self/other closeness. This ambiguity is an important gap in the relational scope and depth of Gutmann's contribution to a comprehensive theory of human development. The issue might be enjoyably limned, even empirically confronted, by posing two versions of Wang Chi's lovely seventh-century poem with which Gutmann introduces a chapter of *Reclaimed Powers*. The poem begins:

> *I ask you, my friend,*
> *What ought a man want*
> *But to sit with his wine*
> *In the sun?*

And my slightly sculpted revision:

> *I ask you, my friend,*
> *What ought a man want*
> *But to sit with his wife*
> *In the sun?*

Preface

I have been turning out papers on the psychology of aging since I was a University of Chicago graduate student back in the early fifties. This collection contains the pieces that, in retrospect, I like best: They track the development of my own thinking *about* development—particularly, the developmental and clinical psychology of later life. The selected articles are arranged in roughly chronological order. The lead-off pieces report early studies, going back to the fifties and early sixties, when the field of developmental geropsychology and myself were still young. The collection ends with more recent writing, where the lifespan, developmental perspective has been applied to the problems of late-onset psychopathology.

But before turning to the articles themselves, I would like to address some issues stirred up by this professional "life review." At the risk of boring the reader, I will use this preface to sort things out, meanwhile taking advantage of the liberation that is one of the incidental gifts of aging. Thus, no longer having a career to build, I can afford the luxury of being honest about personal matters that are only hinted at (or denied) in the pieces that follow.

So the collection opens with this confession: To begin, I am not now nor have I ever been a committed gerontologist; that is, I have never been excited about the field of aging *per se* or about the aged themselves. Whereas most recruits to my field are gerophiles—they were once rescued by their grandparents and now they want to repay the favor—there does exist an underground community of gerophobes, among whom I count myself. I cannot speak for these gerophobic colleagues, but in my case, two powerful motives, ambition and fear, pushed me towards a career in developmental and clinical geropsychology.

First, the "ambition" motive: Although I was indeed a striving youth, I was also (and continue to be) an indifferent library scholar. I do however seek out and learn from direct experience: in the field, from my patients, even from myself. However, most of the geropsychology literature puts me to sleep. But when I first looked for a specialty field, geropsychology did meet my bottom-line requirements: It was a promising but relatively empty field, with only a *small* bibliography. In those bygone days, the aging process was a *Terra Incognita* on the map of psychodynamic theory. Freud—himself clearly a gerophobe—had insisted that true psychological growth ended in adolescence, with the descent of the testicles; only Erik Erikson, Teresa Benedek, and Carl Jung had the guts and the status to challenge his dogmatism in favor of early development. But lacking any empirical basis save for their own clinical observations, they could only speculate about the possibilities for new growth in the later years. So here was my chance to score: While avoiding the library, *I* would create the absent literature; *I* would name and map for the first time the still unscouted territory—the country of the old.

Fear of aging, the second motive driving my early choice of a gerontological career, has only become really salient in my latter years. But I did come by my gerophobia honestly. My father feared aging, and for good reason: Like my mother, he died much too young. I was shocked by his tragically early death and inherited, as my patrimony, his fear of getting old. Some of us study what we are afraid of; moved by that logic, I was attracted to gerontology for a classic gerophobic reason—to avoid getting old. My fantasy was that the study of aging would protect me against the processes that I studied. My elder *subject's* assignment was to get old and to suffer the attendant insults; my job was to study, to advise, to sympathize, to treat—but certainly not to share my client's fate. Trained as a clinician, I had early on acquired the Doctor's delusion: that the role boundaries set between clinician and patient would form an immune barrier against the patient's disorder. But as I become geriatric myself, that fantasy is revealed for the delusion that it really is. My older patients and research subjects are not my portrait of Dorian Gray—and they never were.

This grudging recognition, that *I* have become the gray Dorian, sets the stage for another confession: As a young man I was already phobic about aging, but in the sunset years I find myself turning against the young as well, including my younger self. Thus, as I selected the pieces for this collection, I discovered some real animosity toward the young author of my early work. From the outset of our awkward encounter, I found little in common with this young Gutmann; moreover, I *resented* him. He seemed so smug, so full of the youthful excitement and arrogance of new discovery.

As a Freudian/Eriksonian psychologist, I realize that the Oedipus is an equal-opportunity conflict: Aging men can be as rivalrous with younger men as young men are with them. However, even Sigmund Freud did not prepare me for *this* particular recognition—that an older man can be rivalrous with his younger self. Worse yet, I felt disadvantaged in this competition: Gutmann the younger seemed smarter than me, and—save for some pretentious language and psychobabble—a better writer. Thus, when that cocky stripling deserted, he left me vulnerable to aging and he ripped me off by taking away my special myth and my youthful—if counterphobic—courage. Finally, it seemed, insult was added to injury: Gutmann the younger's work was done, but *I* had to put together a book to highlight that young punk's accomplishments.

But my older psychotherapy patients, who regularly present me with complaints similar to mine, have taught me that resentments like these can mask frustrated affection and a wish for unity among divided portions of the psyche. These senior clients share my condition: They too feel alienated from their younger selves, and they try to recontact—at first, in the person of the therapist—that lost, youthful ghost. Their recovery often begins when they realize that their younger part, which they concede to and then revisit in the therapist, does not really dwell in his consulting room but is still an active though unacknowledged part of their current personality.

So what my patients attempt via psychotherapy, I perhaps attempt through assembling this book. Like them, I am trying to knit together the young and the old, trying to resolve the mutual antipathy between the young Gutmann, who studied aging so as not to get old, and the old Gutmann, who has become what the young man feared to be.

In my case, the gap between these parts of self has deep roots and involves more than differences in age. Psychology has changed drastically since the days when Gutmann the younger was socialized as a behavioral scientist, and the aging Gutmann has—however grudgingly—changed with it. The culture wars have come between us. Thus, when young Gutmann started out, the field of psychology appealed mainly to young men. The personnel and legendary figures were predominantly male, and the language of dynamic psychology was, barely disguised, the language of war: *drive, conflict, defense, splitting, repression, confrontation, resistance, boundary, breakthrough.* Predictably, the clinics and institutes were staffed by veterans of World War II and with ex-Communists for whom their Marxist god had failed.

But as the field changed, psychology has become feminized: in its personnel, in its conceptual emphases, in its politics, and in its language. Instead of conflict doctrine, attachment theory reigns supreme and "relationships" has become the master term. In this new dispensation, neurosis stems not from contending forces within the self but from external dislocations; conflicts are located *out there*, between a needy, victim self and an unsympathetic world. According to attachment theory, love *is* enough.

Meanwhile, the normal life-cycle changes in myself have matched the shifts in the psychology zeitgeist. Obedient to my own theories, I have become conceptually androgynous, I have played footsie with attachment theory, I have even used the "R" word, and I have become the stay-at-home clinician rather than the adventurous field worker. Clearly then, the affect of *shame* is the splitting wedge between Gutmann the younger and Gutmann the older.

The blunt truth seemed to be this: Junior has not abandoned me, quite the contrary; the old Gutmann has abandoned what we both stood for. The ego ideals that both of us hold in common condemn me for getting soft, and for slipping away from the stern language of the warrior and from the challenges of field work. Theory builders are supposed to be exceptions to their own doctrines, but I have become a mere footnote to my own papers on postparental androgyny. Predictably, my shame gets projected: In my fantasy this young and fictive Gutmann is disgusted with old Gutmann, he has taken back my best qualities, and he has left our common house of self empty and split. In this convenient fiction, the fault is not with me, but with him.

Is there a moral here? I think so, and it is this: The young Gutmann does me no harm by staying young, and I have committed no sin by getting old. If anything, we add to each other. Better yet, we *are* each other. There are in reality no warring intrapsychic factions of young and old, no internal community of diverse, multigenerational homunculi. This too is a fiction of the New Wave, with its psychobabble of the "inner child." What we humans *do* have are various appetites, potentials, identifications—sometimes conflictual, sometimes unified—all active within the same, overarching person. If the conflicts are tempered and there is at least a temporary truce, then the result is an expanded rather than a fragmented self. In writing this preface I do seem to have accomplished—at least for now—just such a piece of conflict abatement. As a consequence, I hope that the reader will discover in these pages a more coherent and useful book.

David Gutmann
Chicago, Illinois

Credits

Chapter 1 originally appeared as "The Country of Old Men: Cross-Cultural Studies in the Psychology of Later Life," Institute of Gerontology Occasional Papers in Gerontology No. 5 (April 1969). Reprinted by permission of the Institute of Gerontology.

Chapter 2 originally appeared as "Navajo Dependency and Illness" in *Prediction of Life Span,* edited by E. Palmore (1971). Reprinted by permission of Erdman B. Palmore.

Chapter 3 originally appeared as D. Gutmann, L. Gottesman, and S. Tessler, "A Comparative Study of Ego Functioning in Geriatric Patients," *The Gerontologist* 13 (Winter 1973), pp. 419–423. Reprinted by permission of the Gerontological Society of America.

Chapter 4 originally appeared as "Alternatives to Disengagement: Aging Among the Highland Druze" in *Culture and Personality: Contemporary Readings,* edited by R. Levine (1974). Reprinted by permission of Aldine de Gruyter, a division of Walter de Gruyter, Inc.

Chapter 5 originally appeared as "Aging and the Parental Imperative," in *Reclaimed Powers: Men and Women in Later Life,* by David L. Gutmann (1994). Reprinted by permission of Northwestern University Press.

Chapter 6 originally appeared as "A Cross-Cultural View of Adult Life in the Extended Family," in *Developing Individual in a Changing World,* edited by K. Riegel and J. Meacham (1976). Reprinted by permission of Aldine de Gruyter, a division of Walter de Gruyter, Inc.

Chapter 7 originally appeared as "The Premature Gerontocracy: Themes of Aging and Death in the Youth Culture," *Social Research* 39 (August 1972), pp. 416–448. Reprinted by permission of the New School for Social Research.

Chapter 8 originally appeared as "The Subjective Politics of Power: The Dilemma of Post-Superego Man," *Social Research* 40 (Winter 1973), pp. 570–616. Reprinted by permission of the New School for Social Research.

Chapter 9 originally appeared as "Aging and Oedipus," in *The Psychoanalytic Review* 73 (1986), pp. 137–148. Reprinted by permission of *The Psychoanalytic Review.*

Chapter 10 originally appeared as "Observations on Culture and Mental Health in Later Life," in *Handbook of Mental Health and Aging,* edited by J. Birren and R. Sloane (1980). Reprinted by permission of James E. Birren.

Chapter 11 originally appeared as "The Father and the Masculine Life Cycle," Institute for American Values Working Paper No. 13 (1991). Reprinted by permission of the Institute for American Values.

Chapter 12 originally appeared as "Psychological Development and Pathology" in *New Dimensions in Adult Development,* edited by R. Nemivoff and C. Colarusso (1990). Reprinted by permission of HarperCollins Publishers.

1 The Country of Old Men: Cross-Cultural Studies in the Psychology of Later Life

This article was first published as a monograph in 1969 and presented, in summary form, the fieldwork that I had been conducting since 1964 among traditional agriculturists: the Navajo of the Western Reservation, the Mayan Indians of Yucatan and Chiapas, and the Druze of Galilee and the Golan Heights.

The work reported here extended the preliminary, culture-bound findings from the Kansas City studies and tested their developmental implications. Based on cross-sectional Thematic Apperception Test (TAT) data, the Kansas City studies had shown that the active, passive (or autoplastic), and magical mastery styles discriminated the American sample by age: Younger men were more apt to be found in the active mastery camp, older men in the passive mastery camp, and the oldest men were most apt to rely on magical mastery styles. The findings were provocative on two counts: They suggested that important features of the American male personality might change in later life and that a universal developmental process, common to all normal adult males, might be driving such changes. In order to rule out cohort effects, the hypothesis of developmental change in personality had to be tested across a variety of human groups, significantly different from each other and from the American setting in which the theory was first generated. And within these cultures the developmental hypothesis needed to be further tested through longitudinal studies of the same subjects over time. This contention, that any developmental theory required comparative studies, secured me—in those palmy days of lavish funding—a ten-year Career Development Award from the federal government. That grant freed up my time for a series of field investigations, blessedly distant from academic libraries, among the middle-aged and aging men of the Navajo, the Maya, and the Middle Eastern Druze. The Druze would not allow a foreign male to approach their women; instead, female research assistants were employed to interview and test a sample of older Druze females.

The following paper reports early findings based on the aggregated data from the various sites, including Kansas City. Reading it now, I find it to be too long, repetitive, and dry. But—as I have to remind myself—let's cut the young writer some slack: He is after all a naturalist, just back from the field, and eager to report all the new birds that he has spotted. Eager for scientific recognition and not yet aware that significance is more than statistics, he seeks the holy grail of the .05 level and clutters the paper with too many tables. In short, because he has not yet found his scientific "voice," and because he is not yet able to distinguish significant from trivial findings, he sets down everything—sometimes twice. So bear with me: The later papers of this empirical section do go beyond reports findings couched in statistical terms to speculations about their larger meanings.

Cross-cultural comparative work aimed at testing developmental conceptions called for variation in study sites but also for continuity of instruments and procedures across sites. The major findings of age-related personality changes in this and other cultures did come from TAT data; accordingly, some introductory comments are called for concerning the rationales for these instruments, as well as their administration and analysis.

Regarding administration, the same basic deck of TAT cards—some of them slightly altered to meet local customs of dress and furnishing—were used at all sites, and their administration was prefaced with the same instructions: "Look at this picture, and tell me a story about what you see there."

In order to ensure that the subjects' responses would not be contaminated by test anxiety—worries about the investigator's motives, for example, or his possible ties to government agencies—my students and I prefaced the actual testing with an open interview designed to explore the subject's life history in his own terms and to put him at ease. As it turned out, these "naturalistic" interviews proved to be our best source of information on male psychology in later life.

The following article reports mainly on the age X theme X culture distributions of the TAT data and shows that these fall roughly in keeping with predictions derived from the Kansas City findings. Thus, though cultures differ in the degree to which they stress one or another of the ego mastery modalities, the age shift in these cross-sectional data is, in all cases, away from active mastery and towards the passive and magical orientations. These cross-sectional findings were, in the Navajo and Druze cases, replicated in longitudinal distributions. Thus, the Time 2 TAT profile of individual respondents was, in most cases, shifted toward the more passive and magical sectors of the mastery spectrum. Furthermore, for both the Druze and Navajo subjects the degree of shift away from the Time 1 profile increased with the age of respondent: The older the respondent, the more marked is the movement towards the passive and regressive positions. A "nearness to death" phenomenon appears to be at work: The closer you come to the waterfall, the faster the current takes you.

Finally, the reader should be warned that "scientific" geropsychologists—and they are by far the majority—will have nothing to do with the projective tests and will ignore any findings based on them. In their view, the projective protocols, because they require "subjective" analytic approaches, are irredeemably unreliable. Worse yet, in their book, the projectives rarely predict to the presumably more reliable readings from the "objective" self-report personality inventories. However, the doctoral work of my Northwestern colleague, Dr. Jordan Jacobowitz (1984), redeems the TAT as a proper tool of science. Having conducted longitudinal studies with a population of middle-aged and senior Israelis, he discovered that the psychological profiles derived from the respondent's Time 1 TAT did not correlate with the findings from the Time 1 questionnaire measures; they did however show respectable correlations with the Time 2 measures derived by the same instruments from the same subjects. In other words, passive tendencies picked up by the TAT will not surface in the subject's concurrent self-report inventory; but five years later these tendencies are no longer covert; they will be openly acknowledged by the same respondents. Clearly, tendencies that will later emerge openly in behavior and attitude are first rehearsed and "detoxified" in fantasy; the mind obeys the rules of the fantasy life and not those of the bureaucratic methodologists. The TAT acts as a kind of early warning system or seismograph of the psyche, picking up the early stirrings at the tectonic bowels of the personality, while these same murmurs are still being ignored by the conscious mind (and unavailable for self-report). Accordingly, the projective instruments are best fitted to a study of developmental transitions. As Bernice Neugarten (1968) has pointed out, these tools are more likely to register change rather than stability of personality. They are then, without apology, ideal instruments for our study of personality transitions in the later years.

Our early cross-cultural forays had succeeded in their first objective: We had successfully replicated the results of the Kansas City studies and had strengthened the developmental hypothesis. As an extra bonus, our interviewers were also picking up signals from our aging respondents that would be amplified in later work. For example, we sensed that older men revive the "oral" interests of early childhood, as well as their yearnings for the maternal persons who first met these needs. Seemingly, as men aged they turned back the psychological clock. In their youth, they pushed away from the mother and became the father's actively mastering son, but in later life they reverse course and become once again the mother's passive mastery "child." Early data in support of this "oral revival" hypothesis is first presented in the following piece and followed up, in greater detail, in Chapter 2, "Dependency, Illness, and Survival Among Navajo Men."

This chapter outlines some results thus far obtained from an on-going program of research on the psychological characteristics of older men undertaken in a variety of mainly preliterate societies.[1] The contention of this study, first developed from urban United States data, has been that certain modes of relating, of experiencing, and of knowing distribute more predictably by age than they do by culture. Put in another way, the contention of this study has been that men age psychologically according to an intrinsic schedule of ego mastery stages that follow a sequence of some fixity, some predictability, across a panel of diverse cultures. In this paper we will describe the mastery stages, as well as the recurrent ways in which they register themselves in the content of fantasy and in the forms of thought, across cultures which themselves maintain differing conventions about these matters.

A Mastery Typology

The studies which led to initial formulation of the mastery typology were undertaken as part of the Kansas City Studies of Adult Life, of the Committee on Human Development, University of Chicago. The research, described in greater detail elsewhere (Neugarten and Gutmann 1958; Gutmann 1964) involved a sample of 145 mentally and physically fit White males, 40 to 70 years in age, all residents of the Kansas City area. The data consisted of Thematic Apperception Test (TAT) stories given in response to selected stimulus cards. Three major types and six component subtypes emerged from the TAT analysis, each presumably representing a special form of relatedness toward the world, and each representing a distinct solution to the ego's task of maintaining internal and external mastery.

As shown in Table 1.1, younger Kansas City men (aged 40–54) tend significantly towards Active Mastery, while older Kansas City men (aged 55–71) favor Passive or Magical Mastery. Thus, the types significantly discriminate age groups, suggesting the possibility that the mastery typology defines a continuum of ego states through which men move as they age. Each mastery type will be briefly discussed in terms of the salient motives, relational modes, and coping styles that it embodies.

Active Mastery

The Active (or Alloplastic) Mastery style seems to be founded on strivings towards autonomy, competence, and control. The Active Mastery individual works within or collaborates with external systems in order to bring some part of them under his control. He is wary of having his actions and choices limited by others, and he is therefore mistrustful of any dependent wishes in himself that would tempt him to trade compliance for security.

Generally speaking, the Active Mastery individual is not much interested in nuances of feeling whether tender or otherwise, either in himself or in others. His sensitivity is turned outwards to the kinds of behavior that can be measured, predicted, and counteracted: and he is not much concerned with the cognitive or emotional counterparts of such behavior. Consistent with their externalizing tendencies, such men also refer potentially troubling inner conflicts to the outer world. Active Mastery men do not ruminate much over inner problems identified

TABLE 1.1   Distribution of the Kansas City Male Sample by Major Age Periods, and by Mastery Orientations

		40–49	50–59	60–71	
ACTIVE MASTERY	Promethean-Competitive	7*	8	3	
		} 17	} 26	} 12	
	Productive Autonomous	10	18	9	
PASSIVE MASTERY	Emphasized Receptivity	8	20	12	
		} 8	} 26	} 23	
	Anxious Constriction	0	6	11	
MAGICAL MASTERY		4	15	14	
		29	67	49	145

*This distribution of the mastery cell subtotals is significant at the .02 level ($\chi^2 = 17.417$; DF = 8).

as such; rather they look for outer agents which represent—or can be held responsible for—what they dislike and fear in themselves. They legislate their inner problems into collective struggles, for example, realistic fights against political abuse, intruding enemies, or some refractory segment of external nature.

The various dispositions cumulate to what we have called an "active-productive" orientation. Like all men, the Active Mastery individual desires emotional and physical security, but he is happiest when he can supply these needs through his own capacities, and when he is a source of security to others. He is most comfortable with resources—be they a business, a flock, or a cornfield—that he has generated for himself and for his dependents out of his own competence, boldness, and disciplined effort.

The Active Mastery orientation includes "Promethean-competitive" and "productive-autonomous" subtypes. These may be found together within some Active Mastery individuals or they may in other cases discriminate between men of this general orientation. The first subtype emphasizes combat and competition; strength and prestige are trophies won from an enemy. The second subtype emphasizes self-reliance and autonomy, enacted through vigorous and productive efforts. In productive autonomy there is less emphasis on external enemies and challenges, more emphasis on living up to high internal standards. One competes, in effect, against oneself.

Passive Mastery

The Passive (autoplastic) Mastery individual also needs to control the source of his pleasure and security. But the Passive Mastery individual does not feel effective enough to create, by himself, his own emotional and physical logistic base. From his standpoint, strong, independent, and capricious external agents control what he needs. The Passive Mastery individual can only influence the powers-that-be indirectly, through what he does to himself. He shapes himself to fit their expectations; he demonstrates mildness rather than challenge; and he tries to expunge those tendencies that might lead him into dangerous conflict. He does not, in the Promethean fashion of the Active Mastery men, try to wrest power from the gods; rather he participates passively in external power by identifying with and complying with those who control it. Humility and accommodation are the keynotes of this stage.

The world of the Passive Mastery individual tends to be closed, bounded by prohibitions that he cannot revoke and by dangers that he cannot survive. Fantasy and rumination precede action and substitute for action; in this world one moves mainly to discover the limitations on movement and to justify staying put. The passive individuals, therefore, retrench. They draw back into those familiar, limited terrains that reflect their schedule, that are still responsive to their will. This is the "tend your own garden" style, and the passive person convinces himself that little value exists beyond the precincts of his garden. This is the style of internal rather than external engineering: the productive style moves inward, toward the cultivation, in a redundant world, of pleasant thoughts, pleasant sensations, and predictable experiences.

This orientation includes anxious/constricted and emphasized receptivity subtypes. Again, these may be found together within some Passive Mastery individuals, while they differentiate between others. In anxiety/constriction, passivity is the consequence of fearful inhibition. In emphasized receptivity, the focus is on nurturance to the self and from the self. One passively accepts what others give; and one passively puts oneself at the disposal of others to meet their requirements. Both positions involve overt gentleness and avoidance of strife.

Magical Mastery

The preceding orientations are mainly centered around aggressive motives which are to be expressed (as in Active Mastery) or controlled (as in Passive Mastery). But for Magical Mastery individuals the receptive motives dominate (as in syntonic receptivity). However, Magical Mastery individuals do not have the capacity to delay gratification or to identify with the pleasure of others that is part of the syntonic receptivity state. Furthermore, in Active and Passive Mastery, instru-

mental actions and realistic cognitions intervene between impulse and gratification. But in this state, rather primitive defense mechanisms substitute for instrumental action either against the world or against the self. Denial replaces instrumental action against outer troubles; threatening agents are arbitrarily seen as
benign; projection substitutes for reformative action against the ego; troublesome
wishes and impulses are conveniently located in others rather than in the self.
Thus, in the magical ego state (particularly at times of stress and arousal), wish,
cognition, and action are mingled, such that the wish guarantees its own fulfill-
ment. Reality is altered through perceptual change, and external agents are seen
to play out roles in a personal psychodrama.

Thus, for Magical Mastery men, the world is seen in simplistic and extreme
terms; the world is full of potential providers (who can never provide enough) and
potential predators. Vulnerability is the keynote of their relationship to the world.

The Mastery Types and Other Measures

These various ego states are not mutually exclusive. The same individual can display them all in different contexts, or at different times within the same context.
They are here presented as exclusive states for heuristic purposes, in order to
highlight real inter-type differences. Moreover, the typology does have an empirical basis: men sorted into these types on the basis of their TAT performance were
also discriminated by interviewers' ratings of overt behavior and affect; by performance on the "Draw-A-Person" test; by the "Life Satisfaction" rating—a validated
scale devised by Neugarten and associates (1961); and by other independent measures derived from interview and observational data provided by these same subjects (see Gutmann 1964, pp. 137–142; see also Williams and Wirths 1963, pp.
209–210). In general, the prediction was that the Active Mastery men would
achieve high ratings on these measures of energy, affective liveliness, and life satisfaction, and that the Passive and especially the Magical Mastery men would receive
lower ratings. In the main, at a statistically significant level, these predictions were
confirmed.

Accordingly, while they may coexist within persons, each mastery orientation
seemingly refers to a distinct psychic system that coordinates, across persons, a
fairly standard panel of motives, attitudes, and behaviors. But the finding that the
types are distinct does not shed light on their meaning and origin. The question remains: Are these types developmental in nature, corresponding to stages of the individual life cycle; or, are they extrinsic in nature, having to do with specific psychological and cultural differences between the generations in United States
society? The major part of this report deals with the steps thus far taken to investigate this question.

The Cross-Cultural Study
of the Mastery Typology

Thus far, the hypothesis considered here—that men age psychologically along a continuum delineated by the Active, the Passive, and the Magical Mastery orientations—has received some support from the findings of other students of aging psychology in American populations. Thus, Schaw and Henry (1956), Rosen and Neugarten (1960), Shukin and Neugarten (1964), and Hays (1952) tend to report findings similar to those cited here.

Working with another urban United States sample, Clark (1967, p. 62) found that the self-conceptions of normal San Francisco subjects, aged 60 and over, were consistent with Passive Mastery criteria, as predicted for this age group.

Confirmatory clinical observations have also been made by psychiatrists (Meerloo 1955; Zinberg and Kaufman 1963; and Berezin 1963). All the above stress the aging American's withdrawal from active engagement with the world in favor of more cerebral, introversive, and self-centered positions.

However, while these independent observations support mine, they do not in themselves support the *developmental* conclusions that I would draw from the finding of age-graded psychological differences in a population of adult United States men. Socio-cultural influences may still account for the observed generational differences. The developmental implications of the United States findings have been tested in four groups of preliterate agriculturalists: the Lowland and Highland Maya of Mexico, the Western Navajo of Arizona, and the Druze of Israel. In this design, we make intergenerational comparisons across a variety of cultural settings. If the same psychological variables continue to discriminate the generations across this range of diverse societies, socio-cultural explanations cannot account for the predicted uniformity, and intrinsic or developmental explanations become more powerful.

The following considerations have governed the choice of study sites: (1) Subject societies should be significantly different from each other in terms of child-rearing practices, important value orientations, and age-grading systems.

(2) It is important to control for those extrinsic, socio-cultural factors that might independently bring about the age difference in ego orientation that are predicted by the developmental theory being tested. Accordingly, the subject societies should have maintained, for some generations, a stable consensus as to what is good and bad, real and unreal, possible and impossible. That is, the subject societies should be tradition-directed; and the means for communicating the tradition should also have remained fairly stable across generations.

(3) The theory being tested proposes mandatory age-graded regression in ego functions, towards Magical Mastery. In order to further rule out extrinsic contributions to this decline, the theory is most rigorously tested in societies which pro-

vide ample ego supports to older men. These are societies where older men are respected, where they have an advisory role towards the young, and where with increasing age they tend to amass political and/or ceremonial power less available to younger men.

Regarding criterion (1), the Lowland Maya, Highland Maya, Navajo, and Druze societies differ from each other (and from Kansas City) in major economic, cultural, and ecological respects. Thus, both Mayan groups are composed of subsistence level, village-dwelling corn farmers who nonetheless show greatly contrasting cultural and personal styles. The Lowland Maya represent the "Protestant Ethic" of thrift, industry, and moderation, while the Highland Maya, a more oppressed and unruly people, rely on external authorities to control the unmodulated rage and envy that they sense in themselves and fear openly in their neighbors.

The traditional Navajo, migratory herdsmen, are notably different from both the Highland and Lowland aspects of the Maya. They turn away from White influences—they do not live in organized villages; and they mingle extremes of suspicion and humor, vulnerability and toughness, pragmatism and superstition.

The Druze tribesmen of the Galilean highland are village-dwelling herdsmen and agriculturalists, accounted heretics in Islam, who have nevertheless maintained their cultural continuity in the Levant for over 800 years, though in the face of much persecution. As might be expected, core features of individual Druze character are stubbornness, piety, and reserve.[2]

Regarding criterion (2), these four groups—although they differ from each other—tend to be generationally homogeneous within themselves. Young men can see in their elders something of what they will become, and older men see in the younger men something of what they themselves have been.

Finally, as regards criterion (3), in each setting the older men are respected and at least formally deferred to. Thus, among the Lowland Maya, old men lack power but are indulged and supported out of a mixture of love and respect. In contrast, the Highland Maya and Druze patriarchs have much political, economic, and religious power. Similarly, older traditional Navajo often remain economically productive, and they also perform, through the medicine man role, important healing and ceremonial functions. Generally speaking, the socio-emotional situation of older men at all the study sites appears to be better than that of their relatively isolated, working-class age-peers of urban America.

For each of the subject cultures, the prediction has been that the age distribution of mastery orientations, as registered in TAT and other data, would replicate the age distribution of these orientations in the Kansas City sample. Mastery orientations that distribute more predictably by age than by culture can be regarded as developmental bench-marks, attributes of the human life cycle, and not as cultural styles that discriminate among the generations within societies.

Data Collection

The approach to data collection tended to vary with local conditions,[3] and as our field competence increased we tended to generate more extensive and intensive data. However, despite such variations, across the four subject societies relatively equivalent sets of TAT data have been gathered under roughly similar field conditions. Prior to TAT administration, subjects were first invited to ask questions of the investigator. Once their curiosity and suspicion had been dealt with, they were intensively interviewed concerning past and present life issues, childhood memories, sources of contentment, causes of discontent, favored remedies for discontent, and dreams. These topics were not necessarily covered in any fixed order but were brought up as they meshed with the respondent's subjective priorities. Interviews were gathered by myself and by students supervised in this "naturalistic" interviewing approach.

Following the interview, subjects were shown a battery of approximately twelve TAT cards, which had as its standard core four Murray TAT cards, and two cards originally designed for an Amerindian population. These basic cards depicted ambiguous situations that had no particular cultural referents; and they were used in their unmodified form at all sites. The remaining six cards presented standard "human" situations, (e.g., family life, cross-generational interaction, etc.) and were altered in detail (though hopefully, not in import) to correspond to the local versions of these events.[4]

While subjects were routinely asked to tell a story about the card, this instruction was often confusing to literal minded, concretely oriented Indian subjects. They could not see the card as an occasion for an imaginative exercise, recognized as such, but automatically assumed that the card presented some specific drama, intrinsic to it, that they were to discover. Accordingly, whenever we encountered this concrete attitude, we shifted our instructions to, "Tell me what is happening there." Probes around introduced content were used to elicit the final "story."

Data Analysis

The original, orienting conceptions of this study came from the TAT, and we have thus far mainly studied the pools of comparable TAT data generated by cards—such as the rope climber of the Murray set—that were presented without modification to all appropriate subjects at all study sites. As with the Kansas City data, the approach to the cross-cultural data has been exploratory and inductive. The basic analytic unit has been the story generated by one respondent, to one card. The goal of the analytic procedures has been to make themes and trends which are (1) implicit in data, and (2) relevant to the ego mastery conceptions, explicit and comparable. This has involved the standard application of interpretive procedures and guidelines, those based on mastery typology criteria, to the data generated by each card in each culture.

Thus, for any card and for any culture, Active Mastery stories were those in which card issues were recognized by the respondent, active stances were proposed in regard to that issue, and vigorous action led to good consequences. Passive Mastery stories were those in which central figures were seen as ineffectual, overwhelmed by external force, or in a receptive position *vis à vis* some external provider. Magical Mastery stories were those in which major stimulus features, particularly those suggestive of conflict and trouble, were either grossly distorted or ignored. Again, for each card thus analyzed, the prediction has been that the age by mastery type distributions would discriminate older from younger men, at any site, along the lines first noted in the Kansas City data.[5]

Card Analysis

Results of comparisons thus far undertaken have been encouraging. In those cases where a particular card has been used at all sites, the age by mastery position distributions from most or all Indian groups have roughly corresponded to the original Kansas City distributions for the same card. Then, too, while some findings have proved equivocal in terms of the predictions advanced, none of the data from other cultures has been grossly discrepant with the original hypotheses of this study.

The analytic methods and some typical findings are illustrated in the following discussion which deals with the data developed by four cards, two of which were used in their original, unmodified form at all sites (including Kansas City) and two of which were used at all Indian sites (though not at Kansas City). Some of the most representative findings emerged from the data of the rope climber card, which has been used at all sites and is discussed below.

The Rope Climber Card

This card suggests to many respondents—in any culture—a vigorous, muscular, and possibly nude figure who could be going up or down a rope. Because the card suggests nudity and strength, and because it does not depict any social agents besides the protagonist (and the rope), the stimulus might be regarded as a representation of the impulsive, instinctual aspects of life. Hence, the latent card issue is presumably "impulsive vigor" and the card presumably asks the respondent, "What *is your* conception of strength, of impulse and where do you locate these qualities?" Accordingly, respondents' estimates of the qualities, goals, and activities of this figure were regarded as metaphors of their personal relationship to their own impulse life. The various phrasings of this relationship were expressed in a set of thematic categories which are presented below, grouped according to their respective mastery orientations.

Active Mastery

A. Promethean

1. Challenge and competition: The hero demonstrates his strength, usually in successful competition. However, the rope may break at the moment of triumph; and the respondent himself may deride the hero as a show-off.

B. Productive-Autonomous

2. Productive effort: The hero strives vigorously, sometimes zestfully, towards a self-determined productive goal. He does not compete against others or flaunt his strength.

Passive Mastery

A. Anxious Constriction

3. Externalized inhibition: The hero is immobilized by environmental agents which do not collaborate with his action, or which block it; the rope is slack, the cliff is slippery.

4. Threat from internal or external aggression: The hero is threatened by destructive external forces (he flees a burning building); alternatively, the hero's aggression is turned against himself (suicide) or is out of control and constitutes a threat to others (the hero is homicidal).

5. Role dominated: The hero climbs, though without much involvement, for conventional purposes. Or, the respondent conforms to his role as subject by giving a minimal though accurate description of the card.

B. Syntonic passivity

6. Somaticized passivity: The hero lacks force to match his purpose; he is tired or ill.

7. Sensual receptivity: The hero has hedonic or security-seeking (rather than productive) purposes, he plays on the rope; he dives into water; he climbs to see something, to get a morsel of food, or to find his home.

Magical Mastery

8. The hero is not erect; or the rope is not a rope (the hero is lying down; the hero is wounded; the rope is a snake, etc.).

The Rope Climber: Age Trends

Table 1.2 presents the distribution of responses by the above card categories, by age, and by culture.

Though societies vary in overall degree of activity and passivity that they ascribe to the rope climber, the intergenerational comparisons within and across cultures indicate that younger men generally favor the more active, productive possibilities, while older men generally favor the more hedonic, inert, less instrumental possibilities. This point is dramatized by Table 1.6, which allows us to compare age cohorts across cultures, for each card. For example, in regard to Active Mastery, Table 1.6 shows that this orientation, as estimated by the rope climber card, is always lower, across cultures, for the 60-year-olds than it is for the 40-year-olds. Conversely, Passive Mastery is always higher for the 60-year-olds than it is for the 40-year-olds; and, except for the Highland Maya, the same is true for Magical Mastery. Despite intercultural differences in mastery preferences, there is a clear and independent age effect in these terms.

Thus, each culture shows age variation in its interpretations, but most of the variation occurs within a thematic band that is characteristic of the culture. For example, younger American respondents mainly propose that the rope climber competes against other athletes, that he demonstrates his strength to an admiring audience, or that he escapes from prison. Many also propose that successful striving has its dangers: at the moment of victory or freedom the rope will break, or the prisoner will be recaptured. Generally, younger United States subjects see a Promethean who strives against dangers that he has, by his own daring, created for himself. But older Americans to a significant degree locate energy and menace outside of this figure: for them the rope climber escapes from a fire or from some similar external threat. The card asks where they locate strength; the older Americans in effect reply: "Force is an external menace, and my job is to keep out of trouble." Thus, as a group the majority of Kansas City men, whether young or old, are more preoccupied than are the Indian respondents with the aggression variable; it is the location of aggression—from inside to outside the self—that is seen to shift with age.

Unlike the younger Americans, the younger Mexican and American Indians do not often regard the rope climber as a Promethean, competing figure. Instead, younger Indian men emphasize a more temperate version of striving. They propose that the rope climber more or less adequately fills an already defined productive role, and they do not suggest that he strives with others. But the older Indians are more blatantly passive. In these three societies, the tendencies to see the rope climber as inert (asleep, dead), as playful ("fooling around"), or as receptive to sensual supply ("he wants to see"), most clearly discriminate the older from the younger men. Thus, the younger Mexican and American Indians appear more passive than their urban American age peers; but, as in the American case, their versions of the rope climber's activities are consistently less inert and less hedonic than is the case for the older men of their own Mayan or Navajo societies.[6]

The trend away from active productivity and towards greater receptivity is especially sharp when we consider all responses to the rope climber card wherein

TABLE 1.2   The Rope Climber Card: Distribution of Stories by Age, Culture, and Theme

		35–49		50–59		60+	
ACTIVE MASTERY							
A. Promethean	Kansas City	21		33		10	
1. Competitive	Trad. Navajo	5	31*	1	36	6	19
	Lowland Maya	3		2		2	
	Highland Maya	2		0		1	
B. Autonomous	Kansas City	4		10		7	
2. Productive	Trad. Navajo	6	15	6	19	10	20
	Lowland Maya	3		2		2	
	Highland Maya	2		1		1	
PASSIVE MASTERY							
A. Anxious Constriction	Kansas City	—		3		—	
3. External inhibition	Trad. Navajo	—	7†	1	4	—	0
	Lowland Maya	6		—		—	
	Highland Maya	1		—		—	
4. External aggression	Kansas City	3		7		12	
	Trad. Navajo	3	8	—	8	7	20
	Lowland Maya	2		1		1	
	Highland Maya	—		—		—	
5. Constriction	Kansas City	1		11		5	
	Trad. Navajo	1	8	5	23	9	26
	Lowland Maya	1		5		7	
	Highland Maya	5		2		5	

(continues)

TABLE 1.2   *(continued)*

		35–49	50–59	60+
B. Syntonic Passivity				
6. Somatic passivity	Kansas City	—	1	—
	Trad. Navajo	—	1	2
	Lowland Maya	— }0†	— }2	— }2
	Highland Maya	—	—	—
7. Sexual receptivity	Kansas City	2	2	7
	Trad. Navajo	3	3	10
	Lowland Maya	3 }12	5 }17	14 }38
	Highland Maya	4	7	7
MAGICAL MASTERY				
8. Magical mastery	Kansas City	—	2	2
	Trad. Navajo	—	—	3
	Lowland Maya	— }1	1 }4	2 }8
	Highland Maya	1	1	1
		82	113	133

Kansas City	N = 143
Trad. Navajo	N = 82
Lowland Maya	N = 62
Highland Maya	N = 41
TOTAL	N = 328

*Chi Square (of cell totals) = 42.558, DF = 12, P < .001
†These cell totals have been combined with those of next lower category for computational purposes.

the hero is portrayed as looking or being looked at. Table 1.3 shows that younger Americans most often propose that the hero is the center of some audience's admiring attention: "He's showing off his strength," or "The audience gets a thrill out of seeing him." A confident, "look at me!" self-conception is projected through such responses. By contrast, older Americans are more likely to propose that the rope climber looks towards the audience for response and for direction: the *audience* tells him if he is doing a good job. Here the shift from confident, assertive inner-direction to cautious other-direction is clear.

Similarly, younger Mexican and American Indians usually suggest that the rope climber's visual activity is instrumental; the hero checks progress towards some goal. But for older Indians, looking *is in itself the goal* of the activity; the hero climbs to see something, to get a better view. (In this vein, a few older—and no younger—Kansas City men see the rope climber as a sexual voyeur.)

TABLE 1.3   Distribution by Age, Thematic Category, and Culture of Watchfulness Responses (Rope Climber Card)

		30–54		55–95	
1. Hero watched (attentively or admiringly)	Kansas City	17		10	
	Navajo	4	25*	6	20
	Lowland Maya	—		—	
	Highland Maya	4		4	
2. Hero is watchful for productive, task-centered reasons	Kansas City	5		2	
	Navajo	6	15	11	18
	Lowland Maya	—		4	
	Highland Maya	4		1	
3. Hero watchful of audience response to his performance	Kansas City	3		8	
	Navajo	—	4	—	8
	Lowland Maya	—		—	
	Highland Maya	1		—	
4. Climbing and un-motivated watchfulness are hero's only activity	Kansas City	6		1	
	Navajo	—	13	2	7
	Lowland Maya	3		1	
	Highland Maya	4		3	
5. Emphasized (erotized) watchfulness: increased visual input is hero's chief goal	Kansas City	1		5	
	Navajo	2	7	7	26
	Lowland Maya	4		11	
	Highland Maya	—		3	
TOTAL		64		79	143

*$\chi^2 = 13.473$ (for all cell totals) Kansas City N = 58
DF = 4, P < .01   Navajo   N = 38
          Lowland Maya N = 23
          Highland Maya N = 24

The Heterosexual Mastery Card

This card of the original Murray TAT battery depicts a young man turned away from a young woman who reaches towards him. Like the rope climber, this card has been shown to male respondents at all sites. In the typical drama, conflict is proposed between an angry, sometimes rejecting man and a solicitous and/or retentive woman. Thus, the card issue concerns the collision between potentially dangerous male energy, and more nutritive, less directly intrusive female qualities.

Accordingly, in deriving the mastery orientation of particular stories, particularly when the respondents are men, we consider such content issues as the deployment and impact of male energy; the locus of forces, internal or external, inhibiting such energy; and the qualities and powers ascribed to the young woman figure. Thus, Active Mastery stories portray a vigorous young man who is intrinsically impelled towards productive, amorous, or combative exploits, and who is relatively impervious to either the tenderness or the fear expressed by the young woman. Passive Mastery stories are those in which significant power is located outside of the young man. A domineering, retentive woman restricts the outward movement of a still assertive young man; or a young man, defeated in or menaced by the outer world, moves back to the comfort and security offered by the young woman. Magical Mastery stories are those in which the usually noted conflict possibilities are overlooked, and the emphasis is instead on some peaceful, though undifferentiated, relationship between the young man and young woman.

Grouped under their respective mastery orientations, the specific categories that accommodated all card data, from all cultures, are these:

Active Mastery

A. Promethean

1. Male aggressive initiatives: Young man's intrinsic sex, aggression, and autonomy needs constitute a problem for a gentle, nurturant young woman, and potential danger for himself.

B. Autonomous

2. Male autonomy needs: The young man forcefully rejects the young woman's nurturance. In some cases, he turns away from the consolation of the young woman to the impersonal consolation of liquor, which also sponsors his aggression.

Passive Mastery

A. Externalized Aggression

3. Female initiatives and dominance: The young man's anger is not intrinsic to him, but is in reaction to the young woman's dominance and/or rejection of him; she is a nagging or a cheating wife.

B. Syntonic Passivity

4. Rationalized male succorance: Menaced by external forces, or defeated in his outer-world striving, the young man looks for or accepts female nurturance and control.

Magical Mastery

5. Untroubled affiliation (or syntonic dependency): Mild, untroubled affiliation between a relatively undifferentiated young man and woman.

The Heterosexual Card: Age Trends

Table 1.4 indicates the age X theme X culture distributions to this card. Again the intergenerational, intercultural comparisons tend to conform to predictions; a later life shift towards the passive and magical end of the psychological spectrum was observed in the data from three out of the four societies studied.

Table 1.4 indicates more clearly that in all but the Highland Maya case,[7] Active Mastery declines steadily across age groups; Passive Mastery rises steadily across age groups, and if Magical Mastery appears at all, it is always higher among the 60-year-olds than among the 40-year-olds.[8]

The psychoanalytic theorist Otto Fenichel explicitly links scoptophilia with oral eroticism: "The eye may represent pregenital erogenous zones symbolically. As a sense organ it may express oral-incorporative and oral-sadistic longings in particular" (Fenichel 1945, p. 227). Accordingly, the striking emphasis among older men in a variety of cultures on "looking" for its own sake is indirect evidence of the hypothesized motivational shift in later life away from assertive productivity and towards pregenital versions of receptivity. The visual zone comes under the dominance of the oral-incorporative modality: the visual inputs of older men no longer serve ego executive functions primarily, but are valued for themselves as sensual supplies. The world is "eaten" through the eyes.

Cultural anthropologists have tended to insist that all organized mental contents are products of prior cultural indoctrination. But the striking similarity in the age distributions, across cultures, of specific imagery with high visual content, suggest that intrinsic, untrained psychosexual modalities may be ubiquitous, and that they can be registered in predictable ways and without prior cultural sponsorship in the content of thought, imagery, and behavior.

In the main, then, in regard to the heterosexual card, the between-age cohorts, across-cultures comparisons tend to replicate the results from equivalent rope climber comparisons, and provide further evidence of the shift away from exuberant and outward-directed male aggression towards more security-seeking, receptive stances. Thus, younger men propose that the male hero brushes aside a beseeching woman and pushes into a dangerous but exciting world of combat, carouse, and mistresses. To the same stimulus, older men propose more anergic, constricted, or pregenital themes. In their version, the young woman tends to domineer; or the male protagonist retreats back to her consolation, and away from a world in which he has known danger and de-

TABLE 1.4   The Heterosexual Card: Distribution of Stories by Age, Culture, and Theme

		35–49		50–59		60+	
ACTIVE MASTERY							
A. Promethean	Kansas City	21		12		10	
1. Male aggressive	Navajo	9	36*	7	20	9	21
initiative	Lowland Maya	4		1		2	
	Highland Maya	2		—		—	
B. Autonomous	Kansas City	1		3		—	
2. Male autonomy	Navajo	4	12	4	14	4	12
needs	Lowland Maya	7		5		7	
	Highland Maya	—		2		1	
PASSIVE MASTERY							
A. Externalized	Kansas City	6		5		6	
Aggression	Navajo	—	9	3	9	9	19
3. Female dominance	Lowland Maya	—		—		2	
	Highland Maya	3		1		2	
B. Syntonic Passivity	Kansas City	—		1		4	
4. Rationalized male	Navajo	—	1	1	3	12	20
succorance	Lowland Maya	—		1		2	
	Highland Maya	1		—		2	
MAGICAL MASTERY							
5. Untroubled	Kansas City	—		—		—	
affiliation	Navajo	1	12	6	16	6	21
	Lowland Maya	3		7		12	
	Highland Maya	8		3		3	

*Chi Square (of cell totals) = 24.643,   N = 70   62   93
DF = 8, P < .005

Kansas City	N = 69
Navajo	N = 75
Lowland Maya	N = 53
Highland Maya	N = 28
TOTAL	N = 225

feat. In either case, initiative and strength have migrated away from the young man toward the young woman or toward vaguely defined external agents which threaten the young man or the young couple. Finally, for many older men, the male protagonist does not reject the nurturance offered by the young woman, but instead dwells with her in happy, seamless harmony. Potential trouble comes from outside, not within, the dyad, and menaces the young man and woman equally.

The Heterosexual Card: Cultural Differences

Regarding the between-cultures comparisons, the culture X theme distributions for the heterosexual card also replicate those refracted by the rope climber card. Again, both younger and older United States men are notable for their common concern with the young man's aggression. While passive definitions of the young male figure increase in later life, they do not, even for the 60-year-old Kansas City group, supersede Active Mastery as the dominant orientation elicited by this card. Younger Kansas City men tend to be more concerned with the outer world, presumably masculine, reactions to their aggression, while older men are more concerned with the domestic reactions (perhaps from their wives). Most Kansas City men, young or old, are concerned with the deployment of their aggression. The primary aggressive orientation stays fairly constant; it is the theater of action that changes with age. It is significant that older Kansas City men never move to the Magical Mastery, nonconflict view of this card. They never propose the unrealistic, total harmony solution.

By contrast to Kansas City respondents of all ages, and by contrast to the younger Indian men, the older Indian men—as with the rope climber card—cluster significantly at the magical end of this card's thematic spectrum. These older Navajo and Mayan men to a striking extent agree that the card mainly depicts harmonious male-female interaction. Thus, as in the case of the rope climber, American respondents of any age are more concerned with the expression, the consequences, and the control of aggression; Indian respondents are generally more attuned to the hedonic and affiliative card implications.[9]

The Rope Climber and Heterosexual Cards: Common Age Trends

To summarize, the two TAT cards that raise for respondents the issue of the nature and deployment of masculine energies outline an age-graded, transcultural consensus around these matters. That is, young men define strength as an ambivalently valued internal resource: the strong, competitive man also stirs up trouble for himself (the rope climber can fall at the moment of triumph; the young man rejects a woman only to get into fights with men). The old men also retain this ambivalent relationship towards strength—it can help them or hurt them—but they see it as lodged outside of themselves, in relatively capricious agencies, institutions, or authorities. Both cards also produce agreement on the age shift to more openly needful and incorporative positions, towards immediate affectional, oral, and ocular supplies. In their apparent need to turn the world into a secure storehouse of consumable supplies, older men will determinedly overlook potential conflicts and troubles that are clear to younger men. Thus, the older men, as predicted, rely on defensive denial, rather than on action, to remove the sense of threat. Instead of "taking arms against a sea of troubles," they may revise their perception, and claim that the outer world holds neither armaments nor troubles.

The Desert Scene Card

The data from the rope climber and heterosexual conflict cards indicate that men relate to the world in different ways, depending on their age-status. Younger men look for challenge, opportunity, and assertion; older men look for oral, visual, and affectional gratuities. These relational shifts also have consequences for the ego defenses. The data from the desert scene card illustrate the predicted age trend towards reliance on the denial defense, which is pivotal to the Magical Mastery ego state. This card (shown only to Indian respondents) portrays a desert scene, gullied in the foreground, empty of people, but transected by a trail and by barb-wire fences.

The majority of Indian respondents visualized in this card one or another version of aridity, and they were judged to be responding to a card issue of "innurturant environment." Category criteria took account of the degree to which respondents recognized this aridity, proposed reasonable human efforts to counteract it, or tried to deny it. Thus, Active Mastery categories grouped those stories in which the reality of a hostile environment was admitted, without palliation and also those stories which proposed restitutive human effort. Passive Mastery categories grouped those stories in which it was proposed that restorative rain or water would appear through some natural agency, not under human control. Magical Mastery categories grouped those stories in which key elements of the scene were misperceived, and it was proposed that water already covered the ground, or that helpful supernatural agents were concretely present on the scene. The particular categories, grouped by mastery orientations, are as follows:

Active Mastery

A. Coping

1. Human agency: Emphasis on human effort in the face of a hostile environment; or on those human systems and structures that might oppose the ravages of nature (fenced fields, road systems, etc.).

B. Realism

2. Innurturance: Emphasis on an arid environment, hostile to life and to human effort.

Passive Mastery

A. Anxious Constriction

3. Perceptual restriction: Emphasis on a few accurately perceived details, but avoidance of total, integrated scene.

B. Syntonic Passivity

4. Fantasied relief from innurturance: Description of arid desert, and suggestion that background clouds might bring rain.

5. Integrated denial of innurturance: Rain actually falls from distant clouds; or the foreground gully forms the banks of a body of water.

Magical Mastery

A. Denial

6. Gross perceptual denial: Arbitrary introduction of helpful, fertile, or nurturant agents—angels, churches, flowers, money, sheets of water.

B. Projection of Threat

7. Uncontrolled natural forces: Floods, marine volcanoes, sea battles, sinking ships, drowning, or dangerous animals.

Desert Scene: Age Trends

Table 1.5 shows a clear age progression in the data, defined especially by categories 1, 2, 4, 5, and 6, away from recognition of card issues, and towards various perceptual metaphors of denial. Forty-eight percent of responses given by all men in the youngest group cluster in categories 1 and 2, indicating the relative readiness of this group to look squarely at unpleasant issues, and even to do something about them. By contrast, 62 percent of responses given by 50-year-olds are found in 5 and 6, the two perceptual denial categories, as are 75 percent of the responses from men aged 60 and over.

Regarding the intergenerational, intercultural comparison of the mastery distributions, Table 1.6 indicates that, across cultures, Active Mastery follows the predicted course, always declining with age from its starting point. Passive Mastery

TABLE 1.5   The Desert Scene: Distribution of Stories by Age, Culture, and Theme

		35–49		50–59		60+	
ACTIVE MASTERY							
A. Coping	Navajo	5		3		2	
1. Human agency	Lowland Maya	5	} 13*	1	} 5	—	} 2
	Highland Maya	3		1		—	
B. Realism	Navajo	7		1		1	
2. Innurturance	Lowland Maya	—	} 9	1	} 3	—	} 1
	Highland Maya	2		1		—	
PASSIVE MASTERY							
A. Anxious Constriction	Navajo	4		5		10	
3. Constriction	Lowland Maya	—	} 6	1	} 7	1	} 13
	Highland Maya	2		1		2	
B. Syntonic Passivity	Navajo	5		7		9	
4. Fantasied relief	Lowland Maya	2	} 7	—	} 8	—	} 9
from innurturance	Highland Maya	—		1		—	
5. Integrated denial	Navajo	5		8		5	
of innurturance	Lowland Maya	3	} 10	2	} 10	1	} 6
	Highland Maya	2		—		—	
MAGICAL MASTERY							
A. Denial	Navajo	1		2		11	
6. Gross perceptual	Lowland Maya	—	} 7	9	} 16	14	} 31
denial	Highland Maya	6		5		6	
B. Projection	Navajo	1		2		6	
7. Uncontrolled	Lowland Maya	6	} 8	1	} 3	6	} 12
natural forces	Highland Maya	1		—		—	
*Chi Square = 38.297,			60		52		74
DF = 12, P < .001							

Navajo   N = 100
Lowland Maya   N = 53
Highland Maya   N = 33

TOTAL   N = 186

does not, however, always conform to prediction, and sometimes falls or stays constant with increasing age. However, we also see that in those cases where, contrary to prediction, Passive Mastery drops off in later life, Magical Mastery rises, and in general, always shows the predicted age-graded increase across cultures. Thus, as regards this card, Passive Mastery in some instances follows the age career that was predicted for Active Mastery; and Magical Mastery follows the course

24

TABLE 1.6   Distribution of Mastery by Card, by Culture, and by Age

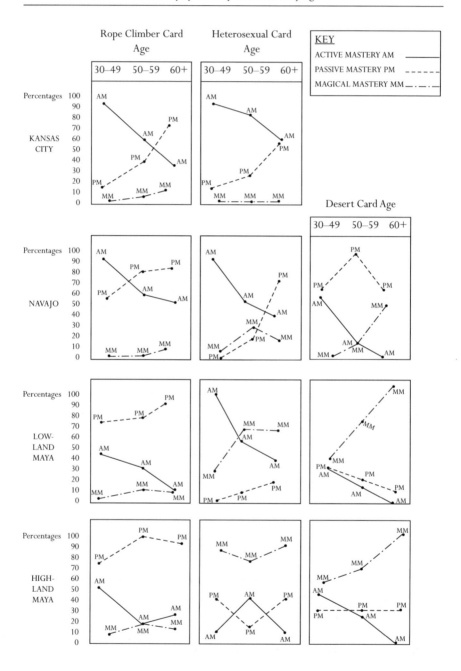

that was predicted for Passive Mastery. That is, the desert scene card, by contrast to other cards, seems to shift all age groups in all the subject cultures, towards the more passive and regressive end of the mastery spectrum, while maintaining the relative distinctions as to mastery preferences between them.

Possibly, this card, which depicts the natural rather than the personal world, picks up in these three Indian societies the preliterate world view towards nature. One can be effective among one's own people, but nature is refractory, and one is either stoic about this, or hopes for the best.[10] And with advanced age it appears that the boundary between wish and reality may break down, such that the wish creates the satisfying perception. Furthermore, while the emphasis on one or another mastery orientation can vary by card and by culture, these card and culture effects tend to be constant, and there is an age effect which appears to be independent of them both. As predicted, and with few exceptions, Active Mastery declines with age, while the percentage of Passive and Magical Mastery stories increases with age, according to the sequence, Active → Passive or Magical Mastery.

This consistency in the age distributions and in the cultural distributions of standardized data—where the original stories were given to different cards and differed as to manifest content—suggests that the mastery orientations have transcultural distribution; and that while cultural influences can amplify or retard particular mastery orientations, these decline or unfold according to an intrinsic *developmental* schedule. These results also suggest that the individual card judgments are reliable, that they measure what they purport to measure, and that the criteria upon which such judgments are based can be standardly applied across different cards and across different cultures.

Analysis of Interview Data

We have thus far reviewed some age changes, across cultures, in the subjective postures of the ego, and have found these to be consistent with the predicted age-staging of mastery orientations. Thus, the cross-cultural TAT data replicate some of the predicted relational and defensive shifts that were found in the Kansas City population and that in their American version gave rise to the developmental theory of mastery stages. We also touched on some serendipitous findings concerning the later life emergence of a visual-sensual modality which is consistent with the theory, though not specifically predicted by it. Furthermore, the analysis of interview data suggests that the subjective shifts from Active towards Passive and Magical Mastery, as revealed in TAT stories, have implications for more overt attitudes and behavior in later life.

Sources of Contentment, Discontentment, and Remedy

In the course of the interviewing that preceded projective testing, Navajo and Highland Maya men were routinely asked, "What makes you happy?" "What makes you unhappy?" "When you are unhappy, how do you make yourself contented again?" Again, categories were devised which integrated the thematic emphases of the actual responses with mastery typology criteria. Tables 1.7, 1.8, and 1.9 indicate various category criteria and the response distributions: by these categories, by age, and by culture. Starting with responses to the question, "What makes you happy?" Table 1.7 indicates that both the younger Highland Maya and the younger Navajo equate pleasure with productive work. They are happy when they acquire livestock, when they bring new cornfields under cultivation, or when they find lucrative wage work. But older men are most likely to define happiness in passive-receptive terms. They are made happy by visits from relatives, by their accustomed food, by pleasant music, by the sight of a flourishing vegetable garden, or by a pretty view. The younger men take pleasure in that which they make or gain and in the activities associated with production, but the older men are made happy by the pleasant sights, sounds, tastes, and friendly sentiments that come to them as earned or unearned gratuities from the outside.

Similarly, as seen from Tables 1.8 and 1.9, younger Navajo and Highland Maya men are mainly made unhappy by work stoppages and their major remedy for any trouble is to get back to work. Older Navajo and Maya are mainly troubled by losses of family, friends, and providers, and they look for remedy to powerful allies (village authorities, saints, doctors) or, again, to suppliers of food, drink, and friendly attention. The older men of both societies clearly visualize themselves in Passive Mastery terms, that is, as receivers; and the younger men clearly visualize themselves in Active Mastery terms, that is, as centers of action, influence, and productivity.

Mastery Orientation and Early Memories

Other interview data suggest that the individual's current ego orientation not only directs behavior and attitude in the present, but also has implication for the reconstruction, in memory, of the past. Given their predominately Passive Mastery orientation, it was predicted that older men, as they recalled their past, would give most attention to the maternal figures associated with the earliest satisfactions (or frustrations) of succorant demands. By contrast, the more Active Mastery, production oriented younger men were expected to give greater prominence to memories of the paternal figures who had provided their first models of a manly competence. As predicted, the percentage of maternal memories spontaneously put forth by tra-

TABLE 1.7   Age and Thematic Distribution: Traditional Navajo and Highland Maya Responses to Question, "What Makes You Happy?"

Age		Productive Work		Maintaining Status Quo		Passive-Receptivity	
30–49	Highland Maya	9	} 13*	0	} 3	4	} 5
	Navajo	4		3		1	
50–90†	Highland Maya	6	} 10	6	} 16	9	} 22
	Navajo	4		10		13	

*χ² = 11.168   Highland Maya   N = 34
DF = 2, P < .005   Navajo   N = 35

†6 Navajo, 2 Highland Maya   TOTAL   N = 69
  S's aged 80 and over.

TABLE 1.8   Age and Thematic Distribution: Traditional Navajo and Highland Maya Responses to Question, "What Makes You Unhappy?"

Age		Interruptions of Production; Enmity of Competitors		Illness		Anaclitic Concerns; Objects Loss, etc.	
30–49	Highland Maya	10	} 17*	1	} 2	0	} 4
	Navajo	7		1		4	
50–96†	Highland Maya	2	} 10	7	} 9	8	} 22
	Navajo	8		2		14	

*χ² (of cell totals) = 14.843   Highland Maya   N = 28
DF = 2, P < .001   Navajo   N = 36
†6 Navajo, 2 Highland Maya   TOTAL   N = 64
  S's aged 60 and over.

TABLE 1.9   Age and Thematic Distribution: Traditional Navajo and Highland Maya Responses to Question, "How Do You Restore Contentment?"

Age		Reliance on Instrumental Action		Reliance on "Omnipotent" Figures		Reliance on Oral (and other) Supplies	
30–49	Highland Maya	8	} 13*	2	} 3	1	} 3
	Navajo	5		1		2	
50–96†	Highland Maya	5	} 11	5	} 15	7	} 19
	Navajo	6		10		12	

*χ² (of cell totals) = 11.066   Highland Maya   N = 28
DF = 2, P < .005   Navajo   N = 36
†6 Navajo, 2 Highland Maya   TOTAL   N = 64
  S's aged 80 and over.
  2 Highland Maya under 35

ditional Navajo interviewees increases markedly with age, while spontaneous memories of paternal figures decrease at a corresponding rate (see Table 1.10).[11]

Mastery Orientation and Orality

The hypothesized association between Passive Mastery, Magical Mastery, and receptivity in later life was further tested through studies of the orality variable. The prediction was that specifically oral interests would increase in later life in conformity with the general increase in Passive and Magical Mastery orientations. To this end, the Navajo interview and projective data were coded for the orality variable. All mentions of eating, food preparation, purchase, or production were assigned weights which reflected the intensity of oral need that they presumably expressed. The orality scores are presently being checked for reliability, but the first assessments differentiate older from younger Navajo and in the predicted direction. More interesting are the findings that the highest proportion of young men's scores derive from mentions of food production, while the highest proportion of old men's scores derive from mentions of eating and pleasure in food. Thus far then, the age variations in the Navajo orality scores tend to be consistent with the age variation in the mastery orientations.

TABLE 1.10   Traditional Navajo Age Group Comparisons: Percentages of Memory Materials Relating to Mothers and Fathers*

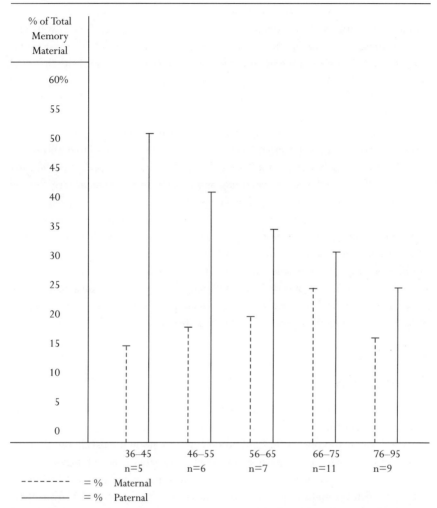

*For this chart and the work that it represents I gratefully acknowledge the efforts of Jeffrey Urist.

Another, unexpected, finding concerns the within-protocols age shifts: as shown in Table 1.11, younger men displayed oral yearnings mainly through externalized, projective forms of fantasy. They dream about people who eat, and they can vividly describe the hunger and nutriment of people depicted in the TAT, but they are not likely to depict their own lives, past or present, in these terms. By contrast, older men are much less likely to ascribe hunger or eating to TAT stimulus figures, but such oral content suffuses interview accounts of their activities and concerns, and is particularly pervasive in their reminiscences of early life. While younger men remember the fathers who trained them for competence, older men dwell with greater frequency on the mothers who fed them, and on the food that these mothers prepared. A common theme in older men's interviews is that of the "lost oral paradise": "When I was a boy there was more green grass and good grazing. Berries and *piñon* nuts for eating grew all over the ground. Now we have to buy all our food from the trading post."

Thus, there seems to be an inverse relationship between reminiscence and the more projective or depersonalized forms of fantasy, at least in regard to oral content: as oral material leaches out of the TAT and out of dreams it reappears in the early memories. Thus, the dependent yearnings appear to be problematic in early life and are therefore repressed, or managed, in fantasy. But in later life there appears to be a "return of the repressed," which restores the oral representations to consciousness. This tentative finding also suggests that reminiscence may in later life take over some of the dynamic functions usually ascribed to dreaming and other fantasy activities. We have observed that our older subjects in the course of their interviews move easily to detailed memories of early life. In so doing, they may rework their past so as to "feed" themselves with experiences that—much like restorative dreams—have the effect of maintaining their present psychic equilibrium.

Conclusion

A mixed bag of evidence, mostly derived from work still in progress and not from completed analytic programs, has been presented. The fragmentary picture thus far developed supports the contention that changes in the psychosexual, relational, ego defensive, and cognitive aspects of personality proceed, in a variety of simple agricultural societies along continua whose tracks were first discerned in data derived from middle-aged and older urban American men. Men from these societies move—though with different pacing and different priorities—through successive Active, Passive, and Magical Mastery ego stages, toward oral definitions of pleasure and pain, toward simplistic defensive tactics, and toward subjectivity of thinking. It begins to appear that aged men across cultures have their own "country of old men," a dominion that they do not share even with their own sons, in their own societies.

However, while it now appears probable that individuals move, in predictable sequence, through the mastery stages, we cannot yet claim that this progression has an intrinsic, developmental basis. Although we can now rule out a strictly cul-

TABLE 1.11 Age Group Comparisons: Mode of Expressing Oral Interests Among the Western Navajo

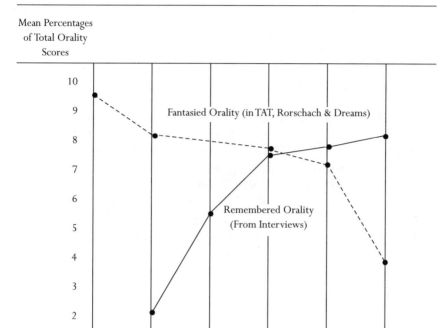

Mean Percentages of Total Orality Scores

Fantasied Orality (in TAT, Rorschach & Dreams)

Remembered Orality (From Interviews)

Age: 36–49   50–59   60–69   70–79   80–90

tural explanation of these findings, we do not automatically prove the developmental theory by refuting the socio-cultural alternative. There are existential necessities that impinge on most men, especially in later life—the exigencies of illness, of failing strength, of approaching death, of reduced opportunity and hope—that are independent of specific cultural circumstances just as they may be independent of any prior psychological or developmental events. These existential imperatives may be the independent variables, the independent engines of psychological change in later life, which set in motion, as dependent events, the universal passage across the mastery continuum that we have described.

Thus, there are those who propose that human beings are not in the end *driven* towards Magical Mastery, but that they *choose* it. These critics would see in the final psychic postures of life not a compelled developmental outcome, but an ego directed response to the imminence of death. In this view, the common reality that unites older men is the universal recognition of death, and not some somatic program outside of human awareness. The seeming regression of the ego towards Magical Mastery does not in this view represent ego debility; it represents an executive act, performed by the ego upon itself, in defiance of approaching death. Passive and especially Magical Mastery recapitulate early ego states. Therefore, faced with its own ending, and lacking any rational, instrumental means for avoiding that end, the ego may regress in its own service, and revive the appetitive, relational, and cognitive climate of its beginning.

Our present data do not allow us to make final choices between the developmental and the more cognitive or "ego executive" explanations of the findings developed by the cross-cultural work. At this time, I believe that there is an interaction, such that developmental variables may regulate the individual's sensitivity to the existential imperatives that we have described, with different consequences for different stages of life. The young man may view the imposed necessity of illness as an arbitrary interruption of his life work; an older man may secretly welcome the same illness because it rationalizes an emergent passivity.[12]

But at this point we only glimpse the interesting questions. More field work may provide the answers, or—this is the more likely possibility—suggest better questions.

Notes

1. The overall program of cross-cultural research has been supported by Career Development Award no. 5-K3-HD-6043-04, from the National Institutes of Child Health and Human Development. Field expenses for Indian studies in Mexico and America were covered by Faculty Research Grants nos. 1344 and 1412 from the Rackham School of Graduate Studies, The University of Michigan; and by grant no. MH 13031-01 from the National Institutes of Mental Health. Field work expenses among the Israeli Druze were covered by grant no. M66-345 from the Foundation's Fund for Research in Psychiatry.

2. The traditional Druze enclaves have been studied; but the Six-Day War and the resultant Israeli mobilization interfered with the transcription of our data tapes, so that the analysis of individual Druze protocols has not yet begun. No formal findings will be reported from this group.

3. Given the realities of field work in remote areas, one cannot be obsessive about meeting criteria for random and representative samples. The particular subjects demanded by a sampling design often turn out to be sick, in trouble with the police, drunk, or working away from the community.

In any event, working in a small village, or in a sparsely settled region, one eventually contacts all those potential subjects who are willing or able to talk to a foreign investigator. Thus, the study sample tends to be coextensive with the local set of possible subjects, and thereby meets the criteria for representativeness, if not for randomness.

We generally recruited subjects by first making ourselves known to men of reasonable reputation, without important disability, in the age range 35–75. In larger villages, where we did not expect to study all possible subjects, we tried to reduce the sampling bias inherent in the use of a single sponsor by patronizing several principal men, hopefully from different village clans or factions. Interpreters of good local reputation were relied on at all sites; these also helped to recruit subjects and further legitimized our presence in the village or on the reservation.

4. The desert scene TAT card is part of a set of American Indian TAT pictures originally designed for research on Indian education. This study was sponsored by the United States Office of Indian Affairs and the Committee on Human Development, University of Chicago. Robert J. Havighurst was primarily responsible for the design of the American Indian pictures. They were first used by William E. Henry (1947).

5. Positive results would validate the original judgments concerning the degree of activity, passivity, of "magical" arbitrariness registered in particular response themes. Also supported is the a priori assumption often contested by anthropologists—that data from other cultures can be analyzed from a conceptual framework not indigenous to those cultures.

6. Note also that the rope climber card not only distinguishes between the Kansas City and the Indian respondents, but that it also distinguishes between the Indian societies in terms of the mastery orientations along lines predictable from their socio-cultural makeup. Table 1.6 shows that the individualistic Navajo, who live in small bands rather than organized villages, who value mobility, and who still remember their Apachean warrior tradition, maintain a higher level of Active Mastery at any age than either of the two village-dwelling, sedentary Mayan groups. And for both Mayan groups, Passive Mastery is always higher than Active Mastery for any age cohort (though this lead increases with age).

7. Both the younger and older Highland Maya men depicted the young man figure as relatively mild and inert relative to the outer world or the young woman figure. But men of this group are very inhibited and fearful concerning sexual matters, and their anxiety may have been reflected in their particularly constricted definitions of the young man figure. Thus, the data generated by this card from this group may not be comparable to data from the other societies where sex is far less problematic.

8. Along the same lines, older respondents again emphasize visual content: 11 Indian men over 50 (and only two men younger than 50) propose that the young couple look out toward some undefined external presence. Again, older men substitute visual intensity in place of the aggression and sexuality stressed by younger men. Findings of this sort, from TAT data, suggest that the visual interests of the aged are scoptophilic in nature—pregenital versions of sexuality.

9. The heterosexual card data not only distinguish the Kansas City from the Indian distributions as a whole, but also replicate the rankings between the Indian

groups first developed by the rope climber card. Thus we see from Table 1.6 that Active Mastery is usually much higher among the Navajo that it is for either of the Mayan groups, and the Passive Mastery is the dominant Navajo later life orientation, while Magical Mastery dominates among the Mayan elders. Indeed, Magical Mastery is lower at any age for the Navajo than it is for the two Mayan groups. Thus, despite the independent, predicted age effects, we find consistent intersocietal differences where, in terms of Active Mastery, Kansas City>Navajo>Maya (Highland and Lowland); and in terms of Magical Mastery (which can vary independently of Active Mastery), Maya (Highland and Lowland)>Navajo>Kansas City.

10. Though the desert card portrays the familiar arid terrain of the Navajo, we see from Table 1.5 that this card, like the rope climber and heterosexual cards, continues to rank the Navajo higher in terms of Active Mastery, and lower in terms of Magical Mastery, than either of the two Mayan groups. Where Magical Mastery is the major Mayan orientation to the desert card for any age group, Passive Mastery has priority among the Navajo, and Magical Mastery only begins to compete with Passive Mastery for dominance among the 60-year-old Navajo.

11. Note that for the 76–95-year-old-group, paternal memories again lead over maternal memories, whereas in the preceding age groups the two phrasings of parental memory had gradually but consistently moved toward equality. This irregular pattern may indicate the unreliability of the measure, but it also should be remembered that any remote-dwelling Navajo who survive into their seventies are unusually hardy men by anybody's standards. Accordingly, the data from this group are not comparable with that from the more typical younger Navajo. The longevous Navajo show an unexpected dominance, reminiscent of younger men, of the independent, productive (hence father-oriented) stance.

12. Thus, among the Navajo, we found a very high incidence of diagnosed psychosomatic incapacity among the "Rice Christians," the passive dispirited Navajo who live near the Indian Agency towns, and near the provident missionaries. These men are, by all psychological measures, a highly succorant group. In their early forties they quit work, live on handouts, on welfare, and on their wives' rug-weaving earnings. Their typical rationale is that they fell off a horse, that they are dizzy, ache all over, and thus can no longer work. The remote-living non-Christian Navajo emerge in the same measures as a counter-dependent group, and their older men will minimize real illnesses, and continue to strive despite them. Obviously the former group amplifies illness in order to justify dependency. Dependency precedes illness, and not vice versa.

References

1. Berezin, M. A. (1963). "Some Intra-Psychic Aspects of Aging." In N. Zinberg, (ed.). *The Normal Psychology of the Aging Process.* New York: International University Press.

2. Clark, M. (1967)."The Anthropology of Aging: A New Area for Studies of Culture and Personality." *The Gerontologist, 7*, 55–64.
3. Fenichel, O. (1945). *Psychoanalytic Theory of Neurosis.* New York: Norton.
4. Gutmann, D. (1964). "An Exploration of Ego Configurations in Middle and Later Life." In B. Neugarten (ed.). *Personality In Middle and Later Life.* New York: Atherton.
5. Hays, W. (1952). "Age and Sex Differences in the Rorschach Experience Balance." *Journal of Abnormal and Social Psychology, 47.*
6. Henry, W. E. (1947). "The Thematic Apperception Technique in the Study of Culture-Personality Relations." *Genetic Psychology Monographs, 35*, 3–135.
7. Jacobowitz, J. (1984). "Stability and Change of Coping Patterns During the Middle Years As a Function of Personality Type." Unpublished doctoral dissertation, Department of Psychology, Hebrew University, Jerusalem.
8. Meerloo, J. (1955). "Transference and Resistance in Geriatric Psychotherapy." *Psychoanalytic Review, 42*, 72–82.
9. Neugarten, B., and Gutmann, D. (1958). "Age-Sex Role and Personality in Middle Age: A Thematic Apperception Study." *Psychological Monographs*, 470.
10. Neugarten, B., Havighurst, R., and Tobin, S. (1961). "The Measurement of Life Satisfaction." *Journal of Gerontology, 16*, 134–143.
11. Rosen, J., and Neugarten, B. (1960). "Ego Functions in the Middle and Later Years." *Journal of Gerontology, 15*, 62–67.
12. Schaw, L., and Henry, W. E. (1956). "A Method for the Comparison of Groups: A Study in Thematic Apperception." *Genetic Psychology Monographs, 50*, 207–253.
13. Shukin, A., and Neugarten, B. (1964). "Personality and Social Interaction." In B. Neugarten (ed.). *Personality in Middle and Later Life.* New York: Atherton.
14. Williams, R., and Wirths, C. (1963). *Lives Through the Years.* New York: Atherton.
15. Zinberg, N., and Kaufman, I. (1963)."Cultural and Personality Factors Associated with Aging: An Introduction." In N. Zinberg (ed.). *The Normal Psychology of the Aging Process.* New York: International University Press.

2 Dependency, Illness, and Survival Among Navajo Men

In the following paper, I concentrated on the unexpected finding first reported in "The Country of Old Men," that is, that across cultures, references to food tend to increase in the interview protocols of older men. In later studies, I traced out in greater detail the implications of that serendipitous finding for a theory of aging personality. The extra effort appears to have paid off: I was able to show the generality of the orality X age distribution across two very different cultures, Navajo and Druze—a finding that supported the developmental hypothesis in regard to these appetites. I found in addition that regional differences in orality within societies were also replicated across these two strikingly different peoples. Thus, as regards oral appetites and concerns, elderly Navajo and Druze who dwell in remote and traditional regions of their domain resemble each other more than they resemble their age peers resident in more secular communities, closer to major roads and cities. In effect, across cultures, the folk-urban continuum replicated, as regards oral interests, the effects of aging: the more remote the settlement, the lower the degree of orality at any age. I still don't know what to make of this finding, which seems to suggest that urban domains attract and/or sponsor oral-dependent character types. Thus far then, the findings concerning the regional distribution of oral character points to a conclusion much favored by cultural conservatives (including the founders of the Republic), namely, that the God-fearing countryside attracts or breeds self-reliant characters, while the cities are nests of needy, demanding welfare bums. That is one possibility. The other, less dramatic possibility, is that urbanized people—by contrast to the sturdy work-ethic agrarians—are omnipotential, more open to a whole range of appetites: They can be simultaneously self-reliant and oral. This latter possibility was never checked out, so for me the question is still moot.

"Gutmann," a splenetic critic of my work once observed, "finds that old men get more interested in groceries. Big deal. What else could they be interested in?" In other words, if sex is no longer an option, old men might as well content themselves with their nums. But in point of fact, one thing is clear: These appetites do play a significant part in the personality of later

life. The data presented in this paper show that oral tendencies are not limited to the zone of the mouth. These are modal *tendencies; they spread across a variety of zones that have nothing to do with the mouth, the gut, or with groceries. Thus, we find that orality behaves less like a specific appetite, restricted to the mucosa of the mouth, and more like a dynamic personality factor: a general tendency to gain the feeling of comfort and security via the intake of pleasant experiences, whether in the form of pretty sights, comforting touch, loving concern, or tasty food. In the reported studies we find orality, so construed, to be correlated not only with age, but also with passive themes in dreams and TATs, with drinking behavior, and—most importantly—with health status and mortality.*

When I wrote this paper, I was still the naturalist, describing the shapes of human nature in later life; only later did I glimpse the forces driving the emerging patterns and use the orality variable to test my tentative theories. Despite these stumbling beginnings, the theory of later life orality has held up over the years, has shed light on the normal psychology of aging, and has proven itself in clinical practice. Nevertheless, it has never, to my knowledge, been cited in any review of geropsychology theories. The conventional wisdom in the geropsychology field has consistently rejected the idea of unconscious motivation, but I never thought that the avoidance would go to such lengths. In any event, the "oral" doctrine of aging fell into the memory hole, and there it has stayed; perhaps, this time around, attention might be paid.

This paper explores the relationship between illness, survival, and the management of passive-receptive character traits in a sample composed mainly of traditional Navajo men. While such relationships can also be studied in our own culture, tradition-oriented and remote living groups, such as Navajo, are particularly suited to a study of the relationship between somatic and psychological states. If such a relationship exists, it can best be observed in men who have less than we by way of extrinsic, medical, and nutritional supports. If these men survive, it is by their own resources, and if psychological parameters are included among these resources, then their contributions should be most evident in these populations.

The hypotheses which guided this study were developed from the results of previous investigations in the comparative psychology of later life, first undertaken among urban Americans and then replicated among middle-aged and aging men of various traditional and preliterate groups.[1]

The data analysis is not complete, but thus far the results from the various studies support the American findings: the active-productive, passive-receptive, and magical orientations distribute more predictably by age in adult male populations than they do by culture. As in Kansas City, the younger Navajo, Maya, and Druze rely on and relish their own instrumentality and the products of their industry; moreover, they see themselves as a source of provision to others. By contrast, older men come to rely on the accommodating techniques whereby they influence external providers in their favor; and the oldest men, especially in time of trouble, manage reality projectively and rely on the less adaptive illusions of security and comfort. In sum, the "species" age shift in men as it emerges from these comparative studies is away from the position of one who actively provides security for others and towards the position of one whose sense of security is based on the good will of powerful providers (see Gutmann, 1969).[2]

By contrast to the younger men's more autonomous stance, the older men are characterized by oral-dependency. In this, my authority derives from aspects of the psychoanalytic character theory and from empirical evidence, which will be presented later. Thus, on the theoretical side, psychoanalysts propose an intrinsic association between the passive-dependent ego-orientations that we have observed transculturally in older men, and the oral needs of the personality.[3] From this theory comes our prediction that the older man's concern with external donations of affection and support, with powerful external providers, and with magical defenses against threat, should be matched by a heightened interest in the production, the preparation, and especially the pleasurable consumption of food.

Accordingly, if old men are more accommodating and succorant than younger men, then their explicitly oral interests should also be higher than those of younger men. Furthermore, since the relationship between the psychosexual and the psychosocial vectors of personality is presumed to be intrinsic and invariant, then we would expect to find that the predicted relationship is transcultural in its distribution: in *any* society, a high degree of manifest orality should predict, on the individual level, to character traits and behaviors that register a high degree of passive-receptivity, relative to local standards.

Empirical support for this prediction is provided by Simmons (1945) who collected ethnographic reports from over thirty diverse preliterate societies bearing on the roles and personal characteristics of their aged members. He devotes his first chapter, (titled "Assurance of Food") to making the point that, across cultures, the aged are particularly concerned with oral supply. He notes, for example, that older men have typically used their prestige to ensure the choicest foods for themselves, by making them taboo for younger men.[4]

Scoring for Orality

In order to further check the hypothesis that oral interests, (like the ego styles of passive and magical mastery) become more prominent in later life, the Navajo and Druze[5] data collected by the author were coded for the orality variable. All references to eating, food preparation, purchase, or production were assigned weights which reflected the intensity of oral need presumably expressed through them. Thus, mentions of food production or preparation received lower scores than mentions of food consumption; and mentions of food consumption by others received lower scores than mentions of food consumption by the respondent himself. In addition, a distinction was made between those oral references embedded in the body of the interview proper, and those found in the subject's projective data—whether from TAT or dream protocols.

The age, cultural, and regional distributions of the various orality sub-scales are reported in another paper (Gutmann, 1971). Here, we will restrict ourselves to the *Syntonic Orality Score* (SOS) which is based on the subject's references to his own ingestion of food or beverage, in the past or in the present, and by his mentions of pleasure in such consumption. Included in this score are references to food and beverage as a remedy against discontent. Examples of statements scored for SOS are: "I feel better about these problems when I drink good coffee," (Druze) or "My relatives bring me the food, sometimes they bring that great big roast rib" (Navajo). Oral references occurring in dreams or in TAT record are not coded as SOS. Because raw SOS could be a function of interview length, which varied from respondent to respondent, it is expressed for computational purposes as a percentage of the respondent's Total Orality Score (TOS), a scale which sums *all* the respondent's references to nutriment (including those having to do with the consumption of food and drink by others).

Age and Regional Variations in the Orality Score

As a further step, the Navajo and Druze samples were divided into three matching regional subgroups: traditional-remote men (residents of conservative settlements, remote from population centers and main roads); traditional-proximal men (residents of conservative settlements, remote from population centers, but close to main roads); and secular-urban men (residents of "modern" settlements, close to population centers). The SOS mean was then computed for each Age X Region X Culture cell, and the resulting distribution is plotted in Figure 2.1. This display indicates that syntonic orality clearly increases as a function of age for both the Druze and Navajo cultures and across the three settlement types. There is a regional effect in that, for any age group, traditional remote men, whether Druze or Navajo, have the lowest SOS, while Druze and Navajo "urbanites" tend to have the highest SOS; but the age effect is clearly independent, both of culture and of settlement type within cultures.

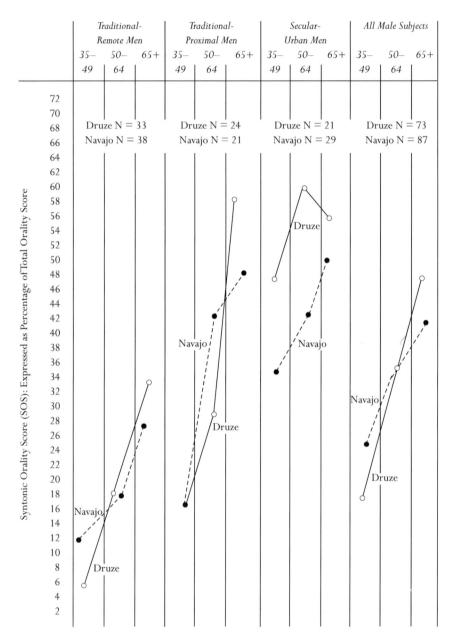

FIGURE 2.1 Comparison of Navajo and Druze Syntonic Orality Scores

The Orality Scores in Relation
to Other Personality Measures

This age effect in regard to syntonic orality was predicted from the prior find-ings concerning the age-grading of passive ego states, and thereby supports the hy-pothesis of a relationship between these variables. However, before we can use the SOS as a valid barometer of passivity, its predictive power vis à vis independent registers of this trait must also be demonstrated. Accordingly, partly in order to test the relationship between SOS and the deeper fantasies of our Navajo subjects, Krohn and Gutmann (1971) estimated the ego position—active, passive, or magi-cal—represented through the formal and content aspects of dreams reported by the most traditional men. Krohn selected a sample of those dreams in which mas-tery orientations were clearly represented through relevant imagery. Thus, active mastery dreams were typically set outdoors and, regardless of dream content, the subject played a central and organizing role in the fantasized action. In passive mas-tery dreams the subject was either absent from the dream scene, or peripheral to it: characters other than himself are the main actors, and in the dream the subject is either inert or at the mercy of arbitrary force. Dreams classified as "magical" had all the passive characteristics, though the dream events tended to be highly improba-ble; and the subject believed that the dream events were portents of specific events in his waking life. Our prediction was that men with active mastery dreams would have syntonic orality scores below the median for the traditional Navajo group; and that men with passive or magical mastery dreams would have syntonic orality scores above that median. The results of the median test, shown in Table 2.1, indicate a significant association in the predicted direction: the subject's mastery style, as portrayed in his dream, predicts fairly well his level of syntonic orality.

Along similar lines, the TAT protocols of Navajo subjects are being analyzed for the central mastery tendency represented in component stories. The hypothesis states that subjects whose syntonic orality scores lie below the median would show a majority of active mastery stories in their TAT protocols, and that subjects with a

TABLE 2.1   Distribution of Navajo Dreams: By Mastery Style and by Syntonic Orality Scores

Mastery Style of Dream	Subject's SOS below Median	Subject's SOS above Median
Active Mastery	17*	8
Passive or Magical Mastery	8	19

N = 52

*Chi-square = 7.641, D.F. = 1, p < .01

preponderance of passive and/or magical mastery stories would have syntonic orality scores above the median. Thus far, a preliminary analysis restricted to remote-traditional Navajo subjects shows a significant association between respondent's mastery type, as represented in TAT content, and his degree of syntonic orality, as shown in Table 2.2.

The Orality Scores and Navajo Drinking Patterns

Finally, many Navajo drink heavily, sometimes so much so that the addiction is noted in the medical records of the Public Health hospitals to which we had access. Again, other investigators, especially Wolowitz and Barker (1968), have noted a significant relationship in American populations between alcoholism and oral receptivity, and it was therefore proposed that a similar relationship would be discerned in the Navajo subjects as well. Accordingly, the Navajo sample was divided into three categories, whose criteria referred to various degrees of alcoholic intake. Category 1 grouped those men who reported no drinking and whose self-reports and medical records also contained no mention of drinking, nor of any injuries sustained in brawling. Category 2 grouped those men who reported that they had given up drinking (usually after a conversion to Christianity or to Peyotism) and those men whose medical records mentioned injuries sustained in fights.[6] Category 3 included all those men who admitted, usually reluctantly, to chronic drinking and those men whose medical records mentioned alcoholic psychoses, or organic syndromes caused by heavy drinking.

TABLE 2.2   Distribution of Navajo Remote Traditionals: By Projected Mastery Styles (From TAT) and by Syntonic Orality Scores

	Subject's SOS below Median	Subject's SOS above Median
Majority of respondent's TAT stories have Active Mastery theme and organization	12	5
Majority of respondent's TAT stories have Passive and/or Magical Mastery theme and organization	6	14

N = 37
p < .05 by Fisher's Exact Probabilities test

Respondents were further sorted, depending on their SOS, into the first, second, or third tercile of the Syntonic Orality Score distribution, and a chi square was calculated for the resulting SOS X Alcohol intake distribution. If we compare only the non-drinkers of all ages to the chronic drinkers of all ages, the resulting chi square is significant at the .10 level. However, Table 2.3 indicates that the SOS discriminates drinking patterns in the case of men under 70 much more sharply than it does for men 70 and over. The percentage of possible, reformed, and chronic drinkers is much lower (19 percent) in the older cohort than it is for the younger men (57 percent). This finding suggests that the older men are a particularly abstinent group—a fact which might account for their relative longevity. Nevertheless, the possibility that cultural factors specific to the over-70 group may in their case inhibit the hypothesized relationship between orality and alcoholic intake allows us to compute a chi square comparing only the younger non-drinkers to the chronic drinkers. In this case, the chi square is at the .02 level.[7]

In sum, the SOS varies with age across two disparate cultures as predicted by theory; furthermore, it varies as predicted with passive fantasy content and with the degree of drinking behavior in Navajo subjects. Accordingly, we can have some faith that this score is a valid measure of passive tendencies in personality, such as might steer overt forms of behavior. We will now investigate the hypothesis that the SOS, considered as a barometer of passivity, is related to the health status of middle-aged and elderly Navajo subjects.

TABLE 2.3 Distribution of Navajo Subjects by Drinking Patterns and by Syntonic Orality Scores

	Without Evidence of Drinking		*History of Brawling or Reformed Drinker*		*Chronic Drinker*	
SOS less than or equal to .08 (First Tercile)	Aged 35–69	18†	8		3	
		23*		9		3
	Aged 70+	5	1		0	
SOS less than or equal to .29 (Second Tercile)	Aged 35–69	9	9		9	
		20		9		9
	Aged 70+	11	0		0	
SOS equal to or above .30 (Third Tercile)	Aged 35–69	7	7		9	
		13		11		10
	Aged 70+	6	4		1	

*χ^2 (of the "without evidence" and "Chronic" cell totals) = 5.027, DF = 2, P < .10.

†χ^2 (for 35–69 years old cell totals in the "without evidence" and "Chronic" columns) = 8.358, DF = 2, P < .02.

Passivity, Orality, and Health Status: The Autonomy of the Traditional Survivor

The hypothesis that passivity, as a personality dimension, might influence the health status of Navajo subjects was based on our interviews with Navajo men aged 70 and over. Given the harsh conditions of Navajo life on the arid, remote Arizona deserts, we considered men living to this age as "survivors," whose longevity—in view of the relative absence of adequate nutrition, housing, and medical care—presumably reflected their superior physical and psychological resources. In our contacts with such men, my students and I have been impressed by the psychological and physical differences between this longevous cadre and most "normal" Navajo men in their late fifties and sixties, those not old enough to merit the classification of "survivor." These differences are most marked in regard to the passivity variable: the presurvival Navajo elder typically expresses the fantasy, cognitive, and behavioral metaphors of passive mastery, but the survivor of seventy, eighty, or even ninety years of age is, particularly in his behavior and ideology, "counter-passive." While the survivor's dreams and TAT's give evidence of passive wishes, these do not find their way into his behavior or value systems. The essential difference between these cohorts seems to reside not in the sheer degree of passive wishes, but in their management. Where the pre-survivor tends to indulge his passivity, to take it easy, and to rely on others for his security, the survivor treats such temptations as a danger signal, even as a precursor of death, and his response is to swing into action: instead of lying down he goes out to herd sheep, to plant corn, to cut wood, or to haul water.[8]

It seemed reasonable to assume that the surviving Navajo were not "normal" men who had undergone a massive character reformation towards counter-passivity after they reached age seventy. Rather, their life histories suggested that these had always been unusually vital men (by any culture's standards) whose proportion increased in the highest age brackets owing to the greater mortality rate of "normal" Navajo. Accordingly, if mortality was highest among "normal" men, those who freely expressed passive mastery, it seemed reasonable that the longevity of the survivor cohort might be related to their counter-passivity. This line of reasoning led to the hypothesis tested in this research stanza, namely, that the health status of middle-aged and elderly Navajo would be related to their management of passivity. If SOS is taken as an index of overt passivity, then low SOS should reflect a successful management of passivity and should coincide with reasonable health. By the same token, a high SOS should reflect inadequate management of passivity, and should coincide with poor health and premorbid conditions.

This hypothesis was tested in the summer of 1970, through a re-study of the panel of Navajo subjects who had first been contacted in the summer of 1966. One hundred and thirteen men of the original sample were either seen for the re-study, or friends and kin-folk of deceased informants were interviewed concerning the circumstances of death.[9] The interviews, whether with our original subjects or with their surviving kin, were focused mainly on health-related topics, with particular emphasis on the subject's health status during the four years since Time 1. Those five TAT cards which had most significantly discriminated age cohorts at Time 1 were also readministered on this occasion.

Furthermore, in all but four cases, we were able to inspect the usually detailed medical records kept by the USPHS Indian hospitals on the Navajo reservation.[10] The Navajo (as is the case with other American Indian tribes) have the use of Indian hospital services, without charge, and accordingly resort to them for minor as well as major complaints. As a result, the individual records are in most cases very detailed and cover an average span of ten years. With some help from USPHS resident physicians it was quite feasible in most cases to make a rough estimate of the subject's overall health from these records and from his self-report.

Drawing on the interview and medical data, the Navajo subjects were sorted into three major health status categories, which define a continuum from relative health to serious disease, as listed below.

Category I

This included all men whose interviews and medical records gave evidence of a continuing state of good health. That is, they were without chronic or crippling disease, and they had mainly complained, if at all, of upper respiratory and gastrointestinal infections, the latter being endemic on the reservation. In some cases there was a record of serious, acute infection, e.g., bronchopneumonia, but these maladies were quickly overcome, apparently without damaging *sequelae*, and had not recurred. Older men grouped here sometimes complained that their "health is down" but in evidence they cited only vague "aches and pains" and "tired feelings" that accompanied physical exertion but were not troubling enough to keep them from their work. In a few cases, these complaints were supported by medical evidence of mild osteoarthritis; but, in the main, the old men grouped here were not identifying a distinct syndrome but were ruefully noting the usual physical symptoms of aging. It was not the pain and fatigue that they minded so much as the loss of vigor and the attendant limitations on their mobility and productivity.

Category II

This was a residual category which grouped all men who had chronic but not fatal disease. They ranged from probable psychosomatic cripples and malingerers to men with cases of severe arthritis, glaucoma, or TB that had either been arrested or controlled. Some of these men seem to have used their illness as an excuse to quit work and get on welfare; others were clearly incapacitated by blindness or degenerative joint disease. But for all of them, illness—whether psychosomatic or organic—was either currently important, or had once been important, in their lives.

Category III

This category included two subgroups—those men who had either died from or were still enduring a major illness (e.g., congestive heart failure) contracted before Time 1; and those men who were apparently in good health at Time 1 but had since developed a potentially terminal illness (with death since Time 1 resulting in three instances). Thus, this category included all subjects whose deaths since Time 1 are clearly traceable to illness and all those who suffered from potentially terminal conditions contracted before or after Time 1.

The Covariance of SOS and Disease

The above sortings were made without prior knowledge of the individual subject's Syntonic Orality scores. These scores were computed from Time 1 data by a research assistant who had no knowledge of the individual subject's Time 2 health status. The median SOS was computed for all subjects in the Time 2 sample, the hypothesis being that subjects with SOS above the median would be found mainly in Category III. Table 2.4 shows the SOS distribution relative to the median, the three health status categories, and the subject's Time 2 age. While a highly significant association between SOS and health status obtains for subjects younger than 70, the SOS does not discriminate successfully between sickness and health for men aged 70 and over at Time 2. In sum, consistent with our prediction, the SOS shows a high degree of association with health status, though only for the "normal" pre-survivor Navajo sample.

Implications of the SOS–Health Status Relationship

The high degree of association between somatic status and a score that presumably registers the degree of psychological passivity does not allow us to assume that passivity as an independent variable precedes illness and death. For one thing, while orality may be the register of a psychic orientation, it is also a synonym for "hunger," a fairly common somatic condition. Thus, the orality of unhealthy Navajo may be only another physical symptom, the expression of somatic illness rather than the expression of some independent psychological "cause" of somatic illness.

TABLE 2.4   Median Distribution of Syntonic Orality Scores: by Health Status and by Age

				Health Status II (Moderate Chronic Illness)		*Health Status III* (Potentially Terminal Illness)	
		Health Status I (Healthy)					
SOS equal to or less than .18 (median)	Aged 35–54	10		8		2	
	Aged 55–69	12	24*	10	25	3	8
	Aged 70+	2		7		3	
SOS equal to or above .19 (median)	Aged 35–54	2		4		8	
	Aged 55–69	3	11	8	19	10	26
	Aged 70+	6		7		8	

*$\chi^2 = 15.167$ (of cell totals)
DF = 2
P < .001

However, appetite is more likely to decline with illness than be increased by it, and so the critique cited above does not really hold up. However, a more sophisticated explanation of the association between orality and illness derives from psychoanalytic theory itself, which proposes that heightened oral need can be reactive to anxiety: the anxious person turns to oral gratification as a form of comfort, as a natural tranquilizer. By this reasoning, unhealthy Navajo, frightened by the mortal implication of their illness, seek magical reassurance by reviving the passive-dependent relationships of the early, "oral" period of development, when food stood for maternal love and protection against inner and outer dangers.[11] Again, in this plausible formulation, oral passivity does not precede the onset of serious illness, but is a side-effect, and illness is the independent event.

Passivity as the Precursor of Disease: Some Relevant Findings

At this point then, we can neither finally affirm nor refute the central hypothesis of this secondary study, namely, that passive ego states, as represented by the SOS, predict to important illness. However, while severe pathology can clearly put even the most autonomous individuals in a passive and dependent frame of mind, there are scattered findings from the Navajo data which support the idea that passivity as a personality dimension contributes significantly to the occurrence of chronic, disabling, or fatal disease.

For example, regional variations in orality and in disease-proneness do support the hypothesis that passivity is prior to disease. Thus, as Table 2.5 indicates, we find that an inordinately high proportion (60 percent) of the healthiest men in our sample hail from the traditional-remote (Navajo mountain) region of the reservation, while the secular-urban sector contributes only 11 percent to that salubrious Type I population. These proportions are reversed for the significantly ill Type III group: 48 percent from the Tuba City area, and 23 percent from Navajo mountain. These striking regional differences in the distribution of significant disease are unexpected, the more so since supportive missionaries, welfare agencies, and especially medical services are much more available in Tuba City, an Indian agency center, than around the remote Navajo mountain/Rainbow Plateau region.

Furthermore, the great majority of the chronically ill Tuba City men were already established residents of their region when their disease revealed itself; they did not first become ill and then move to Tuba City in order to be close to a hospital. Accordingly, the finding that the frequency of Navajo illness increases in step with the availability of supportive agencies may be related to the special characteristics of the population which is attracted to welfare services even prior to the onset of serious disease. As an administrative, trading, and road center, Tuba City has attracted many of the most vigorous and talented Navajo on the reservation; but it has also either attracted or generated a significant number of the more passive, dispirited "Rice Christian" types. Thus, it is in this secular urban population that we are most likely to find early retirees, dependent on welfare payments, on the provident missionaries, and on their wives' rug-weaving income. They are in marked contrast to those hardy remote-living Navajo who choose to maintain personal control over the sources of their security by following the traditional life-way of the semi-migratory sheep-herder around

TABLE 2.5   Regional Representation in Navajo Health Status Categories

Regions	Type I (Healthy) (N = 35)	Type II (Moderate Chronic Illness) (N = 44)	Type III (Potentially Terminal Illness) (N = 34)
Remote-Traditional	60%	41%	23%
Outlying Areas	29%	25%	29%
Secular-Urban	11%	34%	48%

Paiute Mesa and Navajo mountain. Our impression that the more passive-dependent Navajo tend to collect around Tuba City is also borne out by the regional differences in SOS, which, as shown in Figure 2.1, are strikingly higher, for any age cohort, in the Tuba City subsample than they are for the Navajo mountain subsample.

In sum, given its special endowment of medical facilities, there are no features peculiar to the Tuba City region which can explain the special susceptibility of its adult male inhabitants to disease. And there are no obvious features of the Tuba population which might account for their special vulnerability except for the high degree of passivity found among many of its members. In their case, passive-dependency seems to be a precondition rather than a side-effect of their disease-intensive community.[12]

Let us be clear: I am not suggesting some mystical "mind over matter" causation of somatic illness; I am not suggesting that passivity is a metaphor of death or that it involves a resignation which by itself brings on disease and actual death. Such dramatic ideas are admittedly attractive to psychologists: we do want to believe that the psychic states which interest us are also the great independent variables of human existence. However, at least in regard to the Navajo, it is quite likely that passivity and disease are related in a fairly straightforward manner, *via* those behaviors which among them express the passive attitude and which are incidentally deleterious to health. Take the matter of exercise, its antecedents and consequences. We have found that counter-passive Navajo survivors force themselves, by sheer effort of will, to herd sheep or to hoe corn. Their intent is to demonstrate their continued independence, but they incidentally keep their cardiovascular systems in tune and probably extend their lives. By the same token, the more overtly passive Navajo, who sends his grandchild out to herd the sheep, may think that he is conserving his energies, but he is more likely contributing to the clogging of his arteries.

Probably most crucial is the relation between passivity, alcohol intake, and disease. Table 2.3 showed a significant relationship between SOS, considered as a measure of passive-dependency, and alcohol intake. Table 2.6 shows a strong positive relationship between organic disease and such intake: 47 percent of the Type III men drink to a significant degree, as against 23 percent of the healthy Type I men. Accordingly, if passivity indeed predisposes Navajo men to disease, the relationship is probably mediated, in a high proportion of cases, by alcohol: the passive-dependent man of high oral needs in a culture that sponsors drinking will be most likely to turn to alcohol as an anodyne against the anxiety and depression to which he is particularly prone; and this chronic reliance on alcohol could result in organic damage and heightened susceptibility to degenerative and infectious disease.

TABLE 2.6   The Relation Between Alcoholism and Health Status

	Type I (Healthy) (N = 35)	Type II (Moderate Chronic Illness) (N = 44)	Type III (Potentially Terminal Illness) (N = 34)
Percentage of Men With History of Heavy and/or Chronic Drinking	23%	29%	47%

If there are other links between passivity and disease, these are masked in the Navajo case by the high incidence of alcoholism that marks this group. If there is a relationship between passive-dependency and disease that works through agents other than alcohol, it can only be revealed through studies undertaken in societies which maintain strong cultural sanctions against drinking. The Druze are such a society, and most of our Druze subjects live by traditional religious precepts which forbid drinking. If our projected Time 2 study of the Druze reveals the same degree of association between SOS and health status that we found among the Navajo, then we can more seriously consider the possibility that there is an intrinsic relationship, species-wide in its distribution, between passive-dependency and somatic morbidity.

Notes

1. The overall program of cross-cultural studies has been supported by Career Development Award no. 5-K3-HD-6043-04, from the National Institutes of Child Health and Human Development. Field expenses for Indian studies in Mexico and in the American Southwest were covered by Faculty Research Grant nos. 1344 and 1412 from the Rackham School of Graduate Studies, the University of Michigan, and by grant no. MH 13031-01 from the National Institutes of Mental Health. Israeli Druze research was supported by grant no. M66-345 from the Foundation's Fund for Research in Psychiatry.

2. The objection has been repeatedly raised that these results represent generational rather than developmental differences. Cultures are changing, so the argument goes, and different age cohorts, within societies, have been exposed to different socializing and child rearing practices. Thus, the "mastery" types X age group distributions could represent the outcomes of different forms of nurture,

rather than positions along a developmental or "life cycle" continuum. This objection has been tested in a second field trip to the Navajo reservation, in the course of which I re-interviewed my original panel of informants, and re-administered those TAT cards which had significantly discriminated age groups at Time 1. Seventy-five Time 2 records were thus obtained, and in the majority of cases, the later profiles show the shift away from the Time 1 profile, in the passive and/or magical direction. Though the predicted shift did not show up in all cases, it is mainly important medicine men or tribal leaders who either replicate or improve on the Time 1 estimate of their mastery status. These results counter the objection that the differences in mastery style that obtain between age cohorts would reflect age group differences in child rearing, degree of acculturation, etc., rather than developmental transitions within individuals.

3. Thus Fenichel (1945, p. 491) states, "Just as the essential connection between the anal-social conflicts and anal-erotic drives have been doubted, so also have the relations between dependence and oral eroticism. But their connection is an essential one. The biological basis of all attitudes of dependence is the fact that man is a mammal, and that the human infant is born more helpless than other mammals and requires feeding and care by adults. Every human being has a dim recollection that there were once powerful or, as it must seem to him, omnipotent beings whose help, comfort and protection he must depend on in time of need. Later, the ego learns to use active means of mastering the world. But a passive-oral attitude as a residue of infancy is potentially present. Often enough, the adult person gets into situations in which he is again helpless as he was as a child; sometimes forces of nature are responsible, but more often social forces created by man. He then longs for just such omnipotent protection and comfort as were at his disposal in childhood. He regresses to orality. There are many social institutions that make use of this biologically predetermined longing. They promise the longed-for help if certain conditions are fulfilled. The conditions vary greatly in different cultures, but the formula, 'If you obey, you will be protected,' is one that all gods have in common with all earthly authorities. It is true that there are great differences between an almighty god, or a modern employer, and a mother who feeds her baby; but nevertheless it is the similarity among them that explains the psychological effectiveness of authority."

4. While Simmons and I agree on the fact of senescent orality, we disagree on the interpretation. Where I see in these developments the tracings of universal psychological laws that, for the most part, operate outside of human consciousness, Simmons explains them as a direct consequence of human awareness, in this case, the awareness of mortality. Simmons' basic position is summed up in this statement (ibid., p. 20): "A dominant interest in old age is to live long, perhaps as long as possible. Therefore, food becomes a matter of increasing concern. Its provision in suitable form, on a regular schedule, and in proper amounts depends more and more upon the efforts of those who are in a position to provide or with-

hold it. And, as life goes on, the problem of supplying and feeding the aged eventually reaches a stage at which they require the choicest morsels and tenderest care."

5. The theoretical basis of this exercise comes from western psychoanalysis; but the two cultures in which the assumptions concerning the increased orality of later life were tested are distinctly nonwestern in their cultural values and social forms. Furthermore, while the Navajo and the Druze groups are both composed of traditionally oriented agriculturists, they are also strikingly unlike each other. The Navajo are herdsmen, migratory within fixed ranges, whose small bands, largely based on kinship, are scattered across the high desert plateau of northeastern Arizona. Their world is dynamic: what are for us neutral events are for them charged with personal, often magical significance. And the Navajo character mingles opposing traits: suspicion and humor, toughness and vulnerability, pragmatism and superstition, apathy and a delight in movement. By contrast, the Galilean Druze are sedentary agriculturists, who live in organized villages. In their values and in their social forms they are similar to other Arabic speaking agriculturists of the Levant; but while they worship Allah, they have a special religion, and they are accounted heretics in Islam. They have survived 800 years of consequent persecution through cultivation of industry, courage in battle, and political sophistication. Where the Navajo character is a blend of opposites, the Druze are almost rigidly self-consistent: their character combines piety, stubbornness, a valuing of rationality over emotion, and a reserve that takes the form of extreme politeness and formality. Despite these marked cultural differences, Navajo and Druze aged have a fairly secure and valued status.

6. The logic being that the Navajo are typically restrained and pacific, except when intoxicated.

7. These findings can be contested on the grounds that respondent mentions of drinking may have elevated their SOS, thereby bringing about an artificial association between SOS and drinking pattern. This is very unlikely: even confirmed Navajo drinkers customarily refer to their own and other's drinking practice in pejorative terms, as leading to imprisonment, fighting, or serious accidents. Such statements do not meet the criteria for Syntonic Orality, and would instead be coded as "Oral Rejection." Accordingly, the SOS, while it can co-vary with overt drinking behavior, is independent of verbal reports of such behavior.

8. The tendency towards active coping as a way of resisting passive wishes in Navajo "survivors" appears to be characteristic of surviving populations in other cultures that I have studied. For example, among the Druze it is customary for older men to sign over their land to their sons, to give up physical labor, and to rely on the support provided by their sons or by the Israeli government in the form of Social Security. But the oldest, "surviving" Druze tend to be "hold-outs" against this cultural design for easing them into dependence: either they refuse to give up their land, or if they do, they continue to interfere in their son's management of it. And when these men reject Social Security payment, they draw their

rationales from the "counter-passive" morality: they refuse to be supported by tax monies that "were not given willingly."

9. Two students, Mr. Jeffrey Urist of the University of Michigan, and Miss Sally Haimo of the University of Chicago, both helped with the interviewing. Also, three members of the Navajo tribe, Mr. Harvey Bilagodi, Mr. Charles Bracker, and Mr. Max Hanley, Sr., helped us locate our subjects, performed interpreting services, and Mr. Bilagodi carried out independent interviews. Such assistance was invaluable and is gratefully acknowledged.

10. I wish to thank Dr. George Bock, Chief of the Indian Health Service of the Navajo Reservation, and Mr. Tony Lincoln, of the Navajo tribe, for granting me access to the medical records kept by USPHS Indian hospitals on our Indian subjects.

11. Should this be the case, one does not need to propose a heightened level of *appetite* in reaction to illness, but only a re-activation of orally-tinged *fantasies*, which is quite a different matter.

12. The possibility that a regression towards passive-dependency and primitive ego function precedes death has also been suggested by Lieberman (1965), who collected longitudinal psychological data from the population of an old age home. He reviewed the premorbid protocols of those subjects whose sudden deaths had not been predicted by medical personnel; comparisons with earlier data from the same subjects and equivalent data from still surviving inmates showed a drastic shift towards dependent imagery and thought processes structured along magical mastery lines in the period prior to the unexpected death.

References

1. Fenichel, O. (1945). *The Psychoanalytic Theory of Neurosis*. New York: Norton.
2. Gutmann, D. (1964). "An Exploration of Ego Configurations in Middle and Later Life." In B. Neugarten (ed.). *Personality in Middle and Later Life*. New York: Atherton.
3. Gutmann, D. (1969). "The Country of Old Men: Cross-Cultural Studies in the Psychology of Later Life." *Occasional Papers in Gerontology*. Institute of Gerontology: The University of Michigan—Wayne State University.
4. Gutmann, D. (1971). "The Hunger of Old Men: Cross-Cultural Studies of Orality in Later Life." *Trans-Action,* vol. 9, Nos. 1–2. 55–56.
5. Krohn, A., and Gutmann, D. (1971). "Changes in Mastery Style with Age: A Study of Navajo Dreams." *Psychiatry*, August 1971.
6. Lieberman, M. (1965). "Psychological Correlates of Impending Death: Some Preliminary Observations." *Journal of Gerontology,* vol. 20, No. 2.
7. Lieberman, M., and Coplan, A. (1969). "Distance from Death as a Variable in the Study of Aging." *Developmental Psychology,* vol. 2, No. 1.

8. Neugarten, B., and Gutmann, D. (1958). "Age-Sex Roles and Personality in Middle Age: A Thematic Apperception Study." *Psychological Monographs,* No. 470.
9. Simmons, L. (1945). *The Role of the Aged in Primitive Society.* New Haven: Yale University Press.
10. Wolowitz, H., and Barker, M. (1968). "Alcoholism and Oral Passivity." *Quarterly Journal of Studies on Alcohol,* vol. 29, No. 3.

3   A Comparative Study
of Ego Functioning
in Geriatric Patients

I include this early clinical paper for two reasons. First, though it is a personal favorite, it has never to my knowledge been cited in the gerontological literature. So this is payback: I will resurrect the scorned work. *The second reason has to do with methods in geropsychological research, rather than my personal* meshugas. *I was an apprentice field worker when I wrote this and had recently learned, from my work among the Highland Maya, that "standard" interview instruments and protocols developed what I came to think of as "bureaucratic" data: conventional, predictable, and insensitive to individual differences. Such "consensus" data is useful to sociologists but not to psychodynamic psychologists.*

It had been brought home to me that rapport—*the truly "standard" interviewing situation—was arrived at in each case via nonstandard approaches, the kinds that were responsive to the concerns and suspicions of naive informants. You have achieved rapport when the subject* wants *to talk to you about matters that are personally important to him and genuinely interesting to you, the interviewer. Standard instruments standardly administered do not activate that crucial process—they block it.*

I applied this thinking to the project outlined in the paper that follows. The goal of our research team was to study the effects of a "total push" program on elderly chronic schizophrenics, long-term patients of Ypsilanti State Hospital. It occurred to me that such effects should be studied naturalistically, through approaches that stayed close to the patients' experience of their enclosed world. Our approach was straightforward: We told each subject that we wanted to learn about their unit and asked for a personal tour. The hypothesis was that the "total push" patients would show us a richer, more complex domain than the custodial care control patients.

As reported here, the hypothesis was borne out, and the "grounded" method was—for me, at least—vindicated. The experimental patients did turn out, as predicted, to be truly activated: They proved to be involved and relatively knowledgeable guides to their world. I doubt that a standard instrument, designed to produce the usual "ego function" rating would have engaged our subjects to the same degree or delivered such convincing results.

So, Dr. Science, score this one for qualitative research.

The emphasis in the social sciences on method and on rigorous testing of *a priori* theories has led to a proliferation of instruments, measures, and indexes, all of which generate the kinds of data to which they were originally calibrated. These approaches give the illusion of purity and certainty, but exact the price of passivity. In some sense, both the investigator and the subject become extensions of the instrument, which also operates as a barrier between them. Furthermore, surprise is ruled out: coerced nature can only say yes or no to *a priori*, theoretically based questions; it cannot suggest a new, unpredicted possibility. But there is something of a naturalistic revolution taking place in the social sciences. Investigators are beginning to sense that risk and methodological vulnerability may be the price of discovery and they are moving out into open situations, wherein they will have to deal wisely, given minimal prior guidance, with events that they have not predicted. As part of this revolution, investigators are remembering that their business is not only to explain the variance in already existing data, but to generate new data, out of events that had no prior cognitive status. And investigators are also, in various ways, asking their subjects to define the variables in terms of which these subjects can be studied and understood.

It was in this spirit that the authors, working under the auspices of the Institute of Gerontology, University of Michigan, began a study of ego functions among geriatric mental patients in an experimental program at Ypsilanti State Hospital. The authors thought of the ego as that persistent system of psychic structures that processes experience, that seeks out or creates optimal experiences, that assesses the meaning of experience from a variety of personal and impersonal perspectives, that coordinates energy judgment and action, and that maintains the boundary between self and other. The authors were interested in the differences in ego functions, so construed, between patients on an experimental and a custodial ward. The hypothesis was that patients on the Institute's high-staff, paid employment, community-oriented, experimental wards would demonstrate more highly developed ego-executive capacities than patients matched as to age, intelligence, and length of hospitalization, resident on the Institute's more custodially oriented control wards.

All patients in the community-oriented ward had originally resided for long periods in custodial settings. But once they were selected for the community-oriented ward, they were exposed to programs grossly different from those that they had previously known. On the experimental wards, there was a high ratio of staff to patients; activities were scheduled throughout the day; and patient participation was expected and strongly encouraged. Patients spent 5 to 6 hours a day assembling small parts for outside contractors and they were paid at an hourly rate. Much stress was put on personal grooming, and for the first time in their hospital career, men and women shared the same ward space.

On the custodial ward, the staff-to-patient ratio was low and typical of the hospital as a whole. The activities program was minimal, and while the patients did some of the routine work of the ward and the hospital, their work had no extramural, community referent, and was not recompensed. In sum, for the control population, hospital life was relatively unchanged, except that these subjects now—like the experimental patients—shared the same ward space with the opposite sex.

In comparing patients exposed to these two conditions, the authors decided not to use some already validated instrument that would produce a score or an index that presumably registered ego functioning. When such tests are used, the ego is treated as though it were passive, other-directed; the assumption is that the ego will give priority to any task that is set for it and that it will bring to bear on that task a full battery of adaptive resources.

The contention of this paper, derived from recent thinking in ego psychology, is that the ego is not passive; that the ego tries to master problems that it has created for itself, or that have been made relevant to it by over-riding necessity. Accordingly, adaptive ego functioning is best studied naturalistically, that is, in relation to those milieux that subjects have chosen to deal with, or feel that they must deal with. *A priori,* pre-coded tests may or may not be relevant to research subjects; they may or may not mesh with their ego priorities. But the subject's psychosocial ecology is always relevant to him; and when the subject is observed in relation to his psychosocial "habitat," and when the regularities in that relationship are noted, then accurate inferences, concerning the adaptive program of the subject's ego, can be made.

As a first and most important step, it is necessary to determine, with the subject's help, his most relevant psychosocial ecologies. The study of the subject's adaptive ego functions can only begin after this preliminary work has been completed. But in the case of the long-term hospitalized patient, this initial mapping task is much simplified. It is safe to assume that the ward and hospital setting to which the chronic patient is confined comprises at least the present context of his ego: the ward has shaped him, the requirements of people like himself have to some degree shaped the ward, and in many cases the patient finds the setting congenial and has made at least an implicit decision to remain there. State hospital and ward environments are relatively impersonal and functional. They are not congenial settings for long-term residence. Yet patients do adapt to them, and in many cases come to value them over more open, community settings. Furthermore, whatever their drawbacks for the patient, the closed residential ward provides an ideal opportunity for the naturalistic investigator: it is precisely in these clearly boundaried, describable and controllable milieux that the adaptive design of the patient's ego can be most clearly observed.

Using the Patient as
a Guide to His World

With these considerations in mind, a naturalistic approach, based on the similarity in physical layout across experimental and control wards, was pretested with both sets of patients. Subjects were told that the investigators were interested in the different ways that people thought about the ward and about hospital life in general. Patients were then asked to tour the investigator around the ward, starting at any point of their choice. At each room or location that the patient pointed out, he was asked a series of questions: "Tell me about this room" (or place); "What kinds of things occur here?"; "Do people come here? For what reason?"; "Do *you* ever come here, and for what reason?"; "When you are here, what happens then?" Subjects were also asked to point out their best and least liked locations, and their reasons for these preferences.

In the course of the tour, a *verbatim* account was kept of questions, responses, and incidental comments. The interviewer also kept track of the sequence of the tour—the order in which rooms and locations were visited. During the tour, the interviewer tried to remain sensitive to the patient's covert reactions—fearful, suspicious, or angry—to the procedures. These reactions were identified and discussed whenever possible, so that they would not inhibit or distort the patient's report of his environment, as he normally saw it. At the end of the tour, subjects were asked to describe a typical and an atypical day, including the kinds of events that they looked forward to, the kinds of events that they dreaded, and the kinds of remedies, if any, that were available to them for dealing with the troubling circumstances that they named. Subjects were also asked to comment about their feelings as to the mixing of sexes on the ward.

Pre-testing indicated that the tour and the associated schedule of questions was generating data that discriminated subjects and that appeared to be codable in terms of ego variables. Accordingly, a sample of 20 men and 20 women was selected, half from the high-staff, community-oriented experimental ward, half from the custodial ward, with equal numbers of men and women. Subjects were in the age range 55 to 69, without chronic brain syndrome, and with at least 4 years of prior hospitalization. The usual diagnosis was "chronic, undifferentiated schizophrenia." Despite this pessimistic diagnosis, all subjects, experimental and control, had achieved scores of 12 or better on an orientation index whose top score was 14. It should be noted that the physical layouts of the experimental and custodial wards were identical, although some experimental ward space had been converted to workshops and storage rooms, functions which did not exist on the custodial ward.

Similar Spaces, but Different Worlds

Analysis of the data tended to confirm our predictions of inter-ward differences in ego functioning; and though some results are equivocal, in no case have the predictions been grossly refuted.

For example, when we consider the interward differences in the ego variable of complexity, we find that the experimental subjects spontaneously toured three times as many rooms as did the controls. This is a highly significant difference ($p<.01$). If we subtract from the experimental patients' totals all those work and storage areas that were not replicated on the control ward and that were given special prominence on the experimental ward, the experimental patients still toured, on the average, 11.6 rooms, while the custodial patients toured only 5.2 rooms, or less than half of the experimentals' mean ($p<.01$).

Moreover, there is a much greater spread in the room preferences of the experimental patients, and 10% of their "favorite room" choices involved interface rooms. That is, they tended to favor those rooms (such as the visiting room, or the porches) where, realistically or symbolically, the outer world meshed with the hospital world. By contrast, the controls had only two choices: the dayroom, where they watched TV or sat; and the dorms that they slept in.

To a significantly greater degree, the tour guided by the experimental subjects had a logic and an order that reflected either some principle, or, more usually, the physical layout of the ward. In 85% of the cases they either moved sequentially, from room to room, or they went beyond this concrete, spatial organization and organized the tour according to some more abstract but communicable principle: they might, for example, visit work areas, then recreation areas, then dormitory areas and so forth, even when the rooms involved in these functions were separated from each other by intervening spaces. But 50% of the custodial patients moved erratically through their environment, starting out for one room, only to lose sight of their purpose and enter the one that they happened to be passing. Compared to the more innerly directed experimental patients, the subjects from the custodial wards were like particles in Brownian motion, given temporary direction by their immediate field.

Every discrete description of a room, of the ward, or of the hospital as a whole was coded independently in terms of its concrete personal or abstract-functional qualities. Personal descriptions were those in which the patient described the room, ward or hospital in ways that related to his or her own needs or concerns: "Over there is where I like to sit at mealtime . . ." Abstract-functional descriptions were those in which a room or space was described in terms of its function relative to other ward functions, and to the needs of the patient population as a whole:

"This is the room where food is prepared for both dining rooms," or "this is the day room where people can sit when they're not working . . ." By contrast to the personal-concrete descriptions, the functional descriptions presumably reflect various components of ego strength: some capacity for objectivity, some capacity to maintain self-other distinctions, and some capacity to make real that which is not immediately pertinent to the self. It was found that the experimental subjects gave a total of 871 codable descriptions, of which 752 (86%) fell in the functional-abstract category. The control subjects gave a total of 453 codable descriptions—only 52% of the experimental group's total—and only 334 (75%) of their descriptions fell into the functional-abstract category. The group difference in these terms is significant at the .001 level.

In sum, despite similarities in physical layout, the control and experimental groups experience their milieu quite differently. Looked at from the perspective of ego psychology, these intergroup differences in the perception and experience of the ward ecology point to differences in ego functioning between the experimental and control cohorts. The experimental patients, by contrast to the custodial patients, had more highly developed secondary process ego functions: they looked out on a richer, more differentiated world; they organized their experience in that world from more abstract, impersonal perspectives; to a greater degree they recognized and related themselves to an extramural world beyond their immediate ken; and they had some insight into the workings of systems extrinsic to themselves. Clearly then, the experimental patients showed a greater capacity to keep their subjective reactions from grossly interfering with their objective judgments. In addition, their intrapersonal and interpersonal boundaries, pivotal to the secondary processes of the ego, were more intact than was the case with the custodial patients.

Results generated by questions concerning daily events, expected events, dreaded events, and versions of possible remedy were less strong statistically but tended to bear out the impressions already developed by the tour. The experimental patients mentioned more daily activities (experimental mean = 12.9; control mean = 8.45, p<.05) and more different types of activities (p<.10). Though these differences were not statistically significant, experimental patients were more likely to mention self-maintaining activities—brushing teeth, making one's bed, etc.—than the controls (experimentals = 25%; controls = 15%). There was also a slightly greater tendency in the experimental group to mention work that had a collective, or ward-maintaining purpose (experimentals = 90%; controls = 80%). Controls were more likely to mention passive-receptive activities, such as eating (controls = 45%; experimentals = 30%) and rest (controls = 30%; experimentals = 15%), as they reviewed their typical day.

Since they reflect the built-in differences in the pace and variety of life on the experimental and control wards, the differences cited above should not surprise us. However, important differences are still revealed by questions which bear on fantasies and expectations, rather than contrasting ward realities. Thus, when asked to visualize a desirable but unlikely event—"suppose you could do whatever you liked for a day"—the custodial controls continued to emphasize passive pursuits—eating, sleeping, watching TV—while the experimental subjects spoke of more active, extramural visits and explorations (experimentals = 55% active choices; controls = 15% active choices).

Important psychological differences, having little obvious relation to the interward differences, were also elicited by questions concerning feared events. Both groups, experimentals and controls, tended to fear illness more than any other trauma, but the custodial patients mainly dreaded the onset of impersonal somatic symptoms (controls = 45%; experimentals = 16%, $p<.05$), while the experimental patients were equally concerned about disruptive inner feelings and their own psychotic ideation (experimentals = 16%; controls = 0%). In effect, the experimental subjects tended to recognize their inner life; and they tended to make distinctions between pleasant and unpleasant, appropriate and inappropriate events in their own subjective domain. By contrast, the custodial patients showed little sense of an inner life and tend to experience it, if at all, in some externalized, somaticized form.

Just as they tended to report a more personal source of trouble—and by the same token a greater sense of personal responsibility—the experimental subjects also reported distinctive ways of dealing with their complaints. Thus, experimental patients were more likely to report using active, motoric remedies for their troubles—"I take a walk around the grounds" . . . "I do some laundry"—than were controls (experimentals = 50%; controls = 18%). To a much greater degree, controls favored passive resignation, or avoidance, as coping strategies (controls = 59%; experimentals = 18%, $p<.05$).

The experimental patients also suggested their superior tolerance for complexity in that, to a somewhat greater degree than custodial patients, they liked or at least tolerated the mixed ward arrangement (experimentals, favorable or tolerant = 75%; controls, favorable or tolerant = 45%, $p<.20$). In justifying their positive attitudes the experimental patients generally asserted that the mixed ward arrangement was more like normal life in the community (experimentals = 60%; controls = 25%, $p<.02$), thereby revealing again their greater extramural orientation.

Ego-Enrichment: A Side-Effect of "Total Push"?

In sum, it appears that the experimental setting had sponsored some development of individuality and of ego-executive capacities beyond those specifically indoctrinated by the ward staff or required by the experimental program. These extrinsic pressures might explain the readiness to tour more rooms, to list more daily activities, and to be more conscious of grooming. But these same extrinsic pressures do not account for the generally more systematic and abstract depiction of the self and of the world, the *appetite* for complexity, and the multi-levelled involvement with community perspectives, on the part of the experimental patients. These are modalities which pervade their thinking, wherever we tap it, even around areas and concerns that the experimental program had not formally or informally sponsored.

Thus, highly staffed intensive programs for the mentally ill, even the aged, chronic mentally ill, which push for limited and specific gains, may incidentally energize, or re-energize a more total process of ego maturation in the direction of adequate functioning. The test is whether these emergent ego functions and structures can remain as resources for the patient once he is removed from the institutional milieu which was his developmental context.

These results also suggest the value, particularly when dealing with schizophrenic subjects, of approaches which make data out of the subject's reactions to concrete ecologies that have priority for him, and at times when he has voluntarily entered into these situations. It is then that the adaptive ego functions—however minimal their contribution—can best be identified.

4 Alternatives to Disengagement: Aging Among the Highland Druze

When I wrote this piece, following field work among the Galilean and Golan Druze, I was just graduating from the naturalistic, butterfly-counting research phase and was allowing myself the luxury of speculation and model-building. The sojourn among the Druze certainly sparked this development. They are a unique and admirable people, and I was introduced to them by Allah's gift to ethno-geropsychology: Kassem Yussuf Kassem, of the mixed Christian-Druze village of Rami (Western Galilee). The oldest son of a leading Galilean Druze family, Kassem had been trained as a psychiatric social worker at Case Western Reserve, and—following the Israeli Six-Day War—he was temporarily at leisure. With him "Koshering" me, all Druze homes of the Galilee and Golan Heights were automatically opened to us. But he was a double agent: Even as he translated my questions and the respondent's answers, he would sotto voce explain what really lay behind the formal language favored by Druze respondents, as well as the cultural background of the respondent's revelations. Needless to say, I was not about to stuff what I had learned from Kassem and our subjects into the usual research accountancy designs.

The Druze material did link up with the growing database from other cultures. Thus, like elders from other sites, the orality of our elderly Druze subjects bloomed on schedule, but they did not become overtly dependent. Instead, among this unique people, the orality of later life contributed to psychological and social development in the third age. Psychodynamic theorists might object to this equation of late-onset orality with late-blooming psychological development. In their camp, oral wishes, particularly when prominent in adults, are regarded as infantile, a clear sign of regression. As they see it, when the aged fall back on the infantile comforts of the mouth, they are moved not by the forces of growth but by potent anxieties, including the fear of death.

These critics do have a point: In clinical populations, fixations at the oral level of development are commonly associated with various addictions and character disorders. In our Older Adult service we have also treated senior men who bring established dependency and character disorders to our clinic, and we do find that their already tenuous adjustment has been compromised by the added burden of late-onset oral regression. But the clinical model of fixation is not appropriate to the phenomenon that we have documented, namely, the emergence of oral modalities in psychologically mature adults, with a substantial history of love and work. New energies, developmental in origin, are like fire: Depending on who uses it and under what circumstances, fire can cook your meal or burn your house. Thus, their own emerging psychic potentials can be toxic to vulnerable adolescents and bring on severe pathology, but the same potentials can, in the case of healthy teenagers, nurture new executive capacities of the personality. The "oral" potentials of later life are equally bivalent: In clinical populations they can sponsor addictions, depressions, and psychosomatic disorder, but in veteran adults they can bring about a new and largely unrecognized expansion of the self.

Consider then the Druze. Among them, the emerging appetite for groceries is not recruited to the service of passive disengagement but instead powers a developmental advance. The traditional Druze Aqil does not burden his wife, daughters, or nurses with his oral neediness, and his religion forbids drink and gluttony. Instead, under the seemly protocol of the hilweh, *the prayer house, he brings his dependency to Allah. The Druze elder becomes God's petitioner, not only for himself but also for his multigenerational clan, village, and people. His own burgeoning oral needs for comfort and security may urge him to the house of worship, but the prayers that he intones in that holy place form the link to God required by the Druze people as a whole. Thus, though fueled by "infantile" needs, the Druze Aqil find a new basis for union with their God and for high prestige among their people. Powered in part by emerging oral appetites, late life development has clearly taken place.*

I originally chose the Druze for study in order to test a standard criticism of my work— not of my findings per se *but of the developmental interpretation that I had put on them. My critics argued that the shift by older men towards passive and magical mastery could be explained by their bleak social, physical, and economic circumstances and not by some autonomous developmental dynamic. "Of course old men are passive and given to unrealistic thinking," they argue. "It is their natural response to their low postretirement status and society's ageism."*

My Druze studies do, I believe, answer that criticism from the "victim theorists": Druze men gain rather than lose social status as they age, and yet they share with less fortunate elders the postparental shift towards oral and passive modalities. True, in their case, the passive personality tendencies provide a platform for the Aqil's special version of social status and social activism, but the underlying tendencies themselves appear on time with a universal schedule, shared with people that the Druze never heard of. The late-rising oral tendencies of the Druze are clearly not driven by a need to compensate for social losses.

This study of Druze gerontocracy helped me understand the nature of male leadership and its regular though paradoxical association with advanced age. More important, I learned that—contrary to the claims of Cumming and Henry (1961)—disengagement is not the natural condition of the elder but an aberration brought on by the secular nature of advanced societies.Where there is a traditional consensus alive among the people, the elders will be its spokesmen and its living face; they do not disengage. Instead, they sponsor, in special ways, the social engagement of the younger adults.

This paper reports some recent results, based on data from the middle aged and older men of the Druze sect resident in highland villages of the Golan, Galilee, and Carmel regions of Syria and Israel. The overall aim of the research of which this study is a part has been to establish, through application of the comparative method, some basis for a developmental psychology of aging. The guiding hypothesis of this research program was originally developed from findings in an urban United States sample. Briefly stated, it holds that important psychological orientations, based around passivity and aggressivity, dependency and autonomy would discriminate age groups within culturally homogeneous societies—in effect, that these orientations would distribute more reliably by age than by culture. Accordingly, it was proposed that younger men across cultures would reveal motives, attitudes, and images characteristic of an active, production centered, and competitive stance, while older men were expected to show the converse pattern. They would give priority to community over agency, to receptivity over productivity, to mildness and humility over competition.

So far, the hypothesis has been borne out, by both cross-sectional and longitudinal data from the United States, Mexican, and Middle Eastern study sites (see Gutmann, 1969). Thus, despite profound cultural differences in our samples, age accounts for a greater part of the variance in the personality measures than does the variable of culture; and this independent age effect points to the contribution of intrinsic, or developmental influences in the psychology of aging men.

Nature and Nurture:
Their Impact in Later Life

But the finding of intrinsic age related influences does not rule out the importance of socio-cultural influences in the psychic life. Men who are partly shaped by intrinsic processes must still find the setting for their development in socially organized worlds; and they are continually influenced by the age norms set by society over their behaviors and attitudes. Covert, universal influences do not make men *less* sensitive to overt social influences, but only direct that sensitivity to particular sectors of the available social norms, usages, and understandings. Thus, younger men might recognize the existence of a religious tradition in their society, and be knowledgeable about its precepts, but their subjective relation to that tradition would differ from their fathers'. The younger men could report—as anthropological informants, for example—on the rules of the religious tradition, but they would not always refer to them for regulation of their behavior. By the same token, the aging fathers of these young men would know a good deal about the social usages that governed the productive life in their society, but would find them less personally relevant than those which organized the religious life, and the relationship to God. Thus, owing to the influence of emerging developmental dispositions, older men would give personal reality to social norms and conventions which had far less impact for them when they were younger.

The nature versus nurture issue is perhaps the central question in the behavioral sciences, and cannot be put to rest by a single study. Nevertheless, the case of the Highland Druze of the Middle East suggests an integrating model: it suggests the ways in which age-graded role requirements and developmental potentials can coexist, as reciprocals and metaphors of each other, in the traditional community. This discussion begins with a necessarily brief description of Druze history, culture, and modal personality.

The Highland Druze: The People

The villages of the Druze, sited on hill-tops for purposes of defense, are scattered through the highland regions of Lebanon, Syria, and Galilean Israel. The Druze people are mainly agriculturists involved in the cultivation of fruits, olives, wheat, and tobacco. However, throughout their history, individual Druze have been prominent in the political and particularly in the military affairs of the Middle East. The Druze are a people who chose a minority status, on religious grounds, within the larger Arab world. They speak Arabic, and their life style is in most respects similar to that of the patriarchal Muslim villagers of the Levant. However, the Druze broke with the Muslim religion on doctrinal points, and thereby let themselves in for the difficulties that go with self-elected heretical status. Over the past 800 years the Druze have suffered many episodes of religious persecution at the hands of the Muslim majority; and they have managed to develop the personal and cultural traits that generally characterize a minority that survives in the face of odds. Since they could not take the goodwill of the majority for granted, they have learned as a group to mainly trust themselves—the courage, strength, and wit of the Druze people. Each individual Druze tends to reproduce in his personality the general stance of the culture. Thus, individual Druze are fiercely self-reliant, and will only allow themselves to depend on their own strengths, or on resources that they themselves have cultivated—the produce of their fields, or the strength of their sons. In effect, they trust very little that comes from outside of themselves as gift or gratuity, and this mistrust of that which is not under self-control extends even to their mental life. Thus, the Druze are extremely stubborn and refractory as individuals, not only against coercion from other's will, but against coercion from their own willfulness, their own spontaneous emotions. They do not allow themselves to become excited; even illiterate Druze peasants give priority to rationality over emotionality. In effect, they value the mental resource that they have created for themselves over the raw emotions that have been "foisted" on them. As part of their self-reliance, they must deny any needfulness, and must hold themselves in the position of the giver, rather than the receiver. Thus, they are unfailingly and sometimes even aggressively hospitable. The harshest Druze insult is to call another man a "hotel-keeper," implying that he charges his guests for his hospitality.

A major political problem for the Druze is the coordination of their own community life, centered as it is around their religion, with the requirements and demands of the non-Druze majority, which has frequently been hostile to their faith. Over the centuries they have learned to blend flexibility and accommodation with firmness and traditional rigidity. In effect, they change and compromise in minor ways which do not touch on the core of their religious tradition, in order to maintain that same core inviolate and unchanged. Thus, they typically raise their sons to be career soldiers and policemen for the majority government—in effect, they trade their sons for political security—and they are usually meticulously loyal to the letter of the secular law. But they will not tolerate any violation, by the non-Druze majority, of the core of their religion or their tradition. They will not for example tolerate any attack on the honor of their women or of their priests. If compliance does not succeed in staving off dishonor and sacrilege, then the Druze will, almost to the last man, go to war. Though their villages have always been scattered over different countries, the Druze say of themselves that they are like a large brass plate: "strike one corner, then the whole will vibrate." True to this motto, the Druze led the post–World War I revolution against the French which gave rise to the establishment of modern Syria. They are famous throughout the Middle East for their ardor in battle.

Druze Age Roles

Since the Druze people form a religious sect, their religion is central to the workings of their society and to the sense of Druze identity. Yet it is kept a secret, not only from the outside world, but also from the younger people of the community. Thus, the schedules which govern admission to the inner circles of the Druze religion also determine the age-grade systems, the social norms and the shared understandings which partially govern the latter half of the life cycle for the typical Druze male. The Druze have learned to treat their heretic religion as a kind of conspiracy within the body of Islam; therefore, the younger Druze—who might rashly reveal their identity to non-Druze neighbors—are not instructed in the religion or even told that they are Druze until they reach the age of discretion. This tradition, of keeping the religion secret from the younger members of the community, has survived even until these more liberal times. Thus, younger Druze men, those not yet initiated to the secret books, are known as *Jahil*, the "unknowing" ones. The older men, those who have been accepted into the religious society and who have received their copy of the secret text, are known as *Aqil,* literally, those who "know." In the more traditional villages some men might become *Aqil* in early middle age, after they have established their family of procreation; and there are even a few *Aqil* youths, seminary-trained sons of famous religious leaders. But for the most part, men are not invited to become *Aqil* until late middle age, after they have led an exemplary life.

As noted earlier, Druze men of any age are generally formal and punctilious, but this manner is intensified after a man becomes *Aqil*. He shaves his head, he adopts special garb, and there is a notable behavior shift toward even greater propriety. Furthermore, he gives up alcohol and tobacco, he devotes much time to prayers, and he is expected to appear at all important social functions. Even the inner life of the *Aqil* is regulated: he is expected to devote himself to good and pious thoughts and to forget his prior errors and stupidities, before he was introduced to true knowledge. It is therefore very difficult to interview an old *Aqil* concerning his childhood experiences. He becomes remote or evasive and at times angry: "Why do you ask me about the time when I was ignorant, before I became close to God? I was like an animal then, I did not think of God, and it is a shame to remember such things!"

In sum, the old *Aqil* purge themselves, consciously at least, of the appetites—and even the memories of the appetites—which do not fit the prescriptions of the religious life. As the typical Druze man passes into late middle life and old age he appears to shunt into the behavioral and attitudinal tracks that have been prepared for him by the age-grade systems of Druze society. His life appears to be almost completely governed by parochial requirements of the sort that have meaning only to the religious Druze.

Universal Trends in Druze Aging

However, the projective data from these same Druze men suggests that their inner, subjective life changes in later years in accord with universal developments as well as with extrinsic, parochial constraints. These data indicate a pattern of psychological changes that is in conformity with those observed in their age peers from radically different cultures, where older men do not necessarily enter a rigorous religious subculture. The comparative analysis of the Druze projective materials, between age cohorts and across cultures, supports the hypothesis of universal psychological patterns in aging, developments which are mandatory regardless of the requirements set by particular cultures.

Thus, if we inspect Table 4.1 and compare the age X theme distribution of Galilean and Golan Druze responses to the rope climber card of the TAT—a card used in its original form at all sites—we find that this distribution replicates that developed by the same card among the younger and older men of the Mayan (both Highland and Lowland), the Navajo, and the United States cultures.

Equivalent age differences in the distribution of Active, Passive, and Magical perceptions are developed by the heterosexual-conflict card of the standard TAT. The card depicts a young woman reaching towards a young man who is turned away from her. Again, as with the rope climber card, younger men locate energy and assertion within the figure, older men locate it in the environment, and the oldest men overlook or deny it altogether. (See Table 4.2.)

The transcultural age trends elicited by the rope-climber and heterosexual conflict cards hold for the majority of TAT cards used at all sites. However, despite the relative thematic unanimity among age-peers of different societies, the criticism has been raised that such age differences in card interpretation reflect cohort differences between generations, rather than intra-individual, developmental shifts. However, longitudinal studies undertaken with both Navajo and Druze subjects indicate that variations over five year intervals in card perceptions *within* individuals replicate those already found between age cohorts in both these societies. Thus, when we contrast the time 1 and time 2 perceptions of the same individuals to the same cards (see Tables 4.3 and 4.4) we find the predicted appearance of more passive or magical imagery at time 2 in a significant percentage of all subjects. Navajo or Druze men who saw the rope climber as moving vigorously for some productive purpose at time 1 may see him clinging anxiously to that same rope at time 2, or as fleeing from some wild beast. By the same token, subjects who saw the young man of the heterosexual-conflict card in some active role at time 1 have in many cases by time 2 come to see him as more subdued, as dominated by his wife, or as gravely ill. Clearly, the statistically significant age differences that we have been picking up

70

TABLE 4.1   Distribution of Responses to the Rope Climber Card, by Age, Culture, and Theme

		35–49	50–59	60+
1. The climber demonstrates his strength, often in the face of competition. However, triumph has its price: the rope may break at the moment of victory.	Kansas City	21	35	10
	Navajo	5	1	6
	Lowland Maya	3 } 42*	2 } 43	2 } 25
	Highland Maya	2	0	1
	Druze	11	5	6
2. The climber acts in the service of relatively limited but productive goals: he searches for a short-cut, for food, or for herds. He trains for future competition. If he is thwarted, it is by the physical environment, and not by other men, or by his own weakness.	Kansas City	4	13	7
	Navajo	6	7	10
	Lowland Maya	9 } 43	2 } 42	2 } 43
	Highland Maya	3	1	1
	Druze	21	19	23
3. The climber indulges his physical weakness, or his wish for pleasure: he rests, he enjoys the view, he dives into water, he plays on the rope.	Kansas City	2	3	7
	Navajo	3	4	12
	Lowland Maya	3 } 13	5 } 20	14 } 41
	Highland Maya	4	7	7
	Druze	1	1	1
4. The climber is menaced by external forces, or by his own weakness: he flees from enemy, beast, or fire; he is too tired to climb, and clings to the rope; he is on a rope, but not in motion.	Kansas City	4	18	17
	Navajo	4	5	16
	Lowland Maya	3 } 24	6 } 35	8 } 59
	Highland Maya	5	2	6
	Druze	8	4	12
5. Either the rope or the climber is grossly misperceived: the climber is lying down, or dead; the rope is a snake, etc.	Kansas City	—	—	2
	Navajo	—	—	3
	Lowland Maya	— } 3	1 } 2	2 } 22
	Highland Maya	1	1	1
	Druze	2	—	14
		125	142	190

Kansas City   N = 143   Highland Maya N = 42
Navajo   N = 82   Druze**   N = 128
Lowland Maya   N = 62   Total   N = 457
*Chi Square (of cell totals) = 48.712
DF = 8, P < .001
**Druze Group includes Golan, (Syrian) Galilean, and Carmel (Israeli) subjects.

TABLE 4.2   The Heterosexual-Conflict Card: Distribution of Stories by Age, Culture, and Theme

		35–49	50–59	60+
1. Male initiative and dominance: Young man's intrinsic sex, aggression, and autonomy needs constitute a problem for a gentle, nurturant young woman, and potential danger for himself.	Kansas City Navajo Lowland Maya Highland Maya Druze	21 9 4 } 56* 2 20	12 7 1 } 33 — 13	10 9 2 } 28 — 7
2. Domestic problems: Problem centered around young man's aggression; but direction, scope, nature of cause, or outcome of this aggression is unclear.	Kansas City Navajo Lowland Maya Highland Maya Druze	1 4 7 } 20 — 8	3 4 5 } 22 2 8	— 4 7 } 20 1 8
3. Female initiatives and dominance: Young man's anger is reactive to young woman's rejection of him, or dominance over him.	Kansas City Navajo Lowland Maya Highland Maya Druze	6 — — } 14 3 5	5 3 — } 13 1 4	6 9 2 } 27 2 8
4. Rationalized male succorance: Menaced by external forces, or defeated in his outer-world achievement strivings, the young man looks for or accepts female nurturance and control.	Kansas City Navajo Lowland Maya Highland Maya Druze	— — — } 19 1 18	1 1 1 } 8 — 5	4 12 2 } 42 2 22
5. Untroubled Affiliation (or Syntonic Dependency): mild, untroubled affiliation between relatively undifferentiated young man and woman.	Kansas City Navajo Lowland Maya Highland Maya Druze	— 1 3 } 23 8 11	— 6 7 } 25 3 9	— 6 12 } 53 3 32
	N =	132	101	170

Kansas City	N = 69	Highland Maya	N = 28
Navajo	N = 75	Druze**	N = 178
Lowland Maya	N = 53	Total	N = 403

* Chi Square (of cell totals) = 42.165, DF = 8, p < .001
**Druze group includes Golan, (Syrian) Galilean, and Carmel (Israeli) Druze.

TABLE 4.3   Longitudinal Changes in TAT Imagery of Navajo and Druze Subjects, Elicited by the Rope Climber Card

	No. of passive images discarded in favor of more active imagery after Time 1*			No. of passive images appearing only at Time 2		
	Navajo	Druze	total	Navajo	Druze	total
Climber's activity is discredited; he does some evil or crazy thing	2	2	4	6	3	9
Climber descends on the rope	8	1	9	13	3	16
Climber flees from beast, fire, flood, or enemy	1	1	2	9	4	13
Tired climber, unable to ascend, clutches the rope	2	1	3	3	4	7
Menaced by external threats, or by his own weariness, the climber looks for help	3	2	5	6	4	10
The climber is dead, sick, or crippled	—	1	1	4	—	4
The climber seeks pleasure: he looks at pleasant scenes, or plays on the rope	4	1	5	7	4	11
	Total no. of passive images discarded by Time 2 29			Total no. of new passive images by Time 2 . . . .70**		

*Time 1–Time 2 interval is four years in the Navajo case, and five years in the Druze case. The Galilean and Carmel Druze, but not the Golan Druze, were re-interviewed for the Time 2 study.

**Note:* These are not independent entries: A single story may be entered under more than one heading.

across cultures appear to be the artifacts of developmental change in later life, rather than socially induced, cohort differences between generations.

The Social and the Personal in Druze Religious Life

If the passive leanings that emerge openly in the TAT protocols of elderly Druze are universal in scope, we can argue that they should also be powerful; they should have a peremptory effect on behavior. Yet, as noted earlier, at least the public behav-

TABLE 4.4 Longitudinal Changes in TAT Imagery of Navajo and Druze Subjects Elicited by the Heterosexual-Conflict Card

	No. of passive images discarded in favor of more active imagery after Time 1*			No. of passive images appearing only at Time 2		
	Navajo	Druze	total	Navajo	Druze	total
Male aggression is in reaction to female dominance	3	1	4	8	3	11
Man is inactive; woman is active and/or dominant	2	2	4	4	7	11
Man and woman both look at troubling or pleasant scene	3	2	5	5	7	12
Man is sick; woman is his nurse, or is concerned about him	1	3	4	6	4	10
Man is tired, or old (woman may be his daughter)	1	2	3	2	5	7
Man and woman like or love each other. No conflict or role distinctions	1	9**	10	8	4	12
	Total no. of passive images discarded by Time 2 . . . 30			Total no. of new passive images by Time 2 . . . 63***		

*Time 1–Time 2 interval is four years in the Navajo case, and five years in the Druze case. The Galilean and Carmel Druze, but not the Golan Druze, were reinterviewed for the Time 2 study.

**2/3 of the Druze reversals in this category towards more "active" imagery occur among men younger than age 65; 3/4 of the new perceptions of an affiliative and un-differentiated couple occur in men aged 65 and over.

***Note: These are not independent entries. A single story may be entered under more than one heading.

ior of the older *Aqil* seems to be completely ordered by his local culture, and not by some species-wide undertow towards passivity. When we look at the conventional behavior of the religious man, we find him going busily from place to place, from one ceremonial visit to another, praying or receiving guests with elaborate hospitality. In his social relations he is not submissive, but even dogmatic and dictatorial, laying down the law to his younger relations. Within the framework of the religious life the older *Aqil* seems to behave in an active rather than a passive fashion.

Thus, when we ask the *Aqil* what he *does* as a religious man, he describes an energetic life. However, when we ask him about the *meaning* that the religious life holds for him, when we ask about his *subjective* relation to the religious life, and to Allah, we get a different picture. It is at this level that the passive yearnings inferred from the TAT seem to make their appearance, and it is at this point that the *Aqil* resembles not only his Druze coreligionists, but also his overtly passive age-peers in other societies. When they talk about their relationship to Allah, fierce, patriarchal old Druze, still dominant over their grown sons, will adopt completely the posture and the tone of the passive, self-effacing supplicant: "Allah is all and I am nothing; I live only in his will, and by his will . . . I do not question his will . . . I do not complain about my illness, because this is from God; and to complain about my illness is to question God. . ." Incidentally, these older men are not playing back the prescription for conventional religious behavior: when we ask young *Aqil* about the meaning of the religious life, they tell us that their task is to seek out sinners, to correct their ways, and through this action to make the village acceptable in the eyes of God. In effect, the younger *Aqil* are social workers for God; their relationship to Allah is mediated by their *action* in his service. It is only among the old *Aqil* that we get the sense of a direct and personal relation to Allah, mediated not by work, but by supplication and prayer. Their job is not to clean up the village, but to redeem *themselves*. Allah is for them an intensely felt and loving presence: as they talk of God their eyes shine, and the voices of these old patriarchs tremble with emotion. They become not unlike the stereotype of a submissive woman speaking fearfully and yearningly of her master. There are no rules in Druze society that tell young *Aqil* to have a relation to Allah that is centered on their own action, and for older men to have a relationship that is centered on the power and actions of that same Allah. Clearly, there is a range of permissible postures towards Allah available to the Druze, regardless of age, but each age-cohort finds certain postures more congenial than others. The younger *Aqil* define a relationship to Allah that is in conformity with the principles of Active Mastery, while older *Aqil* enact the themes of Passive Mastery; and these age preferences reflect intrinsic rather than social coercion. Evidently then, the religious role of the *Aqil* allows the passive strivings noted in the older man's TAT to find their overt, dramatic expression.

This example illustrates the relatively seamless fit that often exists between particular roles and developmental potentials in the traditional community. As we have seen, the older Druze shares with his age peers in other societies the tendency toward the androgyny of later life. However, in his case he does not need to make some final and conflictful choice between active and passive, "masculine" and "feminine" ways of relating. The traditional religious sector of society provides a particular psychosocial niche in which he can live out passive and covertly "feminine" strivings, even as he continues to domineer his sons and influence community policy. Thus, the religious role requires and gives definition to those psychic potentials which are released by the older man's withdrawal from the active tasks of parenthood and production. The yearnings that men in secular societies might experience in the form of neurotic symptoms, the old traditional Druze experiences as his worshipful linkage to God.

The Social Utility of Passive Mastery

While the religious role fits the special needs of older men, their tendencies towards mildness and accommodation are equally fitted to the requirements of the religious role. In the preliterate mind, life-sustaining vitality or power does not originate in the mundane, everyday world. Life-sustaining power has its ultimate origin in supernatural, extracommunal sources—in the spirits of ancestral dead, in totemic animals, in enemy, and particularly in the Gods. The particular source of power varies by cultural prescription, but the idea that the prosaic world is kept real and vital by power imported from the supernaturals is general across the preliterate world. Wherever this world view is institutionalized specially anointed figures are required to live on the interface between the mundane and supernatural worlds, so as to "attract" the benevolent aspect of supernatural power, to contain it, and to make it available to the life forms of the community and its ecosystem. The old man's emerging humility and submissiveness fits him to live on the dangerous interface between the gods and the mundane community, and, through his prayers, to bring life-sustaining forces into the community, so as to maintain and increase children, flocks, and crops. The passivity that could lead to vulnerability, depression, and psychosomatic illness in other settings becomes in the traditional society the very core and pivot of the older man's social prestige and personal identity.

Disengagement or Role Transition?

The theory of later life disengagement put forward by Cumming and Henry (1961) is perhaps the most prominent conception in the social psychology of aging. In essence, it proposes a mutual disengagement whereby the agencies of society withdraw their attention from the aged, and the aged withdraw from society's normative restraints, to become more idiosyncratic, but also more "liberated." Though the theory was developed exclusively from United States urban studies, and was not tested cross-culturally, its authors claim that disengagement is both mandatory and universal. As such, disengagement is a developmental event; the older person who sets himself to oppose this dictate of nature is fighting a losing battle, and may even do so at his peril.

Cumming and Henry partly justify the case for a developmental (hence universal) underpinning to disengagement by relating this process to another presumably developmental event—the emergence in later life of passive ego states. Thus, various associates of Cumming and Henry (the present author among them) scored the TAT protocols from their Kansas City subjects on various indicators of the passive state, and found that older subjects scored consistently higher on these: they were more likely than younger subjects to introduce Passive Mastery themes into their stories, they were less likely to infuse stimulus figures with assertive energy or emotional intensity, and they were less likely to introduce outside figures or conflict possibilities (see Cumming and Henry, 1961, Chap. 6). Since the age trend towards TAT metaphors of passivity matched the age trend on other social barometers towards disengagement in the study population, Cumming and Henry concluded that the two trends were linked into one developmental event, such that the increased passivity of later life represented the inner, subjective correlate of the total disengagement process. However, the case of the Druze *Aqil* indicates that disengagement need not be compulsory, and it particularly demonstrates that passivity is not inextricably tied to disengagement. Quite the contrary: in the Druze case—and probably in the case of other traditional folk societies of strong religious orientation—the so-called passivity of the older man can be the central, *necessary* component of his engagement with age appropriate social roles, traditions, and associated normative controls.

Clearly, the older Druze *Aqil* switches his allegiance from the norms that govern the secular-productive life to those which govern the traditional and moral life, but in this transition he does not stray from the influence of normative controls as such. If anything, they gain increased influence over him. The older Druze may detach his interest and allegiance from those social codes which are no longer congenial to his passive needs, but he certainly does not detach himself from society *per se*. Rather, he links himself subjectively to the religious dimension of his society, and in so doing plays out the theme of Passive Mastery—the need to be in personal touch with a powerful, benevolent, and productive agency. He relinquishes his own productivity, but not productivity *per se*. Instead of being the center of enterprise, he is now the bridge between the community and the productive, life sustaining potencies of Allah. The old *Aqil* now carries forward the moral rather than the material work of the community. Thus, guided by needs and sensibilities which reflect his emerging passivity the older Druze transits from one normative order to another *within* his society; in that transition he becomes, quite completely, the instrument and the representation of the traditional moral order that he has adopted and that has adopted him. He is not disengaged: he is re-engaged.

Incidentally, what is true for the Druze is also in general true for the men of other tradition oriented societies. As Roy Simmons (1945) reports in the *Role of the Aged in Primitive Society,* the traditional elders of preliterate groups do not usually disengage from the social order and its normative prescriptions; on the contrary, as we found among the Druze, they often become the interpreters and administrators of the *moral* sector of society. They become the norm bearers. Thus, the disengagement that Cumming and Henry found in our society does not generalize to all versions of the human condition; indeed, it is the exception rather than the rule. The disengagement that Cumming and Henry found is only the first step in a total process of *transition;* a process that can reach its natural terminus, that is, *Re-Engagement,* in a traditional society, but that is interrupted or aborted in a secular society. Thus, it may well be that disengagement is only an artifact of secular society, which does not offer the old man a traditional moral order to re-engage with once he has decoupled from those social norms which regulate the parental and productive life periods.

In sum, it is the movement towards Passive and Magical Mastery that appears to be universal, but it does not necessarily lead on to disengagement. The Druze case shows that the inexorable psychic developments of later life are not a necessary prelude to social withdrawal and physical death; given a society which recognizes the emerging dispositions, values them, and articulates them into powerful offices, the so-called passivity of later life can provide the ground for a later life revival, for a kind of social rebirth.

References

Cumming, E., and W. E. Henry
1961. *Growing Old: The Process of Disengagement.* New York: Basic Books.
Goldstine, T., and D. Gutmann
1972. A TAT study of Navajo aging. *Psychiatry* 35: 373–384.
Gutmann, D.
1964. An exploration of ego configurations in middle and later life. In B. Neugarten (ed.), *Personality in Middle and Later Life.* New York: Atherton.
1966. Mayan aging—A comparative TAT study. *Psychiatry* 29: 246–259.
1967. Aging among the Highland Maya: A comparative study. *Journal of Personality and Social Psychology* (1, pt. 1): 28–35.
1969. The country of old men: Cross-cultural studies in the psychology of later life. In W. Donahue (ed.), *Occasional Papers in Gerontology,* Ann Arbor: Institute of Gerontology, University of Michigan.
Krohn, A., and D. Gutmann
1971. Changes in mastery style with age: A study of Navajo dreams. *Psychiatry* 34: 289–300.
Róheim, G.
1930. *Animism, Magic and the Divine King.* London: Kegan Paul.
Simmons, L. W.
1945. *The Role of the Aged in Primitive Society.* New Haven: Yale University Press.

5 Aging and the Parental Imperative

Though the Druze fieldwork continued, by the late 1970s I was satisfied that the developmental hypothesis had been adequately supported. I could entertain this working assumption: that later life was the stage for a significant evolution towards a sexually bi-polar or androgynous condition. Men took on some of the nurturing, pacific qualities they had once relegated to women, and women took over some of the combative properties that they had once sent out of the "demilitarized" house with their husbands.

But while I had dutifully counted the butterflies and had traced the natural history of this transition, I still did not know what drove it. By now though, I did know where to look for answers. Clearly, a universal psychological development should have an equally universal stimulus. That is, it should be brought on by factors common to us all, and by this logic we should look to the human body and to biological science for our answers. The endocrinologists did confirm that psychological androgyny has hormonal parallels: With aging, the relative male monopoly on testosterone is broken and both sexes acquire a more equal share of this heady stuff. Relative to his declining testosterone, the estrogenic level of the aging male increases.

But as a dedicated social sciences chauvinist, one who prefers to think that we psychologists control the independent variables, I am suspicious of the scientific reductionism that automatically concedes independent status to biological over psychological factors. Moreover, I was reluctant to turn my hard-won findings into a footnote for endocrinological biologists. In this case, I wondered, could the reverse be true? Perhaps psychosocial phenomena are the independent forces, and these stimulate the shift in hormonal balance towards elderly androgyny. So I continued to search for psychological processes, sufficient in universality and dignity to bring about the observed age changes in the emotions, the behaviors, and even the hormones of older men and women.

The answer came—as these revelations often do—when it was least expected, my attention being elsewhere. While presenting my findings to a group of mental health workers and chatting up an attractive young nurse, an image suddenly possessed my inner mind: Blinking on and off, the word **PARENTHOOD** lit up and became the center of a moving hologram of the human life-cycle. I saw a double helix, formed out of twisting strands of yang and yin, *masculinity and femininity, coiling together in the child, parting decisively at the latitude of parenthood and then recombining in postparental hyperspace to form the androgynous older individual. Clearly, my covert wish for an amorous connection with the pretty nurse had been sublimated to bring about this integrative but still hectic union of ideas, findings, and observations.*

This initial display was multimedia: mainly non-verbal, textural, and illuminated. But then my secondary process thinking took over; it generated an acceptable "linear" translation and, following that, a lecture that I inflicted on the appreciative young probationer: "The universal requirements of human parenthood determine the degree of gender differentiation between the sexes . . . blah, blah, blah." I went on to explain that the sexes are most differentiated along conventional lines when the sense of parental emergency is at its peak, but as children mature and take over the responsibility for their own physical and emotional nurture, both parents can then relax and reclaim those strands of their sexual nature, yang or yin, that they had temporarily conceded to the spouse during the emergency period.

The rest was commentary. As reported in the following paper, I still had to work out the details and test this rather ambitious set of ideas. Though to some degree this project succeeded, there is still a piece of unfinished business: I never did get to thank the young nurse whose charms had inspired the organizing "Parental Imperative" insight.

But, despite my own sense of closure, the Parental Imperative idea has attracted various critiques. Gender feminists for example are offended by the suggestion that mere "breeding" can powerfully affect human development in early, middle, and late adulthood. Cognitive geropsychologists are offended on different grounds: They prefer to think that development is not preemptive, not the by-product of the human unconscious and the messy body that it hangs out with. Instead, they hold that we are created by our own creations: our own self-crafted personal narratives, or the social role models, cohort effects, economic pressures, etc., that humans themselves have brought into being. In these designs, all explanatory power is conceded to the social and idiosyncratic narratives of development; as is the fashion now, the universal, species *narrative, is ruled out.*

It is comforting to believe that my critics' objections have trendy rather than rational, "scientific" sources. Nevertheless, to the degree that criticisms are couched in cogent terms, they have to be taken seriously and responded to in kind. In the next piece, following a presentation of the basic parental imperative argument, the various subsequent tests of the theory carried out by myself, my students, and my critics are described and discussed.

In previous publications, my reports on the psychology of aging have been devoted mainly to description: they have traced the expressions of the three great relational modes: aggressive (Thanatos), affiliative/communalistic (Eros), and narcissistic (omnipotential, omnisensual) as these vary by age, by sex, and by culture.

Generally speaking, we have found that, as they age, men give *Eros* priority over *Thanatos;* aging women give priority to *Thanatos* over *Eros;* and both sexes, moving toward omnigratification, become more narcissistic. These species regularities point, quite decisively, to a developmental staging of the aging process.

But the work remains uncompleted: a developmental effect has been demonstrated, but not its nature and causes. We are still faced with a crucial question: What is the dynamic of change? What engines power the developmental movement of individual lives along the tracks that we have mapped?

Species Freedom and Parental Servitude

Any species-embracing developmental sequence must in some important respects be guided and orchestrated by inherited factors. These biological agents preserve, within the human gene pool itself, the evolved resources that characterize the hardiest members of our species. A review of the human properties that make for individual hardihood and species survival convinces me that individual and species success are both judged against parental criteria: the hardiest individuals are those who survive at least long enough to raise viable, potentially parental offspring. Species success likewise depends on parental success, across numberless generations. Ultimately a species can survive only when its parenting aptitudes, as genetically directed, ensure the survival and maturation of children who will in turn raise their own viable children to be successful parents.[1]

The human concentration on parenting is determined not only by our low offspring-to-parent ratio but also by the special vulnerability of human children. The centrality of parenting in human affairs (and in primate affairs, generally) is based on a paradox: It is an inescapable consequence of liberation, of the relative human freedom from the tyranny of "old learning," of inflexible, "wired-in" instincts. By contrast with all nonprimate species, our children are born with very few instinctually guaranteed, reliable skills. They are blind, the nervous system is not morphologically mature, and save for the inborn capacity to orient toward and suck the mother's breast, the human neonate lacks a fixed, reliable behavioral repertoire. Instead, it has a large reserve of unformed cognitive and social potentials, each of which requires special tending, by special sponsors, if it is to develop from the original, diffuse state to its sculpted outcome as an executive capacity of the individual. In the human case, genetic determination chiefly accounts for the surgent phase of development, the arousal of diffuse potentials; special social nurture is required, at each subsequent stage, to complete the maturing process for any given capacity.

Human infants are tremendously vulnerable but also tremendously gifted; instead of relying on fixed, inherited old learning to get them through infancy and childhood, we have awesome potentials for new learning stored in the neocortex. Our species has traded the old, "prewired" brain for the *tabula rasa* of the neocortex, the result being a learning explosion that is registered in each successive generation and that has, in a few millennia, made our species the masters of this planet and its near-space environs. But if we are to reap the evolutionary advantage of the human cortex, the parents' matured functions must serve to keep the child alive until its own matured brain can come on stream to embellish the general store of new learning. Our species' freedom from the restrictions of old learning commits the young to a long childhood and the human adult to a long period of parental servitude. Mothers and fathers must meet the child's need for physical and emotional security until their offspring are ready to supply these requirements for themselves, and ultimately for their own children.

Parenthood and Adulthood: An Equation

The dialectical relationship between infantile freedom and parental constraint is registered by most successful human groups in that they bring about a clear identity between mature adulthood and parenthood. Indeed, contemporary American society is one of the few in which a major attempt has been made (outside of monastic orders) to split adulthood from the parental condition. Most human societies are like the Kota of India, in which David Mandelbaum (1957) found that a Kota man does not think of himself as fully human until he has had children, "until there is someone to call him father." Similarly, Levy (1977), who studied adulthood among the Newars and in Tahiti, found at both sites that "a responsible parenthood (the keeping and rearing of children) produces a shift in *informal social definition* to adulthood, confirming the earlier ritual definition at marriage" (emphasis in original). And Lowenthal, Thurnher, and Chiriboga (1975), who studied the psychological effect of important life-span transitions, found that even in our contra-parental American society, "Family centeredness is a dominant theme in the protocols, and parenthood is the main transition envisaged by the young. Work, education, and marriage were viewed largely as a means to that end. Although we saw signs of expansiveness, experimentation, and interest in personal growth among the young men, they primarily hoped to emulate the styles of the parents' generation, and it would appear that they would eventually accede to the nesting inclinations which make up the major goals of the young woman."[2]

I became intuitively aware of the equation between adulthood and parenthood in the course of my field interviews. While the announced purpose of these was to study the psychology of later, postparental life, my male subjects vigorously impressed on me the importance that parenthood had played in shaping their adult life and character. In the beginning, I did not interview my Navajo, Mayan, or Druze informants about parenting issues; nevertheless, in the course of my unstructured interviews, the parental *motif* asserted itself time and again. The interviews were open-ended, exploratory; they were not formed around any predetermined priorities of my own, but were shaped to elicit informants' subjective priorities and concerns. Thus unprompted, the parental theme in the lives of younger subjects (in their late thirties and forties) is stunningly clear: Time and again, younger male subjects linked their pleasures, complaints, and remedies to their situation as parents and to the welfare of their families. Predictably, in unstable as well as stable societies, men told me that they had been wild in their youth, but that marriage had shifted their character dramatically toward greater responsibility, selflessness, and moderation: "I used to hell around; I didn't care for myself or anybody else." (I see that you are not like that now. What happened?) "You know how it is: I got married; I had kids."

Also striking is the degree to which younger men define both their pleasures and their pains in terms of their family's welfare. As we observed earlier, younger men equate contentment with good health and with a sufficiency of food—not for themselves, but for their dependents. Thus I ask a Highland Mayan father, "What is it that makes you happy?" His answer, fairly standard for his younger age group, is quick: "When there is corn and beans for my family. . . . When things are bad we always think, 'Where can I find work? Where can I find the pesos to buy corn and beans?'" And a Druze father in the same age range will tell me, again quite routinely, that he is contented when there is "peace in the home, my family is healthy, and there is peace in the village."

The main message from the middle-aged fathers was that marriage, and particularly parenthood, ended the fun and games of young manhood, and that these pleasures were largely unregretted. Many of us have heard and even rendered the same wry judgments on parenthood, but their repetition across the whole cultural range transforms a seeming banality into a human universal of some dignity. The transcultural reach of such statements points again to the universal importance that parents, including fathers, attach to the fact of their own parenthood. In short, fatherhood seems to mobilize profound emotions and sentiments, and these find standard expression across disparate societies. If I make parenthood central to my own thinking about aging, it is because, without quite expecting to, I found it to be central in the lives of my aging informants.

I also found that parenthood, as a central human concern, sponsors standard comprehensions about parenting across cultures. While developmental psychologists may argue about the importance of early experience versus the "here and now," illiterate peasants did not think it strange that, in my life-cycle interviews, I focused on such matters as weaning, toilet training, sibling rivalry, or the impact of a stepmother on early character development. They already knew about the effect of these contingencies on a child's feelings, on the family's mood, and on the child's later development. I do not think, when it comes to parenting, that any reasonably successful child-rearing regime is inconceivably strange to any human group. Regardless of culture, my informants could discuss child-rearing arrangements other than their own (and including mine) with true psychological sophistication, agreeing as to the range of possible practices, from harsh physical discipline to laissez-faire permissiveness, and as to the developmental consequences of these various styles. As a powerful and standard experience, parenthood seems to enforce its own universal norms and understandings, despite the widest disparities in cultural belief systems. Again, co-existing with cultural and personal scripts, there is a species narrative of parenthood: Like war or love, it has its own stern, preemptive aspect; it is an experience that speaks to and reveals the common nature in all of us. And the compelling nature of the parental experience is demonstrated by the common understandings, concerning the ways of parenting, that this state kindles in those who have shared this experience, however much their lives may vary in other ways.

Gender Differences in Parenting

As a primary experience, parenthood enforces not only common understandings but also a stern discipline. As noted earlier, parents foot the bill for our freedom from instinctual coercion, and for our opportunity, as humans, to create new intellectual forms, to create new social forms, and even to take control of our own evolution. Accordingly, while societies have different ideas as to the developmental end points that they want to reach through their child-rearing methods, they nevertheless maintain common understandings about the basic needs that must be met by any child-care regime. And there is general agreement that parents will, as part of their assignment, accept deep restrictions on their own needs and deep revisions of their own psychological makeup, in order to meet their children's essential needs. There also appears to be general agreement as to the nature of these basic needs: If it is to thrive by any developmental criteria, the vulnerable human child must be assured of two kinds of nurturance: the provision of physical security and the provision of emotional security.[3]

The qualities of gender capture and memorialize the processes of evolutionary selection whereby the necessary capacities were assorted by sex, so as to assure the provision, to children, of physical and emotional security. Let us first consider the masculine responsibility for physical security. In the species sense, there is always an oversupply of males, in that one man can inseminate many females, but women, on the average, can gestate only one child every two years during their relatively brief window of fruitfulness. The surplus of redundant males, those over the number required to maintain viable population levels, can be assigned to the dangerous, high-casualty "perimeter" tasks on which physical security and survival are based. The more expendable male sex, armed with large muscle and a greater store of intrinsic aggression, is generally assigned to hunt large game; to open, maintain, and defend distant tillage; to guard against human and nonhuman predators; or to raid other communities for their wealth.[4]

By the same token, the sex on whom the population level ultimately depends is less expendable. The sex that has breasts, softer skin, a milder nature, the sex that fashions the baby within its own flesh, is generally assigned to secure areas, there to supply the formative experiences that give rise to emotional security in children. Indeed, under conditions of guaranteed physical security, the mother's provision of emotional nurture to the baby can be seen as an extension of her intrauterine care to the fetus. The mother's extrauterine nurture to the infant consolidates its psychological structures, just as her own body once formed and consolidated its physical structures.

The basic division of parenting duties is coded by gender, and that code is universal enough to be understood by most human societies, dictating the assignment of men not only to warfare but to almost any "perimeter" based activity. For example, George Murdoch's (1935) tables, based on ethnographic data from 224 subsistence-level societies, indicate that any productive or military activity requiring a protracted absence from the home—hunting, trapping, herding, fishing (particularly deep-sea fishing), the pursuit of large sea animals, offensive and defensive warfare—is performed almost exclusively by males. Activities carried out closer to home—dairy farming, erecting and dismantling shelters, harvesting, tending kitchen gardens and fowl—are sometimes exclusive to men, more often exclusive to women, but are in many instances carried out by both sexes. However, hearthside activities, particularly those having to do with preserving and preparing food, are almost exclusively the province of women (and the occasional "re-domesticated" old man).

Clearly then, it is not the capacity for hard labor that distinguishes the sexes but the site at which the labor is performed. Women can work, often harder than men, at tasks that do not take them away from the domestic zones; but even idle young men, telling dirty jokes in some barracks off in the bush, comprise a military force. Even in idleness these warriors on the periphery guarantee the domestic center, so that women may carry out, in safety, their vital work. Just as the living cell requires a nucleus and a boundary wall, so does the small human society require its warm, affective core and its stubborn, flinty redoubts. If parenthood is to go forward, in despite of the usual human conditions of relative danger and scarcity of resources, then two distinct groups, usually assorted by sex, are required to maintain these distinct but coacting structures.

Cultural rules may carry some of the burden of maintaining these structures and of assigning men and women to maintain them. But the basic division of labor by gender is an aspect not only of human but of general primate nature. The lower primates share with the human species the protracted period of childhood vulnerability; this blunt fact of primate existence seems to have fostered an equivalent division, by sex, of parenting roles. The primate horde—particularly the more vulnerable ground-dwellers, such as the baboon—is protected by a defense force composed mainly of males who move out to the perimeter when predators approach and who form a scouting line when the troop is on the move. Breeding females look mainly to adult males to provide physical security for themselves and for the offspring who cling to their fur, and the best fighters, the Alpha males, have privileged sexual access to them. Their sexual primacy is not only enforced by the stronger males but is granted by the fertile females themselves. In effect, females bribe males, by the promise of sexual access, into using their superior strength and ferocity for defensive and ultimately paternal purposes.

Despite the vast differences between humans and lower primates, there is a central commonality, having to do with the vulnerability and dependency of offspring, that brings about across species an investment in distinct parental roles. In both humans and apes, adult life is circumscribed by the stringent requirements of primate fatherhood and motherhood. Among the larger primates, the demands of parenting dominate and define adulthood, as well as determining the allocation, by gender, of parenting roles. In early life, human development goes forward because offspring receive parenting; the thesis of this chapter is that the parental imperative orders not only the maturations that precede the reproductive years but also those that come about when that period has ended.

Gender, Early Socialization, and Parenting

If human development is organized by two great principles—being parented in childhood and being parental in adulthood—then the child's reproductive destiny should organize even aspects of its early experience and the forms of rearing that it gets. And we do indeed find that human socialization protocols, as enforced by parents and teachers, underline surgent, genetic dispositions, preparing males for the wide ranging perimeter roles of adulthood and preparing females for the domestic center. Thus Herbert Barry, Marvin Bacon, and Irvin Child (1957), having abstracted early socialization data from 110 distinct, marginal-subsistence communities, report a striking pancultural consensus: Despite the usual intercultural differences, human societies recognize not only the gender distinctions of adult parenthood but also the gender distinctions of childhood. Standard parental requirements not only dictate men's and women's assignments in adulthood, they also give content and meaning to the play, the education, and the indoctrination of boys and girls, long before their entry into actual parenthood. The gender roles of adulthood do not only entail particular behaviors; if these are to be predictable and trustworthy, they must rest on a sound base of psychological structures: tendencies and motives that are inculcated and fixed long before specific parental behaviors are required.

Barry, Bacon, and Child find that societies routinely prepare males for the perimeter and females for the domestic center. For example, males are almost universally socialized toward achievement and self-reliance in a world they never made, the lands beyond the perimeter. The themes that underlie male socialization are most vividly dramatized in puberty rituals, in *rites de passage*. Whatever their specific form and choreography, these always involve some form of ordeal for the young, aspirant male, who—usually at the hands of senior males—is scarified, humiliated, frightened, or all of the above. In this fashion, the elder males test the courage and endurance of the young male. If the young candidate passes the test without crying, without in effect calling for his mother, then he has made it as a man. He has demonstrated that he already has or is likely to mature the qualities of endurance and courage that are called for on the perimeter. Whether as trader, hunter, soldier, rebel on the run, itinerant merchant, or worker, the candidate for manhood moves from the inward, central location of the mother's world to the outward perimeter of his father's world. The puberty ritual marks the rebirth of the young male, from being his mother's child in the home to being his father's son on the perimeter. And in addition to strengthening his ties to the fathers, the young candidate confirms his ties to the "brothers," the age class of boys who endure the ritual with him. The puberty ritual thus strengthens male bonding and introduces the boy to the comrades, mentors, and father-gods who will be his companions and comforters on the road. The ritual gives him male allies, the special portion of the community that he can take with him, even as he leaves the larger community on his sorties beyond the perimeter, and away from the mothers.

Just as societies quicken the traits that will make men perform reliably on various frontiers, so are women urged to cultivate the qualities that will fit them for their role as providers of emotional security, within the heart of the family and the community. The data compiled by Barry, Bacon, and Child make it clear that the central themes in female socialization across cultures are nurturance, responsibility, and, to a lesser degree, obedience. This is not to say that women are not potentially aggressive or that men are not potentially nurturing; but responding to the mingled social and species coercions, each sex amplifies only a limited sector of the potentials available to it. In their socialization practices, societies are guided by two main criteria. They fix on those psychological potentials that are native to the particular sex and that are at the same time germane to the parental roles that men and women will play out.

The Entry into Marriage

In effect, the socializing practices of stable societies undercut the individual's narcissistic illusions of omnipotentiality. By and large, they do not permit individuals to enjoy and amplify the full range of psychological possibilities, *yin* and *yang*, "masculine" and "feminine," that are potential within them. But men and women can regain externally, through mating, what they have lost internally, through repressive socialization. That is, men and women can rediscover outwardly, in their mates and sexual partners, those qualities that have been ruled off-limits internally.

Those self-qualities that are inconsistent with the gender identity change from bad to good as they cross the self boundary, to be experienced as qualities of the other. Thus the wife or lover provides an external medium, a kind of projective screen through which younger men can recontact, appreciate, and vicariously live out the qualities of nurturance and tenderness that complete them, that restore their lost duality, but that can no longer be tolerated within the self. By the same token, women can discover and appreciate in men those qualities of aggression and dominance that are blocked from expression within themselves. They can admire and even sponsor male aggression (so long as it is directed away from themselves and their children), living out their own desires for exploit and competitive success mainly through their husbands' achievements.

The young woman gives up her more assertive strivings in the interest of domestic harmony and in the service of her future parental role, to be a provider of emotional security to children and of emotional comfort to the providing husband. If she kept title to these qualities, if she permitted free expression of her aggression toward demanding, draining offspring, she might end by abusing and damaging her children emotionally and even physically, as well as driving away the provident husband. Having relinquished the dominating qualities that could interfere with her parental role and be destructive to her children, she rediscovers them, and enjoys them, in her mate or lover, often choosing precisely those men who best depict the unruly potentials that she has surrendered for herself. This adaptive restriction—as managed by the representatives of culture and the structures of the psyche—serves parenthood in two ways. Within each sex, it closes out psychological tendencies that could interfere with adequate parenting, and it leads individuals to seek their completion, their lost omnipotentiality, not within themselves but through procreant alliances with the heterosexual other. In order to regain the lost sense of omnipotentiality, men and women must seek completion through intimate liaisons, and these lead on, quite naturally, to reproduction and parenting.

The Chronic Emergency:
The Onset of Parenthood and Its Consequences

While the necessary sex-role training begins early in life, its consequences are not fully evident until the actual onset of parenthood. With the coming of the first child, there also comes a chronic sense of emergency, and a general mobilization, in men as well as in women, along the lines suggested above.

Prior to parenthood, and despite their early sex-role training, young men and women are allowed, in most societies, some freedom to indulge a wide range of psychological potentials. Thus prematernal women are often tomboys, flirtatious one day, actively competing with men the next, while young men, including prepaternal husbands, may live out the extremes of their nature toward violence on the one hand and tenderness on the other. Before parenthood, young men and women are allowed some freedom to live out their narcissistic strivings toward omnipotentiality—toward conserving, for the self, all possible potentials and options, no matter how mutually exclusive these might seem to be. However, the entry into the condition that I like to call the "chronic emergency of parenthood" leads to an energizing, in young parents, of the structures that were laid down during early gender socialization, as well as a muting of the claims toward omnisatisfaction in all domains. After children come, dedicated parents can never completely relax into self-absorption or self-indulgence. From then on, most rest becomes a nurse's sleep, the parent vigilant for the child's cry or the alarm in the night.

Both men and women respond to their emergency state by instrumentalizing themselves to meet parental requirements. Thus young fathers become an extension of their hardened, functional tools and weapons. In this service, they tame the extremes of their nature, deploying aggression toward production, curbing passive tendencies, and generally accepting, even with good humor, the responsibilities and sacrifices that come with the productive stance. By the same token, young mothers divest themselves, quite decisively, of the aggression that could put their vulnerable children at risk.

Having identified her own submerged aggression with the more flamboyant assertiveness of her husband, the wife further removes herself from those dangerous promptings by figuratively sending them out of the house, out to the perimeter, with him. Typically, across history, it is the women who have sung and cheered their garlanded warriors off to battle: Men go to war in large part because women respond amorously to uniforms. When men go off to battle, they are not only following some sexist bent of their own; instead, men become the exporters of aggression for both sexes. They carry on their swords and spears the sharp edge of their wives' hidden wrath, as well as their own. And even as they target their anger against other communities, they export dangerous aggression away from the vulnerable heart of their own settlements.

Further Reactions to the Parental Emergency: The Transformations of Narcissism

We have considered the realignments of "masculine" and "feminine" qualities, aggression and maternal love, in response to the parental emergency. But if we think of the parenting, conjugal family as a kind of organism, an extrauterine extension of the womb specially crafted to favor the psychological and physical growth of children, then it becomes clear that narcissism, the third great relational cement, must also be transformed and relocated. Clearly, the overarching familial structure could not be generated out of the union of a man and a woman unless both partners mutually renounced and transformed major portions of their own self-love and self-idealization. Indeed, unless parents were willing to forgo their narcissistic investments, their claims to omnisatisfaction and omnipotentiality, they would not undertake the necessary divestments—of sensual receptivity in the case of men and bridling aggression on the part of women—on which the family system is founded.

The nurturing organism of the family cannot come into being unless parents are willing to surrender many of their personal goals in favor of system goals, to become coacting parts—protective rind or nurturing core—of the family structure. If narcissistic goals were maintained unmodified by husbands and wives, the periphery would go undefended, aggression would be rampant within the sensitive domestic core, and nurturance would be reserved for the self rather than directed toward needful offspring. If narcissism is not transformed, redirected away from the self by both parents, the necessary family construction does not come into being, and children are gravely at risk: emotionally, because of their parents' unconcern, and physically, because of their parents' undeflected wrath.

While psychoanalytic theory mainly restricts the significant transformations of narcissism to the periods of early development, implicating them chiefly in the formation of self and superego, any naturalistic review that is unfettered by an exclusive bias toward early development must convince us that new parenthood brings about one of the most potent transformations of narcissism in the entire life cycle. The difference between this and earlier conversions has to do with the fact that the parental transformation is not aimed at forging the adult self but is instead aimed at bringing about the psychological formation, the selfhood, of the offspring. New parenthood marks the point at which the conjugal couple routinely and—if things have gone as they should—automatically surrender a large piece of their narcissistic claims to personal omnipotentiality and immortality, conceding these instead to the child.[5] The result is the routine, unexamined heroism of parenting, which even renders mothers and fathers willing to die in their child's stead.

Finally then, parenthood does (or should) mark that point at which mothers and fathers revise their relationship to their own mortality. They may come to accept the natural staging of the life cycle, the inflexible order which dictates that they should predecease their children. Parents still fear death, perhaps more than ever, but now, more than their own demise, they fear the obscene possibility that the child might predecease the parent. Thus orthodox Jewish men introduce their first-born sons as their *kaddishle,* naming him with an affectionate diminutive as the one who will read the Kaddish, the prayer for the dead, over them at their burial. They thereby indicate their acceptance of their own finite life cycle, and even their pleasure in an order of things which holds that fathers, if all goes as it should, will die before their sons.

Indeed, the narcissistic transformations in response to the parental emergency are so profound that they force us to reconsider the ultimate significance of narcissism itself. Typically, we think of narcissism as being conserved for the individual, to provide emergency rations of self-love when there is no love from others. And narcissism does indeed buffer individual self-esteem against the slings and arrows of daily existence. But its major function is not to protect the adult's *amour propre;* rather, sighting on narcissism from the parental perspective, we see that this tendency has been studied mainly in its immature and reflexive forms, before it is recruited and stabilized to its true evolutionary and adaptive purpose: the preservation, by the parent, of the vulnerable child.

The Entry into the Parental Emergency: Empirical Studies

Parenthood brings about major reorganizations of adult personality, and these should be particularly evident at two major transition points: the entry into and the exit from the state of active parenting. In this section, I present research evidence from various sources, all bearing on the psychological changes wrought in men and women by the onset of the parental emergency.

Also based on cross-cultural data, the work of Niles Newton (1973) helps us to better understand the reasons for these crucial parental transformations. She argues that coitus, birth, and lactation—the three neurochemically regulated expressions of female sexuality—while they are vital to successful reproduction and child-rearing, are also strikingly vulnerable, prone to shut down in the face of outer threat. In order to proceed toward their reproductive goal, these activities all require external buffering and protection, most often provided by men. In this vein, Newton cites ethnographic descriptions of young mothers in South America, the Middle East, and China, all pointing to a standard pattern of maternal engrossment with the infant, in an intense bond that can persist through the first years of the child's life. At all these sites, the infant sleeps next to mother, is nursed at the first sign of restlessness, and nursing takes precedence over any competing activity. It is not surprising that, across most societies, young men protect wives who are so engrossed in the reproductive process and rendered vulnerable because of it.

An interesting if limited study done under my direction picks up the surgent changes set in train by first parenthood. Thus Gary Kupper (1975) interviewed and gave projective tests to newly parenting and nonparental married student couples, and found the predicted shift among the parental men toward disciplined careerism. Their goals, no longer inflated by narcissistically grandiose expectations, were more realistic and more attainable than those set by their nonparental age peers. Most interesting are the results from the intergroup projective test comparisons. The Heterosexual–Conflict TAT card was shown to both the parental and the nonparental groups, and the resulting thematic distributions by parental status demonstrated differences in the subjective management of male aggression, along predicted lines. While most subjects see tension and discord in the scene, they vary by parental status in naming the sources of the couple's trouble. For the nonparental subjects, the scene is one of domestic squabbling: The young man and young woman are not sharply differentiated by their personal qualities or by the intensity of their aggressive feelings toward each other. In the stories from the parental group, strong male-female distinctions appear, particularly in regard to the location and management of aggression: Tension no longer divides the couple; instead, these accounts feature extradomestic challenges—there is a war; there is a job that needs doing; another man has insulted the woman—and the aggressive response to these challenges is concentrated in the young man. His action is centrifugal: away from the woman, away from the domestic center, and toward the enemy or the opportunity that he glimpses on the periphery, beyond the actual card boundaries.

Conversely, any fearful concern over the young man's boldness is not found in him; instead, it is concentrated in the young woman figure, who tries to restrain the young man's reckless action. If he is all thrusting exuberance, then she is turned against such aggression and is afraid for its potential victims. In other words, as predicted by our model, for the parental group the young man figure has become a creature of the perimeter, whose job it is to concentrate the dangerous intradomestic aggression of both partners, to export it away from the vulnerable center, and to discharge it beyond the periphery against human or inhuman enemies, or against the agencies of impersonal nature.

But if parental informants see the young man as moving out of the domestic zone, to station himself aggressively on the perimeter, they also see women as moving back into the domestic zone. Consider the responses to the Farm/Family scene, a card that shows, in a bucolic setting, a man who plows the soil, a pregnant woman who leans against a tree, and a young woman who stands in the foreground, half turned toward the farmer and holding a book in her hand. Typical stories told in response to this card usually center on the actions and motives of the young woman. She is seen to be either moving away from the farm in pursuit of her own independence, or moving, usually motivated by guilt and filial concern for her family, back toward the domestic center, to be with and to help her parents. Our sample of nonparental subjects were prone to see the young woman as ambitious and centrifugal, but the parental subjects quite decisively placed her in the world of household and motherhood. Thus young parents move male figures away from the household, and by the same token they remove women away from the periphery, returning them to the center of the domestic world.

Katherine Ewing (1981), an anthropologist with psychoanalytic training, also probed beyond the level of custom and behavior, to explore the subjective side of Pakistani mothers' reactions to their own parenthood. She found that their investment in maternal behavior is matched by an internal repudiation of their own aggression, which is seen as dangerous to their offspring. In Ewing's experience, young mothers, afraid of the harm that unchecked aggression could cause their children, chastise themselves for their own uncontrolled outbursts of anger. The duty of the young mother is to submit to her mother-in-law and to control any anger over this servitude, for the sake of domestic harmony and for the sake of her children.

The predicted parental shifts are also noted for new American fathers. Thus Douglas Heath (1972) found that first-time American fathers are significantly more calculating and achievement-oriented than their nonparental age peers. By the same token, they are less emotive and less affectionate than married nonfathers in the same age range. In other words, young men move into parenthood by focusing on the role of provider and by damping out the sentimentality that could interfere with that vital role. But these young fathers are not totally abandoning their capacity for warmth; rather, they are putting it on hold and giving over the feeling function to their wives. In effect, they become more stereotypically "masculine," not in the service of male chauvinism, but in the service of their children's need for a reliable provider: a father who will be able to leave the household when necessary, and without crippling homesickness.

Studies of couples in early parenthood yield similar findings. Thus Richard Perloff and Michael Lamb (1980) found that, following the onset of parenthood, both marriage partners show increased sex-role stereotypy, while Elizabeth Menaghan (1975) claims that men without offspring are more passive than fathers of the same age, as well as possessing a higher capacity for intimacy. In effect, childless men, not yet stimulated by the parental emergency, show a "softer" personality style, in which feelings are given priority over unsentimental efficiency.

These Western-based studies tell us that the disciplined mobilization of the young man following marriage and especially parenthood is not exclusively a by-product of sexual training in preliterate traditional societies. Thomae (1962), citing studies of adulthood and aging among West German men, reports that younger men are impressed with the changes in their own personality that are consequent on parenthood: They find themselves "to be more stable, more of a homebody." George Gilder (1973) has also argued, from observations in American society, that men are tamed and "made social" only when they bond themselves to a woman and accept her procreative, parental purpose as their own. Until then, unmarried young men may be charming, dramatic, and attractive, but, except as warriors, they are socially surplus.

Standing Down from the Parental Emergency: The Emergence of Contra-Sexual Potentials

We have seen how nature, society, and culture can meet, to support the conversion of sexually mature individuals into parental adults, those who will in their turn oversee the growth of healthy children. But as time passes, once-helpless children go on to demonstrate their viability by exercising for themselves the security giving functions that had previously been exercised by others in their behalf. Children increasingly prove their capacity to provide physical security for themselves and others by demonstrating a marketable labor capacity, and by passing the endurance and fitness trials set by puberty rituals; they demonstrate their capacity to provide their own emotional security by developing a circle of tested friends, and by entering into intimate arrangements of some permanence. They emerge from their long period of dependency and helplessness, and they take over from the parents the executive functions that had been held in escrow for them.

As the parental emergency phases out, fathers and mothers have less need to live in the altruistic conjugal manner. The child is safely launched and no longer needs to be protected, whether magically or realistically, by endowments of parental narcissism. In the postparental years, adults finish paying their species dues: They no longer have to meet the psychological tax that is levied on our species in compensation for human freedom from the programmed rigidities of instinct. Having raised the next generation of viable and procreant children, the parents have earned the right to be again, at least in token ways, omnipotential. As a consequence, postparental men and women can reclaim the sexual bimodality that was hitherto repressed and parceled out between husband and wife. Because the restoration of sexual bimodality to each spouse will no longer interfere with proper parenting, senior men and women can reclaim, for themselves, those aspects of self that were once disowned inwardly, though lived out externally, vicariously, through the mate. They can afford the luxury of elaborating the potentials and pleasures that they had to relinquish early on, in the service of their particular parental task.

In this later development, as we have already observed in the cross-cultural data, a significant sex-role turnover takes place, in that men begin to live out directly, to own as part of themselves, the accommodative, or Passive Mastery, qualities: sensuality, affiliation, and maternal tendencies—in effect, the "femininity" that was previously repressed in the service of productivity and lived out vicariously through the wife. By the same token, across societies, we see the opposite effect in women. As documented, they generally become more domineering, independent, unsentimental, and self-centered—asserting their own desires, particularly toward social dominance, rather than serving the emotional needs and development of others. Just as men in late middle life reclaim their denied "femininity," middle-aged women repossess the aggressive "masculinity" that they once lived out vicariously through their husbands. The consequence of this internal revolution, this shift in the politics of self, is that the sharp sex distinctions of earlier, parental adulthood break down, and each sex becomes to some degree what the other used to be.

Thus, with their children grown, wives can tolerate and even enjoy the aggressiveness that once might have terrified their children and alienated their male providers. By the same token, men are freed up to recapture the latent duality of their own nature: they live out again the extremes of their psyche, tolerable now that their aggression is biologically reduced, and taking a peevish rather than a murderous form. In effect, besides claiming some of the cast-off parts of the feminine psyche, men also reclaim title to the full spectrum of affects that their now grown-up children have in their turn abandoned. Fathers can now be childish: needful, querulous, indignant, or all of the above.

In sum, as the parenting establishment is demobilized, the senior individuals take back into themselves the qualities that had been portioned out into the various parts of the supraindividual family structure: Men take back the sensuality and tenderness that they once left behind at the domestic center, while women take back the aggression that they, through their husbands, had once shipped off to form and defend the communal periphery.

Finally, both parents reclaim the quotient of narcissism that had been converted away from the service of self, and to the service of children and the child-tending family. As that social structure is dismantled, narcissism again becomes available to the postparental self. Depending on the social circumstances under which it emerges, that fund of narcissism can become the basis of new self-idealizations (as well as new vulnerabilities), or it can be recruited to the service of new, more extensive social bonds. These can tie the generations to each other, or they can link the community to the gods.

The Exit from Active Parenthood: Empirical Studies

In recent years, research findings have documented the relationship between parental status and late-blooming features of personality. While a number of researchers have reported sex-role changes in the postparental years that conform to predictions from my model, I will consider in detail only those that control for the effects of chronological age, thereby highlighting the psychological effects directly traceable to life stage, to the exit from active parenting.

As with the studies that covered the entry into the parental state, those studies that trace postparental changes at the deeper levels of personality will be reviewed first.

The Druze Case: A Cross-Cultural Test of the Parental Model

Druze Orality Scores

The Druze research provides an opportunity to test the universality of the relationship between the parental stage and the psychological changes of later life. As we have seen, in later life the focused, "phallic" organization of masculine personality tends to shut down in favor of a more diffuse spectrum of erotic possibilities, including those that were foremost in the earliest years of life. For example, oral-erotic interests, evidenced by the pleasure in eating, show the same prominence in later life, across the Navajo and Druze societies, that they presumably showed in early childhood. To test the possibility that parental status has an effect, independent of age, in determining the variations in orality (and, by extension, in passive-dependency), a scale was developed to quantify the levels of parental involvement among Druze men. On the basis of interview data, Druze informants were classified as to whether they were actively involved in parenting, with young children in the home; were phasing out of active parenting; or were fully into the postparental period, with all children "launched." Figure 5.1 shows the distribution of orality scores by age and by stage of parenting, and indicates the powerful effect that male parenthood plays in determining the oral, passive toning of Druze personality. Thus, for any age, men who are still actively parenting show lower mean orality scores than the postlaunch men. While the level of orality remains relatively constant across age groups for those men who still maintain dependent children in their households, these same orality scores go up, dramatically, across all age groups, for the Druze "empty-nest" men. Again, it is not chronological age that brings on the psychological signs of aging; in the more inner and subjective sense, aging comes about when men demobilize, and stand down from the parental emergency.

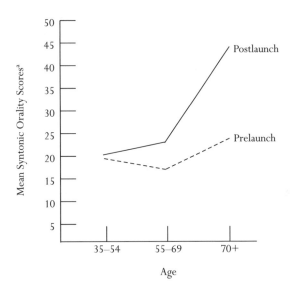

FIGURE 5.1 Variations in Druze Syntonic Orality: By Age and Parental Status

[a]The mean difference between the prelaunch and postlaunch scores is statistically significant at the .065 level by Analysis of Variance (F test).

Druze Ego-Mastery Scores:

Similar results are achieved when we consider age and parental status as independent variables, and distribute the TAT-derived ego mastery scores of Druze males against these dimensions. These TAT ratings express in numerical terms the proportions of Active, Passive, and Magical Mastery responses in the individual test records, the hypothesis being that parental stage would prove more powerful than chronological age in accounting for the variations in these proportions. Specifically, I believed that the cessation of active parenthood (marked by the absence of dependent children in the subject's household) would predict, more significantly than age *per se*, to reduced scores on Active Mastery and to elevated scores on Passive and Magical Mastery modalities. As Figure 5.2 indicates, these expectations were borne out to a significant degree: Analysis of variance tests reveal that prelaunch, still-parenting Druze men score significantly higher on Active Mastery than their postparental age peers.

Most significant is the finding that men in the 55-and-over age range who still parent score even higher on Active Mastery than younger postparental men in the age range 35–54. Though there are independent parental stage and age effects, the stage effects are most significant, by statistical test.

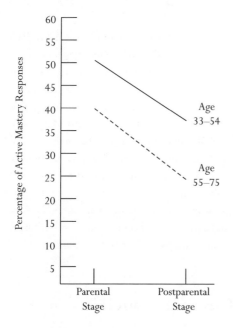

FIGURE 5.2 Variations in the Percentage of Active Mastery TAT Responses among Druze Men, by Age and Parental Status

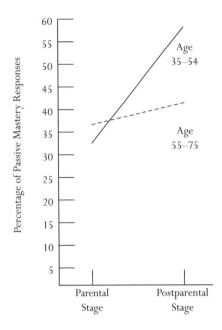

FIGURE 5.3 Variations in the Percentage of Passive Mastery TAT Responses among Druze Men, by Age and Parental Status

The predictions from the parental model are also borne out in regard to Passive and Magical Mastery, though there is an independent age effect registered in the sequencing of these mastery styles. As Figures 5.3 and 5.4 indicate, most post-parental Druze men, regardless of age, show reductions in Active Mastery; but younger postparental men shift from Active into Passive Mastery, while older post-parental men, as they exit from Active Mastery, shift directly into Magical Mastery, bypassing the intervening Passive Mastery stage. Again, the major thesis of the study is borne out, though somewhat qualified in form. The postparental transition does release, in Druze men, a renewed narcissistic demand for the kinds of sensory pleasures and egocentric thinking that they had previously muted in the service of their parental assignment. However, as an independent factor, age determines the choice of postparental modalities—toward dependency and diffuse sensuality (Passive Mastery) for younger men and toward primitive thinking (Magical Mastery) for older men.[6]

American Tests of the Parental Model

Three American researchers who recently undertook similarly explicit tests of the parental model generally confirm these impressions. Comparing late fathers

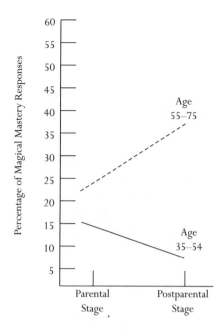

FIGURE 5.4 Variations in the Percentage of Magical Mastery TAT Responses among Druze Men, by Age and Parental Status

(both the continuing and the late starting) to a matched sample of postparental men, Linda O'Connel (1980) found that the former group showed the typical signs of the younger, Active Mastery stance on most of her instruments. The TAT protocols of the late fathers showed a higher percentage of Active Mastery themes, the relationships that they reported with their wives were marked by clear, stereotypic sex-role distinctions, and they tended to give priority to work and achievement over sentiment in their daily lives.

Donna Ripley (1984) of the Illinois Institute of Technology carried out a dissertation study of sixty midwestern male industrial workers sorted into four groups: younger fathers, younger "post-fathers," older fathers, and older "post-fathers" (for both postparental groups, the last child has been launched). These men were given projective tests and interviews from which an overall "Gender" score—ratings that reflected the degree of Active Mastery orientation—could be derived. Supporting the parental imperative hypothesis, Ripley finds that Gender Index Scores reflecting an active, "masculine" stance are highest for parental men, regardless of age, and lowest for the older and younger postparental men.

Kathryn Cooper and I (1987) carried out an equivalent TAT study of employed female teachers, matched as to age and distinguished by parental status; half were prelaunch, and half were postlaunch. The prediction, that postlaunch women would show the signs of being more aggressive, confident, and even masculine, was borne out (see Figure 5.5) for all but one TAT card, at statistically significant levels. As a result of their liberation, the postlaunch women, far from grieving over the emptied nest, now fill the TAT figures with energy and single-minded purpose. For example: for the prelaunch matrons, the young woman of the Farm/Family card is torn between the wish to leave home on her own career mission and guilty concern for the hardworking parents who would be left behind; but for the postlaunch women, the same girl takes off on some legitimate career mission without a backward look. The shifts in other cards are along the same "self-actualizing" axis.

Although they will not openly admit to these ambitions publicly for some years, at this surgent level of communication the postlaunch women are telling us that they are finished with overseeing the growth of others and are entering the phase of self-development, of tending their own growth. This personal flowering may take place in the context of a caring profession, such as clinical psychology, or at the executive levels of the extended family, but the emphasis in midlife is on the professional and careerist aspects of the role, rather than on the provision of care for its own sake.

Using the TAT as a seismograph to pick up early rumblings in the guts of the psyche, Cooper has explored the surgent events set in train by postparenthood. Using more "public" methods, aimed at getting at more finished and sculpted outcomes, Suzanne Galler (1977) studied professional women, much like the women in

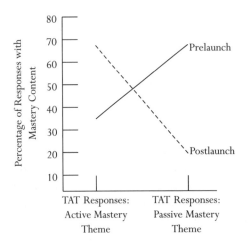

FIGURE 5.5 Pre- and Postlaunch U.S. Women: Distribution of TAT Responses by Mastery Style*

*I am indebted to Kathryn Cooper, Ph.D., for the research data on which this figure is based.

Cooper's sample, the difference being that Galler's subjects are already some years into their "self-launching." Not surprisingly, Galler found that female midlife returnees to professional work had always been achievement-oriented, but that their dormant ambitions had been quickened by the phasing out of active parenthood:

> Women in the professional student group describe themselves as having kept their personal ambitions in the background for many years, supporting, instead, the career aspirations of spouses who are themselves professional or academicians, as well as investing themselves in child rearing and adjunctive community activities. The "it's my turn now" attitudes verbalized by many of these returnees express a self-assertive rather than an other-directed attitude, an acceptance of their current limited interest in domesticity.

Using the recall of early memories as a projective technique, Harvey Peskin and Norman Livson (1981) conducted a particularly significant study, carefully sorting out surgent psychological changes attributable to the parenting stage per se, as distinct from those attributable to chronological age (and the social expectations that pertain to age). Inviting parental and older postparental adults to reminisce about their adolescent years, they found, as expected, that current parental status apparently shaped the recall of earlier experience. Regardless of age, actively parenting women tended to recapture memories clustered around nurturant and sentimental themes, while "empty-nest" women, again regardless of age, were more likely to stress memories that were charged with themes of power, dominance, and autonomy. Thus the memories of actively parenting 40-year-old women were like those of actively parenting 30-year-olds, but unlike the memories of their postparental age peers. Similar effects were observed for men. Actively parenting men remember their adolescent years as a time of competition and training for leadership, while postparental men in the same age range centered their memories of adolescence around milder, more affiliative themes: campfire sings, rather than drag races. Again, the memories of parentally involved 40-year-old men were like memories of 30-year-old parents, and unlike those of postparental peers from the same age cohort.

Studying the more proactive and sculpted aspects of women's roles, the anthropologist Sylvia Vatuk (1975) studied the Rajput Raya, finding again that parental stage counts more than age in demarcating the divisions of their later lives. Thus women enter the age grade of "old age," regardless of their actual years, when their children, particularly their sons, get married. However, the Raya women's transition into old age brings with it social gains rather than losses. Her son's marriage may "age" her in the social sense, but it also brings her daughters-in-law who are pledged to her service; in particular, they do the "inside" work, while the older woman now occupies herself with "outside" work, on the interface between the family and the larger community. Vacating the classic woman's role at the domestic center, the postparental Rajput women move, like younger men, to their society's perimeter.

Also working with the more social fabric of personality, Shirley Feldman, Zeynep Biringen, and Sharon Nash (1981) used the BEM Sex Role Inventory (BSRI) to study fluctuations in the sexual orientations of California men and women across the stages of life from adolescence to grandparenthood. While the BSRI, as a self-report questionnaire, is not designed to tap the surgent, unconscious attitudes and motives that are perhaps most important in determining sexual orientation, and while it could be particularly vulnerable to respondents' "social desirability" concerns—their wish to appear appropriately "nonsexist" to liberal social scientists—the authors nonetheless report positive findings:

> The speculation that instrumental and expressive attributes are better understood as specific to stage of life rather than as traits affixed to one sex or the other receive some support from our data. . . . The largest sex differences (on expressive factors) occur during the active parenting stages when in traditional families they serve to promote effective primary child care. The sexes describe themselves more similarly by the time that all their children have grown up and left home. . . . With the alleviation of the role constraints of active parenting, both sexes perceive themselves as having more cross-sex-typed assets yet do not feel they are any less masculine as men or feminine as women.

What is most striking here is that the young parents in the United States, despite the massive pro-androgyny rhetoric aimed at their generation, nevertheless demonstrate the sex-role differences during the actively parenting years that are predictable from our model: the same polarizations that occur on schedule in more traditionally "sexist" societies.

In the more general or species sense, the studies reviewed in this chapter suggest that the psychological qualities called "masculine" and "feminine" are more tied to the seasons of parenthood than they are to biological sex. It is the balance and scheduling of these qualities (rather than their exclusive possession) that distinguishes men from women. Men comprise the sex that is univocally masculine before reclaiming a feminine component; and the female sex reverses this staging. But despite these life-span changes in the mix of masculine and feminine qualities, both sexes are alike in that men and women maintain their core sexual identities over the years. As in other areas of life, the socially-derived names, such as "man" or "woman," have more endurance and are less changeable than our ever-shifting biological weather.

The Fate of Eros in
the Postparental Years

The reported findings also suggest that genital primacy is not (as the psychoanalysts would claim) the end point of sexual development. In the genital stage of erotic development, the capacity for pleasure, hitherto distributed over the entire body and its organs, is claimed more exclusively by the genitals, to serve the purpose of species procreation as well as individual pleasure. The libido, the capacity for pleasure, is fettered, restricted to the genitals and to the occasional, fleeting ecstasy of the orgasm. During adulthood the utilitarian, species-preserving principle of the erotic life dominates the pleasure principle. Thus, contrary to Freudian doctrine, genital primacy is not the final goal of *eros* but a kind of transient deviation in its course. It is a grudging response to the parental imperative that is undone when the species requirement—"be fruitful and multiply"—has been met. The final development of *Eros* comes about in the postparental period—the matured capacity for genital pleasure is retained, but the receptive pleasures of the mouth, eyes, and skin are regained. Given reasonable health and opportunity, a more complex, varied, and interesting consolidation of the erotic life is finally attainable in the later years.

Conclusion: Legitimizing the Field
of Life-Span Human Development

Finally, those studies that point to a parental armature of psychological change in the later years, though far from complete, do suggest a productive direction for life-span developmental psychology and a hopeful redirection for geropsychology as a whole. For example, they provide refreshing alternatives to the catastrophic view of the aging process, which holds that all later-life changes, in men and women, are ultimately last-ditch adaptations to imposed loss and inevitable depletion.

Equally important, if new potentials are indeed released in later life according to some developmental design, then geropsychologists can begin thinking in new ways about services to the aged and their delivery. Instead of thinking about the aged as hapless recipients of services over which they can have little control, they can begin to study the ways in which postparental *potentials* can be transformed—into resources and capacities—not only for the elders, but for us all.

Notes

1. Many piscine and insect species send forth their hordes of untended off-spring; in such cases, the statistical probabilities, rather than parental concern, may guarantee the survival of enough offspring to maintain population levels. But human females have a relatively short breeding span and rarely birth more than one child at a time. In our case, individualized parental care becomes particularly important in securing the survival of viable, potentially parental descendants.

2. Responding to the contemporary denigration of parenting, Erik Erikson recently asserted—much like this author—that there is a parental imperative. Despite its association with the sexual drives, the surgent drive to be parental is a potent and independent motive that is now coming under repression in Western society, when sexual drives are liberated from procreative goals. Just as sexual repression characterized the Victorian era, there is currently a "real danger that a new kind of repression may become a mark of adult life." Erikson urged psychoanalysts to be alert to the potential harm of such repression.

Indeed, his warning appears to be well-taken. At Northwestern University Medical School, in our studies of late-onset psychiatric disorders, we find that childless older women are represented in the population of first-onset psychotics far beyond their representation in the population as a whole. Replicated in British and Scandinavian samples, these findings suggest that the childless state can have malignant consequences long after the original contra-parental decision was first made. Like any other important motive, parenthood can be denied or repressed but only at one's peril; the subjective will to denial does not negate the objective importance of the denied wish.

3. This folk wisdom is borne out by more sophisticated psychological studies. Thus the experiments of Harlow and Mears (1979) with young chimps raised on terry-cloth "mothers" as well as the observations of Rene Spitz and Margerie Wolf (1946) on institutionally reared foundling infants demonstrate very clearly that physical security does not, by itself, guarantee the survival of the equally helpless, equally vulnerable human or nonhuman primate infant.

Harlow's baby chimps, for example, had all the food they needed, as well as tactile comfort of a sort. But while they survived to physical maturity without emotional nurture, they could not be parents. Male chimps raised without mothers did not know how to approach females, and similarly raised females would not accept the male for coitus; even when artificially inseminated, they would reject their own offspring. In their case, physical nurture without emotive caring had guaranteed individual but not species survival. In the second case, as reported by Spitz, the foundling infants, tended by efficient but unsentimental caretakers, often developed clinical depressions and were very prone to die of minor children's diseases that normally reared infants routinely shrug off. In their case, what appeared to be adequate physical care did not guarantee even individual survival. Thus feeding and blanketing are not enough; the infant who does not experience a loving welcome into the world probably will not thrive or grow to be the adequate parent of viable children.

In normal child-rearing practice, physical and emotional care imply and complement each other. Adequate physical care can come only from a concerned caretaker—truly adequate emotional care requires a physically secure environment. Love alone cannot comfort a baby who is chronically cold, wet, hungry, or in pain. And the mother cannot do her job, of comforting the child, unless she has, usually in the husband, a reliable provider of physical security.

But while the two forms of security, physical and emotional, are mutually supportive, the primary providers of these must, to a large degree, be distinct from each other. The fossil record now suggests that our species has had as many as four million years in which to evolve our distinctive ways, and particularly our unique parenting practices. To be successful, human parenthood, despite any local variations, had to take account of the unique vulnerability of the human child, and the environmental threats menacing that child—from animal predators; from human enemies; from severe weather; from famine, drought, and plague. Under these stringent conditions, which still hold for a large part of the earth's population, the parent responsible for physical security cannot provide adequate emotional security, and the parent responsible for the provision of emotional security cannot guarantee the logistics of physical security.

The exclusivity of parenting roles is rooted in a fixed, necessary distinction between the placement of the protectors and the protected: Physical security is not guaranteed within the home range, but on its perimeter. Under average-expectable human or primate conditions of marginal food supply and external threat, adequate nourishment cannot be found or even produced within the immediate domestic precincts. Under conditions of foraging or marginal agriculture, local food sources may be quickly exhausted, and providers must fan out, far beyond the home site, to find new game preserves or to open up new lands for herding and cultivation. But even when there is settled agriculture, with some guarantee of adequate food supply, physical security requires that human and natural enemies be kept at bay, and as far from the community core as possible. A community whose defense line is pitched close to its center is, by definition, at chronic risk.

It follows, then, that the physical security of the infant can be guaranteed only by the parent, the father, who is ready to leave home if called on, as hunter, as slash-and-burn agriculturist, or in defense of an outlying borderline. Clearly, those assigned such responsibilities would be violating the basic criteria for physical security if they packed vulnerable children with them on their forays; nor could they adequately perform these vital tasks if they stayed homebound, within the range of a child's cry. Hovering close enough to provide the kind of emotional security on which the child's sense of basic trust is founded, they would inevitably fail to provide the same child with adequate physical security.

The same sorts of iron limitations that dictate that the protected must be separated from the providers of physical security hold also for the provision of emotional security. Whatever else she might be doing, the provider of emotional security should remain within sight and sound of her children or at least be in contact with alternate caretakers who are maintaining that immediate touch. She cannot depart too far from the domestic zone, from those familial settings in which the child's sense of basic trust is generated. Moreover, if the child is to feel relaxed and secure, the mother must feel relatively safe and cherished as well; accordingly, she should carry on her maintenance activities in some relatively protected domestic enclave, one in which her own sense of security can be communicated to her children.

4. I do not mean to disparage women's martial courage or to conserve bloodlust exclusively for men. While women have fought in many wars (usually on a voluntary basis), there is an unwritten though universal law about battle: "When it comes to slaughter, you do not send your daughter." As a consequence, at least a thousand men fall every day, around our planet, in one or another version of armed combat: border scuffles, attempted coups, terrorist raids, tribal wars, duels, fights between criminals and police, as well as fights among rival gangs. Idealistic women sometimes enlist in revolutionary bands, but they are otherwise spared our species' routine work of slaughter. This daily blood tax is levied mainly on young unmarried men, and for a good reason: A large proportion of community males can be sacrificed to warfare and other risky activities before there is a significant fall off in the next generation's replacement rate.

5. These speculations are to some degree confirmed by Martin Hoffman (1970) and his associates. They found that new parents move away from high ideals in favor of amoral familism. The child's needs and potentials are exalted over the more abstract claims of the larger community.

6. We can propose only a tentative explanation of the significant effect that age plays in determining the choice of postparental mastery styles. It may be that late fathers have always been invested in the denial defense—particularly, denial of their own aging—and that they maintain such postures in their late middle years through protracted parenting. In later life, facing an enforced retirement from parenthood, they may refuse the "feminine" alternatives represented by Passive Mastery, and instead continue to maintain their denials in the more extreme form of Magical Mastery; that is, they may elect to ignore the troubling realities of aging that they can no longer avoid or change through direct action.

References

1. Barry, H.; Bacon, M.; Child, I. (1957). "A cross-cultural survey of some sex differences in socialization." *J. abnorm. soc. Psychol.,* 55: 372–432.
2. Cooper, K. L.; Gutmann, D. L. (1987). "Gender identity and ego mastery style in middle-aged, pre- and post-empty nest women." *Gerontologist,* 27(3): 347–352.

3. Ewing, K. P. (1981). *The crisis of marriage for two Pakistani women*. Unpublished manuscript, Department of Anthropology, University of Chicago.

4. Feldman, S.; Biringen, Z.; Nash, S. (1981). "Fluctuations of sex-related self-attributions as a function of stage of family life cycle." *Devl. Psychol.,* 17: 24–35.

5. Galler, S. (1977). "Women graduate student returnees and their husbands: Study of the effects of the professional and academic graduate school experience on sex-role perceptions, marital relationships, and family concepts." Unpublished doctoral dissertation, School of Education, Northwestern University, Evanston.

6. Gilder, G. (1973). *Sexual suicide*. New York: Quadrangle Press.

7. Griffin, B. (1984). "Age differences in preferences for continuity and change." Unpublished doctoral dissertation, Division of Psychology, Department of Psychiatry and Behavioral Sciences, Northwestern University Medical School, Chicago.

8. Gutmann, D. L. (1964). "An exploration of ego configurations in middle and later life." In Neugarten, B. (Ed.), *Personality in middle and later life*. New York: Atherton Press.

9. Gutmann, D. L. (1967). "Aging among the highland Maya: A comparative study." *Pers. soc. Psychol.,* 7: 28–35.

10. Gutmann, D. L. (1969). *The country of old men: Cultural studies in the psychology of later life*. Institute of Gerontology, University of Michigan, Ann Arbor.

11. Harlow, H.; Mears, C. (1979). *The human model: Primate perspectives*. Washington, DC: V. H. Winston.

12. Heath, D. H. (1972). "What meaning and effect does fatherhood have for the maturing of professional men?" *Merrill-Palmer Qtrly.,* 24: 265–287.

13. Hoffman, M. L. (1970). "Conscience, personality and socialization techniques." *Human Development,* 13: 90–126.

14. Hrdy, S. B. (1981). "'Nepotists' and 'altruists': The behavior of old females among macaques and langur monkeys." In Amoss, Harrell (Eds.), *Other ways of growing old: Anthropological perspectives*. Stanford: Stanford University Press.

15. Kupper, G. (1975). "Exploring the impact of parenthood on young college students." Unpublished honors thesis, University of Michigan, Ann Arbor.

16. Levy, R. I. (1977). "Notes on being adult in different places." Unpublished manuscript, Department of Anthropology, University of California, San Diego.

17. Lowenthal, M. F. (1975). "Psycho-social variations across the adult life course: Frontiers for research and policy." *Gerontologist,* 15: 301–307.

18. Lowenthal, M. F.; Thurnher, M.; Chiriboga, D. (1975). *Four stages of life*. San Francisco: Jossey-Bass.

19. Mandelbaum, D. (1957). "The world view of the Kota." In Marriott, K. (Ed.), *Village India*. Chicago: University of Chicago Press.

20. Meneghan, E. G. (1975). "Parenthood and life satisfaction in later life: A comparative analysis." Unpublished paper, Committee on Human Development, University of Chicago, Chicago.

21. Murdoch, G. P. (1935). "Comparative data on division of labor by sex." *Soc. Forces,* 15: 551–553.
22. Neugarten, B. L.; Gutmann, D. L. (1968). "Age-sex roles and personality in middle age: A thematic apperception study." In Neugarten, B., *Middle age and aging.* Chicago: University of Chicago Press.
23. Newton, N. (1973). "Psycho-social aspects of the mother/father/child unit." Meetings of the Swedish Nutrition Foundation, Uppsala.
24. O'Connel, L. (1981). "Late parenthood and personality change in middle-aged men: An examination of the developmental hypothesis for adulthood." Unpublished doctoral dissertation, University of Chicago, Committee on Human Development.
25. Perloff, R.; Lamb, M. (1980). "The development of gender roles: An integrative life-span perspective." Unpublished manuscript, Department of Psychology, University of Wisconsin, Madison.
26. Peskin, H.; Livson, N. (1981). "Uses of the past in adult psychological health." In Eichorn, Mussen, Clausen, Hann, and Honzik (Eds.), *Present and past in middle life.* New York: Academic Press.
27. Ripley, D. (1984). "Parental status, sex roles, and gender mastery style in working-class fathers." Unpublished doctoral dissertation, Department of Psychology, Illinois Institute of Technology, Chicago.
28. Spitz, R. A.; Wolf, K. M. (1946). "Anaclitic depression." *Psychoanalytic Study of the Child,* 22: 313–342. New York: International Universities Press.
29. Thomae, H. (1962). "Thematic analysis of aging." In C. Tibbitts and W. Donahue (Eds.), *Social and psychological aspects of aging: Aging around the world.* New York: Columbia University Press.
30. Vatuk, S. (1975). "The aging woman in India: Self-perceptions and changing roles." In DeSouza, J. (Ed.), *Women in contemporary India.* Delhi: Manohar.

6 A Cross-Cultural View of Adult Life in the Extended Family

At this relatively late date, I can no longer remember, with any precision, what drove me to write this particular piece. I do recall (as later selections will show) getting caught up—but from the Right, rather than the Left—in the climate of political activism that dominated the Ann Arbor campus in the 1960s and 1970s. I was in effect a premature neo-conservative, and for a while my evolving insights into lifespan psychology were dedicated to the service of that counterrevolutionary position. In this case, I recall becoming annoyed by Germaine Greer's trashing—from her misapplied feminist perspective—of the nuclear family in favor of the extended family. A selection from her article leads off my response, which attacks the implicit—and simplistic—moralism of her position: "Four or more parental figures GOOD! Two parents BAAD!"

My own field experience in rural Indian and Arab settings had taught me that such politicized moralism corrupted the reality and blunted investigation. There exists a broad range of human family arrangements, and their differences are not to be judged against some absolute scale of moral values. Human proclivities and human institutions appear to have coevolved, and so it appears that each familial type is particularly valid for a particular season of the life-cycle. Thus, a village dominated by an extended family could be Edenic for a small son of that clan, whereas that same boy, grown into randy adolescence, might yearn for a more anonymous setting. He might even "light out for the territories" and migrate to a city, where he could make love to a girl without risking death at her brother's hands.

By extending this relativistic notion, the paper that follows attempts to put the nuclear versus extended family debate into a new and clarifying context: that of the species life-cycle, particularly in its later stages.

The Extended Family as Hero

The social sciences have become, in David Riesman's term, "Other Directed." They are less interested in internally based, intrapersonal sources of security—

conscience, identity—and more interested in those externally based, interpersonal sources of security that are found in the various forms of collective life. Thus, many social scientists now study, generate, and celebrate those collective enterprises in which inter-individual distinctions and rivalries are blurred over or dissipated in favor of some harmonious "group process." What is studied is also valued; and we now find that many social scientists assert the superiority of collectivist over individual enterprise: the encounter group is valued over individual psycho-therapy; Maoist collectivism is valued over democracy; the communard is valued over the entrepreneur; and the extended family is valued over the nuclear family. Thus, partially in deference to the ideas of Women's Lib, social scientists have begun to disparage the nuclear family as though it were the nuclear bomb. It is stigmatized as a hot-bed of sex-ism, double-binding, age-ism, capitalist ethics, and generational discontinuities. By contrast, the extended family—largely found in rural settings—is eulogized. The extended family takes on the pastorale mystique and is depicted as a panacea against human woe. Thus Germaine Greer is so taken by the extended family that she even accepts the patriarchal rule that usually accompanies it:

> The head was the oldest male parent, who ruled a number of sons and their wives and children. The work of the household was divided according to the status of the female in question: The unmarried daughters did the washing and spinning and weaving, the breeding wives bred, the elder wives nursed and disciplined the children, and managed the cooking, the oldest wife supervised the smooth running of the whole. There was friction but it had no chance to build itself into the intense introverted anguish of the single eye-to-eye confrontation of the isolated spouses. Family problems could be challenged openly in the family forum and the decisions of the elders were honored.

In this Rousseauan and essentially "outside" view, the extended family is seen to give, automatically and without stint, the kinds of love and security that the nuclear family either withholds or poisons. If the nuclear family represents an authentic circle of hell, then the extended family is our life in Eden, before the fall from grace.

Inside the Extended Family

However, this public relations picture of the extended family is not always corroborated by its members. For the past several years I have done field research into the comparative psychology of aging and have interviewed Navajo, Maya, and Druze subjects—all of them residents of one or another version of the extended family. But my middle-aged and elderly respondents (in the age-range 35–95 years) have reported grave difficulties in family living, as well as bonuses of the sort noted by social scientists. My subjects mention the support provided by relatives; but these admittedly helpful relatives might also be involved in family feuds. Complaints about mother-in-laws, stepmothers, or heavy handed older brothers come as easily from the members of each form of family, extended or nuclear. Furthermore, across cultures, younger subjects are likely to chafe under the heavy weight of social control: The extended family in the small village is the ideal repository of tradition, and woe to the adventurous spirit who enters into an unsanctioned marriage or some deviant line of work. In the folk society the deviant is not only "bad" in the moral sense, he is also eerie, not quite human. Accordingly, the tradition breaker who stays in or returns to his native village risks much trouble; he, his wife, and children will be the target of unrelenting gossip, even witchcraft accusations.

Clearly, then, the extended family—which typically gives power to the older generation over the younger—is not receptive to innovation. Thus, while younger men defer publicly to their fathers, they will often complain behind his back, calling him an obstacle to progress. Incidentally, revolutionary regimes typically regard the extended family as the major enemy of the new order that they are trying to build; and they work ruthlessly—as in the case of Red China—to disband it.

Comparing the Nuclear and Extended Families

In sum, judging from the accounts of actual members, the extended family is not a piece of our lost perfection or a reproach to our urban venality. It is not a philosopher's stone for transmuting human hate into human love. The extended family and the nuclear family do not represent moral polarities, but contrasting human arrangements, each of which has its own optimal social setting, its distinctive evolutionary history, and its distinctive functions. Each form of family life stresses and delivers the benefits that the other tends to neglect. For example, when we assess the nuclear family for its strengths and weaknesses, we do indeed find important deficiencies. The nuclear family is centered on two parents, and this limited personnel cannot provide a deep sense of security or help children whose love is tangled with their hate to resolve the terrible problem of ambivalence. But, by the same token, the reduced complement of the nuclear family is the basis of its particular strength. Because it is centered on a few members, individual differences are underlined; the nuclear family is not composed of replaceable social parts, but of unique individuals. Accordingly, the nuclear family sponsors individual differences, the sense of personal uniqueness and individual initiative. In effect, the nuclear family is packaged for physical and social mobility, and it prepares its children for successful adaptation in new and unpredicted environments. The child reared in the nuclear family carries the ultimate sources of his security within himself, but he must leave home in order to discover and lay claim to his strength. By contrast, the resources, prestige, and logistics of the cumbersome extended family are inevitably tied to and identified with a particular place, a home range, and the individual member who might want to explore new horizons is in for trouble: He cannot introduce innovations within the tradition-hallowed rigidities of the family; yet if he leaves, he must risk complete up-rooting from his accustomed psychosocial ground. Thus, while the nuclear family erodes the sense of collective resource lodged in the group, in the land, and in the household gods, it does replace it with a sense of individual resource lodged within the self—the kind of resource that is vital to mobility and discovery.

Clearly, these contrasting arrangements, the nuclear and the extended families, fluctuate in value according to historical circumstance, cultural values, and the life cycle position of the component members. The nuclear family tends to be valued over the extended family by emerging societies, by societies which value individual initiative and by those individuals—particularly the young—who are interested in exploring new life ways. The extended family is valued in rural settings, in cultures which resist change, and which value stability over innovation. Furthermore, the extended family tends to be valued by those who give priority to conformity over expressiveness; and within the life cycle, it is valued either by the very young or by the old.

The Comparative Psychology of Adult Life

I am not against the extended family *per se*; I am only against those who would take it out of its socio-historical framework and turn it into some object of cult worship. A determinedly relativistic approach informs the rest of this paper, which outlines some ideas, based on field work, concerning the coordination of the extended family system with the stages of the male life cycle in the middle and later years. We will consider the ways in which the various themes of the adult life stages mesh, or fail to mesh, with the extended family system in which these themes emerge and are expressed.

Once the period of chronic emergency that we know as parenthood has passed, and children can demonstrate their own capacity for active mastery, the massive repression of passive-dependency in the male and aggression in the case of the female is no longer required. As a result there takes place in both sexes a transcultural "return of the repressed." By contrast to younger men—and to their younger selves—the older male subjects (those in the age range 55–95 years) reverse the usual "masculine" priorities; they become more dependent, more diffusely sensual, more sensitive to the incidental pleasures and pains of the world.

By the same token, older women reclaim the aggression that can no longer hurt their young. Even in the patriarchal Druze culture older women become more intrusive, more domineering, and less sentimental. In effect, with the phasing out of the gender-specific emergency reactions that we call sex role behavior, each sex becomes to some degree what the other used to be, and there is ushered in the normal unisex of later life.

The Stages of Adult Life in the Extended Family

However we characterize these transformations, it is clear that they involve important age-shifts in relating styles; we are describing sex and age related changes in the mode of relating to others, in the satisfactions derived from social relationships, in the expectations and demands that are brought to relationships, and in the relative importance of human relationships as against other sources of security and satisfaction. Clearly, given the magnitude of the age change in the inner orientations that individuals bring to their social investments, there should be corresponding shifts in the subjective involvement with that pivotal system of intimate relationships, the extended family, as its members age. Again, my field observations were mainly confined to men, and I will only try to delineate the age changes in masculine priorities within the extended family. Turning first to the younger men, we find that their favored ego style—that of Active Mastery—has important consequences for their relations to and within the extended family. In general, younger men seem to be at best ambivalent towards the ready-made forms of security provided for them by their parents and relatives. True enough, younger men love their kin, and they appreciate the various forms of support that the family provides, but they are at the same time very conscious of the price—in autonomy, in authority, and in privacy—that they have to pay for the security blanket of their family. They are quite often aware that the family's support is bought at the price of free marital, residential, occupational, and religious choice. Furthermore, within the confines of the extended family the future is already predicted. Within its daily rounds, the family presents the picture of the way life has been, will be, and should be. Though the future is depicted as secure, it may contain little room for a younger man's fantasies of challenge, innovation, and high achievement. Accordingly, while many younger men do remain in the ancestral village, accept their place within the family, work their portion of the father's land, and wait to inherit, there is always a minority of restless ones—both married and unmarried—who hive off, who leave the secure but confining life. Some of these out-migrants are clearly motivated by economic necessity: There is not enough land for all the brothers. But others are driven by some inchoate ferment within the blood: They are urged away from the safe harbor precisely because it is too secure. In Shakespeare's words, they are driven "by the winds that blow young men through the world, to seek their fortunes far from home, where small experience grows."[1]

The extended family may look good to us, the rootless children of rootless pioneers. But we must remember that cities are founded and settled by the young refugees from the extended family. We are constantly reminded, as part of the new sentimentality, that the city is a harsh and alienating environment, but the critics of the urban experience forget that while the city alienates the individual it also frees him. The usual charge against the city is that one can drop dead in public without being noticed, but the corollary is that one can enjoy any legal or even para-legal life in the city without being restrained, or gossiped over. In the city the refugee from the extended family can experiment with vocational, religious, political, and sexual possibilities without suffering the usual social consequences of his explorations, and without making final choices. He is not surrounded by a review panel of concerned and keenly observant relatives who will not forget his past sins, and who treat his tentative sexual experiments as though they were final life choices. Thus, if the extended family offers community at the price of freedom, the city offers freedom at the price of community. In effect, the priorities of the city match the priorities of young men. Accordingly, it is not strange that younger men often leave their parental village and their extended family for some strange city halfway around the world.

However, just as young men leave village and family for the rootless city, many older men leave the now lonely and frightening city and cycle back to their native village and kinsmen. In the apt Indian term, they "return to the blanket." Increasingly, the village becomes the retirement community for the older man who has had a moderate success in the city and who has come back to buy the house, the land, the herds, and the prestige that he could not afford in his youth. Clearly, the prospect of being a big shot, of being a big frog in a small puddle, will draw many men back to the village of their birth and to their family of orientation.

The Recycling of the Future

Thus, by providing a haven, the extended family meets the personal needs of those older men who cycle back to their origins at the end of life. But there are many men who have lived out their lives, and reached middle age, without ever leaving the confines of village and family. In their case, as they reach middle life, the extended family and the village ambiance serve to convert some of the personal, intrinsic developments of later life into transactions that have great social utility. This mediation of the life-cycle is very evident in regard to a characteristic phenomenon of the middle years: "the re-cycling of the future." By this I refer to the readiness of older traditional agriculturists to concede their own future hopes and plans to their maturing sons. This development is facilitated by the patterning of interpersonal experience in the small traditional community, and by the blurring of interpersonal boundaries that takes place there. The redundant lifestyle, the high degree of consensus and the pooling of individuals into larger mergers of village, clan, and tribe, reduces self-boundaries and sponsors a fractionating or distribution of the elements of self into their outer exemplars or representations. As regards intergenerational relations, this phenomenon of the "distributed self" makes for a strong sense of identification and relatedness between fathers and sons, across the generations. The father can re-experience his younger self in his son; the son can see his future self represented in the father. This trans-generational homogeneity becomes particularly useful at that point—usually in his early fifties—when the father concedes that he has "peaked," and that he cannot expect his remaining fantasies of wealth or power to be realized in the future. Typically, the middle-aged peasant looks to a future in which his strength for meeting the continuing demands of the agricultural life will decline. However, while his own future closes off it is possible for the peasant father, within the extended family, to transfer his personal hopes and fantasies from himself to that son with whom his own ego is blended. The father joins the future through his younger self, his son, and therefore finds it easy to concede the future to him. On the filial side, while sons may grumble about the father's authority, or his old fashioned methods, they do tend to share his overall values and goals. Accordingly, there is little evidence in extended family relationships of the so-called "Generation Gap."[2]

The Old Man as Hero

But identification across generations is not the only feature of life in the traditional community facilitating the "recycling of the future." The older traditional father can concede the future to his son because doors to particular forms of prestige and power have opened to him that are largely closed to his son. That is, in the traditional community, as the man ages, he may disengage from the technical-productive order (which he concedes to his son) but he tightens his linkage to the traditional order, the moral core of the society, and thereby gains a privileged status largely closed off to the younger individuals who have not yet lived a full life under the discipline of the tradition, and who have not yet proved their moral worth.

In effect, the older man in the traditional society gives up the idea that he is the center of executive action in exchange for a refreshed sense of junction with the executive powers of the Gods (Gutmann 1973). The traditional order of society provides the institutional structures and practices through which this sense of connection to the vital powers of the Gods can be enacted. The older man is humble; therefore his prayer is particularly acceptable to the deity and serves to bring his sustaining powers into the life-forms of community and its ecology. In effect, the social structure of the traditional society acts so as to translate the normal male passivity of later life into the very pivot of the older man's renewed prestige in the community at large.

The Recovery of the Past

The older man's enhanced moral prestige allows his son to inherit the future; and it also allows the old father to regain the past. Having dispensed with the future, he can begin to again enjoy the pleasures of the past that were ruled out in the service of productive parenthood. Within the larger community, in his public aspect, the old man is a sort of hero; but within the extended family he can live out some of his wishes to be the recipient of that which he used to provide to others. As these yearnings emerge or re-emerge, the older man quite naturally turns back to that setting wherein he received his first provisions of affection and support: he turns to the family. His parents have long since passed on; but the family which included the subject and his parents still persists relatively unchanged. The extended family relates the past to the present; therefore the old man in the bosom of the extended family can relive his own past as a child through his participation in the present life of the family; he can recapture the sense of being again included in a "parenting" milieu.

By helping him to relive his beginnings the extended family also aids the old man towards his central goal—the denial of the end. The parental or "species" function of the old man has ended; weakness, disease, and the death of peers remind him of the end. His natural impulse, since he cannot project himself into the future, is to deny the end by returning to his own beginnings. His wish is to deny the end by creating some of the weather, some of the ambiance of his own inception as a protected and relatively indulged child. The extended family supports his denial by providing the human raw materials out of which the old man can reconstruct the early world of attentive and reliable kin. Furthermore, the members of the extended family offer automatic, unquestioned respect to the older man; and by so doing they help to revive childhood memories of total and unconditional acceptance. The extended family gives to the older man a panel of caretakers—

daughters-in-law, daughters, nieces, sons, and sons-in-law—around whom he can live out some of the fantasies and expectations that he once held towards the older parental figures of his childhood. Thus, the extended family allows some of these unfolding developments of later life to take place in benign circumstances, in a setting which accepts the "childish" needs of the old man as these emerge.

In effect then, the major "social ecologies" of the folk society—the formal, traditional institutions and the extended family—between them provide settings in which the older man can live out discrepant aspects of his nature, without these coming into painful conflict. Within the prayer house he can be the autocrat with special *entree* to the deity, and he can look down on the younger men, who do not share his special knowledge; but within the family he can live out and enjoy his need to be indulged and taken care of. Having access to both these settings, he does not have to make some final choice between being either the patriarch or the child.

Finally then, when we view the ways in which the structures and usages of the extended family interface with the changing themes of the adult male life cycle, we do not find guaranteed integration and harmony between social pressures and personal needs. Quite the contrary, it appears that the extended family as an institution is quite discordant with the periods of young adulthood and early middle age—those in which the sense of individual agency and responsibility are being developed, tested, and enacted. These are the age-grades which are most likely to generate refugees and drop-outs from the extended family. On the other hand, the extended family is well fitted to the later stages of the life cycle during which individual agency, individual responsibility, and orientation to the future are being abandoned and turned over to others. The extended family is particularly useful to men who are preparing to relive the past rather than shape the future. Perhaps those social scientists who romanticize the rural and communal past find the extended family attractive for the same reasons.

Notes

1. Thus, the usual rigid sex-role distinctions of young and middle adulthood serve to convert dangerous inter-community male and female aggression to useful extra-communal, outwardly directed aggression. That is, via his role as husband and father, the younger man deflects the wife's aggression away from their children, and his own aggression away from the community as a whole. He "removes" it from within the domestic precincts to the outer defense line of the community.

2. Perhaps the generation gap is a product of urban society and the nuclear family, both of which sponsor a higher degree of individualization in all its members,

including fathers and sons. The self-aware person is likely to cling—well into middle life—to the idea that his future goals will be realized, *by himself*, at some later date. Accordingly, urban fathers are not as likely as traditional fathers to concede the future to their sons. They often continue to work on their own career long into middle and even later life. By the same token, the individualized son, product of nuclear family and urban experience, will not easily accept his father's idea of what the future ought to be. He will not accept or strive towards some vision of the future that was foisted on him by the past. Accordingly, in the nuclear family and in the urban society, fathers and sons tend to fight each other for the ownership of the future. We call this struggle "the generation gap."

References

Gutmann, D. (1973). "The Subjective Politics of Power: The Dilemma of Post-Superego Man." *Social Research,* 40(4): 570–616.

7 The Premature Gerontocracy: Themes of Aging and Death in the Youth Culture

This paper started as a comic piece and was completed under deadline for Social Research *in a Druze village of the Western Galilee. My observations of older men across various cultures had by this point cohered into a generic portrait, focused around the passive traits that distinguished the senior from the younger men. Between field trips, I was teaching psychology at the University of Michigan in Ann Arbor, a city frequently referred to as "Dope Capitol of the Middle West," and was witness to the rise of the counterculture in all its manifold variety, from activism expressed in student takeovers to activism expressed as pot smoking and endless pseudo-philosophical victim-babble. Watching this circus, it struck me that the hippie traits announced as the new revelation for youth closely matched those that, in my findings and in the species narrative, distinguished aged men from young men. The only difference was that the elders came by their psychological makeup more or less naturally, whereas the hippies sometimes reached a similarly geriatric state with the help of chemicals. At first I thought of these parallels as a kind of sidebar on the campus "revolution" and only cited them to twit my earnest liberal colleagues who—in defiance of the rationality that they were supposed to uphold—were busy celebrating the counterculture in all its forms.*

In this spirit of mockery, I presented my critique to a meeting of the Tuesday Night Supper Club, a graduate student gathering (scheduled, of course, for Wednesday evenings) at which faculty speakers appeared by invitation to give funny talks—bluntly put, to be clowns for their students. But good clowns are dangerous: While seeming to ridicule themselves, they manage to ridicule their audience. In this generous spirit, I told the graduate students that the sanctified hippies—the standard bearers of their generation—were, in the psychological sense, premature old men. I didn't get my laugh. Rather, my audience suddenly got very quiet, quickly formed themselves into a research seminar, and asked penetrating questions about my methodology.

At that point, I realized that my "heresy" against the counterculture was more than a joke: I knew I was on to something, and I decided to turn what had started out as a piece of dog-gerel into a paper for Social Research. *In retrospect, I am reassured that this project was justified. Events have proven me right about the death hunger of prematurely geriatric hip-pies. In the name of "life" the counterculture accelerated aging and death for too many of its members—and for our culture as a whole.*

At the time I wrote this piece, the minor goal was to continue bashing the hippies and their adult supporters; the major goal was to drive home a point about the psychology of older men. If young men, with a young man's biology and a young man's future, can nevertheless replicate the passive tendencies and oral appetites of older men, then that same condition is not neces-sarily the incidental side effect of a worn-out body. The condition shared by old men and the chronologically young sixties hippies is—by this logic—explicitly psychological in nature, arising from prior psycho-cultural causes. If so, then its pathological manifestations—in the old as well as the young—are amenable, when necessary, to psychological treatment. They are, if not reversible, at least available for many new expressions. They can enliven the self or pre-pare it for death. The body does indeed age, but as the longevous survivors that I describe in this piece show us, nowhere is it written that the spirit must decompose with it.

Introduction:
The Youthful Fixation on Death

The young people of the counter-culture now obsessively use the terms "life" and "death" to make political, moral, racial, and even generational distinctions. Thus, "life-loving," "life-enhancing," or "of the camp of life" are used to refer to those who are young, black, left-wing, or proletarian; while "the camp of death" includes the bourgeois, the white-skinned, the politically liberal or conservative, and the middle aged (though not the old). This rhetoric has its uses: it takes away the horror of death by presenting it as an invention of the establishment, a side ef-fect of an outworn *Zeitgeist*. In addition, this language reduces the moral ambiguity of revolutionary politics—it is comforting to believe that the killing that is a nec-essary part of revolution is done in the name of nothing less than *life* itself.

But the "life-death" rhetoric does more than justify violence or defend narcis-sism: it is expressive as well as defensive. It seems to express fears, preoccupa-tions, perhaps even fascinations with death, on the part of a young, liberated, and usually gifted cohort. And when we look at the rising number of casualties among the new youth from drug over-dose, serum hepatitis, and SDI, then we have to consider the possibility that some of our most promising children are driven to risk death, and even to suffer it. Behind the "kids'" strident accusation that the establishment forces them towards various forms of death, there may well be some unacknowledged lethal impulse of their own.

This tragic paradox, that those who stand at the beginning of life should share the concerns of those whose lives are ending, is usually explained by the probability of destruction in an atomic war. No doubt this fear plays a large part: young people, with all their lives before them, have the most to lose in a holocaust, and so are most depressed by the sense of doom. However, it appears to me that there are other, less rational and less apparent reasons for the youthful preoccupation with death. These have to do with the psychological resemblance between the very old and the youthful counter-culturists that have impressed me in the course of carrying out research on the comparative psychology of aging.

The Normal Psychology of Aging: A Background Summary

This argument—that there is a psychological equivalence between the new youth and the old men—calls for a short review of the psychological events in normal aging. Accordingly, I will lead off with some observations and findings concerning the psychological traits which seem to be most characteristic of older men, those aged 60 and over, regardless of culture. The cited research into what might be called the species psychology of aging has occupied me for the past eight years, and has involved intensive interviewing and projective testing of men from various ethnic and cultural groups: urban, middle-class white Americans; Mayan Indians of Yucatan and Chiapas; traditional (Western) Navajo Indians; and Druze agriculturists of the Galilee and Golan Heights.

Such comparisons, between age cohorts and across cultures, tell us something about a piece of refractory human nature—the generic psychology of aging. Aging is also the prelude to death, and to the degree that death is also a personal, psychological event, the study of the normal psychology of later life may also tell us something about the normal psychology of dying. Finally, if there are some fundamental parallels between the themes of aging and those emerging in the youth culture, this comparative analysis may provide some insight into the meaning of that much debated sub-culture; and by extension, into the death-consciousness prevalent in its youthful members.

The Phasing Out of Aggression

The methods and the results of the various cross-cultural studies summarized here have been reported in detail elsewhere. This paper will report only a summary of the major results. Turning to these, the firmest findings point to the almost universal phasing out of aggressive motives in men during late middle life, and their replacement by more tender, affiliative sentiments. Thus, we find that older men abjure competition, avoid provocation, and mainly enter into conflict situations as peace-makers. However, while older men may become less aggressive in their behavior and attitudes towards others, their concern with aggression *per se* does not end. It is still something to be reckoned with, but now as an external rather than as an internal threat. This is in contrast to younger men who are more preoccupied with the management of their own rather than others' aggression. For my younger subjects, aggression is *internal,* and potentially at their disposal. It is energy, and, as such, capable of good or bad, constructive or destructive uses. As the younger men see it, their job is to maintain internal controls in order to ensure that their energy will be put to good rather than bad uses. For older men, energy still mingles both beneficial and destructive potentials, but now it belongs to external agents—their grown sons, the priests, the gods, witches, village authorities, even their wives—who can help them or harm them at their pleasure. The older man's job is to manage power in its external forms, to ensure that the good powers will intercede in their behalf against the bad powers that menace and frighten them. Accordingly, the aging man often moves away from a provocative, confronting stance and towards one that is, outwardly at least, accommodating, propitiatory, and even humble, particularly towards the holders of power. Their implicit message to power-bearers is: "I am no threat, and I deserve your helpful intervention."

The Turn from Productivity to Receptivity

Younger husbands either create or take charge of the resources vital to their own security and the security of their dependents. Apparently, the experience of marriage and fatherhood gives them the incentive to make the difficult switch from a combative to a more disciplined and productive deployment of their vital energies. Instead of fighters and potential destroyers, they become builders. But with older men, the current sets in the opposite direction, towards pacifism. Older men are counter-aggressive; and they also tend to be counter-productive. Instead of being a source of security to others, they come to rely on various forms of security, emotional and material, that are provided for them by others. Thus, they become dependent on the productive activity of their grown sons, their wives, the priests, supernatural helpers, social agencies—the particular nature of the nurturing agent has to do with local customs, and with personal circumstances. The important thing is that older men turn—whether with pleasure, with shame, or with apprehension—towards a receptive and away from a productive position.

The Sensuality of Later Life

Older men are not only receptive to love and support from human providers; they also supply themselves from the impersonal world. For example, *concerns* about food become increasingly important to aging men; they think about food, they reminisce about it, and while their actual intake may decline, they become increasingly picky about their grub. Older men tend to become food faddists, and they become particularly addicted to foods like those that they first received from their mothers, in early childhood.

Younger men mainly love what they have produced, but older men respond to all the small pleasures that nature provides: pleasant sights and sounds, soothing textures, warmth and sunshine. Thus, younger men looking at their corn field will see a cash crop; they see money growing. Older men will look at their corn field in less utilitarian, less instrumentalized ways. They report the beauty of the fresh green leaves, the softness of the corn silk, and the plumpness of the kernels. Young men see a product, a piece of security that they have generated; but old men take pleasure in the corn itself, through all their senses.

A Developmental Theory of Adulthood and Old Age

One clear conclusion that can be drawn from the observed age differences is that young men repress their sensuality, they delay gratification, and that older men are less likely to impose these restraints on themselves. In these relatively affluent times we are likely to appreciate the sensual "switched on" old man over the utilitarian, "tuned out" young man. But psychoanalytic theories of development hold that the forms of repression maintained by younger men are vital to survival, particularly in the face of the average expectable human condition of scarcity and necessity. Briefly stated, Freudian theory holds that young men transform their bodies into tools and weapons by developing the capacity for delay of gratification, that is, by clearing their muscles, skin, and sphincters of sensitivity to pleasure. Sensuality is fenced off, relegated to the genital zone, there to be experienced intensely but briefly and in the service of procreation. If this process of repression, of internal boundary-building succeeds, then young men are able to face the challenging and often dangerous world of enemy, prey, or hard work without being distracted by too much longing for comfort or security. By and large, they can be trusted to do what has to be done, or what their elders and leaders tell them has to be done.

This repressive process is strongly stimulated and reinforced in men by the experience of parenthood. The needs of vulnerable children seem to be a formidable stimulus to fathers as well as to mothers—paternity as well as maternity has its imperatives—and the standard reaction for each sex is to surrender to the other the qualities that would interfere with the provision of their special form of security. Men, the providers of physical security, give up the sensual dependency that would interfere with their courage and endurance; and women, the providers of emotional security, give up the aggression that could frighten or hurt a vulnerable, needful child.

An Outcome of Normal Development: The Unisex of Later Life

In any event, the period of chronic emergency passes; children grow up, develop their own capacity for active mastery, take over the responsibility for providing their own security and, in some particularly orderly and traditional societies, the security of their parents. The general consequence is that both sexes can afford, in later life, the luxury of living out the potentials and pleasures that they had to relinquish early on, in the service of their particular parental task.

The consequence of this mid-life involution is that the sexes move closer together, psychologically, each partner becoming what the other used to be, and there is ushered in the unisex of later life. Thus, the loss in later life of boundaries and distinctions within the self is matched by the blurring over of inter-sex distinctions, and by the fading out of the tensions that once charged sexual relationships with their sense of drama and excitement.

The Religiosity of Later Life

Since women are reputed to be more devout than men, the "feminization" of older men may partly account for their evident swing towards religion. Even in societies without a pervasive religious life, we can see the development, in dreams, or in responses to our projective tests, of a *sub rosa* religious orientation among older men. Thus, when younger men look at a TAT picture of a man with his arm extended, they say that he is threatening or hitting somebody. But older men, even in cultures which do not sponsor a formal religious role for their age-grade, see this same figure extending this same arm beseechingly, and in prayer. Along similar lines, old men are more apt than younger men to believe that *particular* deaths or misfortunes are caused by witches or other supernatural agencies, even in societies where the belief in such agents is general across age groups. In the relatively primitive Mayan and Navajo cultures, old men see life as a drama between the evil spirits and the good influences that can be called up, through prayer and humility, to serve as buffers against the malignant powers. The more sophisticated Druze do not fraction external power into good and bad agents, but see all events, whether lethal or benign, as coming from the same Allah, whose purposes are unknowable but also perfect. In both cases, Indian and Druze, older men are taking a humble, deferential stance towards great power, which is seen to be outside of themselves, and to which they need to be allied. Where young men seem to feel that they must—by effort and risk—generate internal power, older men seem to feel that they can *cajole* external power to their cause through postures of submission, and demonstrations of weakness. In prayer they pantomime the postures that the gods would require of them.

Religion as Vicarious Production

But the religious bent of older men has its sources in the ego as well as in the id. Their need to be in touch, whether in active or passive ways, with good and productive forces does not end as the individual life-cycle turns towards its final station. As men sense the ending of their own individual cycle, they tend to identify themselves with cycles that do not end with death, but that persist through *and because of* alternations of death and rebirth. Thus, older men tend to move away from defining and implementing their own productive purposes, and they put themselves at the service, at least in token ways, of the productive forces of the universe, as these are represented in their culture. Where young men live out their passivity vicariously, through their wives, old men live out their active productivity vicariously, through their association with the gods. Specifically, I find that old men are interested in growing things, not solely for purposes of profit but in order to feel that they are agents of some larger productive principle that is manifested through themselves. Thus, older Navajos, as mentioned earlier, will see beauty in an ear of corn, not because it represents money or sustenance, but because it grew from a seed. Moved by the same sentiments, aging executives in Kansas City will turn to the cultivation of rose bushes.

Older men also become more tender and "maternal" in their relations with young children (the "grandfather syndrome"). This probably has to do with the previously discussed "femininity" of later life; but older men—who are trying to escape from the sense of the *end*—also appreciate children because they stand at the *beginning*. Thus, in their involvement with children, old men seem to revive the climate of their own beginning.[1] But at the same time, through their concern for children, old men revive the sense of what Erikson has called *generativity*—the sense that they are agents in some larger process of natural growth.

I would submit that as older men try to identify with versions of productivity that lie outside of themselves, they become, in the best sense of that word, religious; and in their attempt to personalize, to give shape and substance to a principle that they only dimly apprehend, they are led naturally towards the religious imagery of their culture, and so into conventional religious affiliation. The paradox lies in the fact that this affirmation of life through care-taking and religious practices is predicated on the approach of death.

The Death of the Ego: Magical Mastery

The religiosity of older men helps them manage their chronic masculine concerns around power and production, though now within the passive voice. But it also contains expressions of an archaic coping style that normally makes its appearance—except among neurotics and psychotics—mainly in later life. This is the mode of *magical mastery*. It is distinguished from the preceding mastery positions by a lack of reality orientation. Central to this stage is an erosion of ego boundaries, of the persisting sense of self/other distinctions. In effect, the world becomes a picture of what the subject fears or wants from the world; the usually persistent boundary placed between the province of the self and the domain of the other becomes unfixed, indeterminate, such that internal content of the self is mingled with and *perceived in* those external agents that pertain to those contents.[2]

Seemingly, the boundaries that the ego normally maintains—though at a high cost in energy—are the outer aspects of the inner repressions and delaying mechanisms on which active mastery and instrumentality are founded. Once the active, instrumental phase of life is past, ego energy can be withdrawn from both the inner and the outer boundaries, and infantile demands for pleasure and security can flood back into the domains that they had previously held in early life. As they move back into skin, mouth, and sphincter the result is the turn towards diffuse sensuality that we noted earlier; and when they come to dominate—as in childhood—cognition and perception, the result is the stage of magical mastery.

Magical Mastery and Religion

The rather vague, mystical religiosity of later life, the sense that one is blended into some larger order of the universe, is an expression of Magical Mastery brought about by the weakening of ego boundaries. For younger men, whose ego boundaries are normally intact, the experience of mystical union, Freud's "oceanic sense," is achieved through artificial means: rhythmic chanting, dancing, identification with hypnotic leaders, or drugs. By contrast, in later life, as ego boundaries fray out and become "porous," the mystical sense of union with some divine order arises naturally.

Magical Mastery and Death

But despite being "regressive," and a recapitulation of early developmental stages, Magical Mastery has a strange utility: it appears on schedule to close the circle, to lead men naturally towards death. In order to avoid the horror of their end, men revive—through memory, through identification with children, through child-like behavior, through the taste of the foods that were first fed to them by their mothers—the weather of their beginning. They thereby magically deny death; but the price is the "death" of the ego. The ego is dissipated, killed off because it will not finally relinquish the awareness of reality, including the awareness of oncoming death; and that act of murder—even though undertaken to preserve the illusion of rebirth and new beginnings—may set the stage for the final death of the body.

These may sound like the mystical speculations of an investigator who has himself given in to magical thinking. But the sequence, magical mastery then physical death, shapes hard data. Psychological data taken from nursing home residents before their medically unpredicted deaths show that their sudden decease was preceded by an equally sudden breakdown of ego functions towards magical mastery. Klaus Riegel's careful work (personal communication) makes a similar point: intellectual functioning does not decline across the adult years; rather, most forms of thinking hold steady across the adult life span, and only decline sharply and suddenly shortly before actual death. Finally, a comparison of TAT records from the same Navajo subjects over a four-year period indicates that the intra-individual movement towards passive and magical imagery is greater for each successive age group, such that 40-year-old men show little shift in the regressive direction after four years, while 70-year-olds show a great deal. Thus, the degree of psychic regression appears to accelerate with nearness to death.

Narcissism and the Wish for Death

But the old man's relation to death includes more than fear and magical denial. There is also resignation, and beyond that a secret welcoming of death. Thus, trans-culturally, men dream of death as an assassin, as an angry beast, as a canyon into which they fall; but they also dream of it and portray it in their projective test responses as a welcoming mother, or as a wide ocean in which they would like to swim. Some Druze men speak of this attraction for death with a passive voice: death is to be welcomed as an expression of God's will—to argue with death is to argue with God. Others speak of moving actively towards death, of forcing its hand: a 75-year-old Druze tells me: "I should die now, when I am at the height of my wisdom and strength and not when I have become weak and stupid, and children laugh at me in the streets." Statements like these may represent resignation; but they may also be expressions, whether voiced in obedient or defiant terms, of the wish for death.

But, if the old man's fear of death is so great that he relies on magical mastery to deny it, then why might he also seek death? This paradox is perhaps resolved if we consider some effects of narcissism, particularly the normal but also fairly pronounced narcissism of later life. In the narcissistic phase of relationships, the self becomes the target of its own hate as well as of its own love. Where we love, we also hate, whether the object of our love is some other, or ourselves. Accordingly, in later life the claims of the self for immediate satisfaction are raised above competing claims from others, from society, and from the reality principle itself; but that same self is also humbled before men and the gods, and death—the final extinction of the self—may be quietly welcomed. Old men dream of assassins; but the murderer they fear is not only in their aging cells, it is in their own impulses, in the dark side of their own self-love.

Active Mastery and Longevity: A Study of Surviving Traditionalists

If the passive qualities that have been found to accompany masculine aging are indeed the out-riders of somatic death, then the reverse should also be true: the more active traits should be associated with persisting life, and the men who favor the active mastery modality over passivity and/or magical mastery should also be those who are, in any age group, the furthest from death. In the absence of elaborate longitudinal data from our subjects, we have indirectly tested this proposition by singling out, for special examination, the sub-sample of Indian and Druze subjects aged 70 and over. Clearly, these men have been further from death than most of their contemporaries, over most of the life-span. If survivors have a distinctive psychic constitution, we should see its traces most clearly among these longevous preliterate men, who have little going for them but their own resources. And in point of fact, we do find that the oldest men of our samples are distinguished from the "normal" or pre-survivor (55–69 years old) cohorts from the same cultures by their counterdependency, by their continued productivity, by their competitiveness, and by their tendency to personalize death and fight it as an external enemy.

Their differences from the normal, pre-survivor cohort are truly striking: I have seen old Navajo men of 95 years literally crawl to their corn field, not because they need its produce to live, but because they claim that their relatives have asked for the corn. At whatever costs, they have to demonstrate—at least in token ways—that they can still be a source of supply to others. Physical movement has particular importance for these longevous men. Inactivity is for them a metaphor of death: they usually do not sleep more than five hours a night; more than that, and their extremities become cold and numb. Feeling death creeping up their limbs, the old survivors fight back: they rise from the bed, the hammock, the sheepskin, and they go out—to visit friends in the Druze case, to clear fields in the Mayan case, to herd sheep in the Navajo case.[3]

These longevous men are prone to the same passive yearnings as the "normal" aged; they also experience the temptation to relax, to take it easy, to get out of the rat race, to consume rather than to produce, to submit rather than to fight. The difference is that where the normal aged accept these urgings, the survivors, much like younger men, define them as a threat, and put themselves in opposition to their own emergent passivity.[4]

The old survivors usually enjoy much social prestige, and this provides them with both the pressures and the rewards for continued activity. They are also aided in their final struggle against passivity by their earliest identifications. Thus, where the normal aged seem to revive their identification with their mothers (and the sense of themselves as needful children), the survivors are more likely to maintain their identification with the father figures who taught them to work, to endure, and to choose active over passive alternatives.

Survival and the Need for an Enemy

While old survivors mainly turn the resistant, *stubborn* posture inwards, against their own "weakness," they also turn it outwards, against challenges from impersonal nature, or from human enemies. I rarely talk to such a man, in any culture, without finding that he is embroiled in a struggle with some real or imagined enemy. For the longevous Navajo, the enemy is likely to be some witch "way over there," who is jealous of their wealth and is making lethal spells against them; and among the Druze the enemy is some neighbor presumably encroaching on their lands. Even where life does not offer evidence of real enemies, old survivors are likely to imagine them and to turn bucolic and potentially peaceful activities into fantasy wars. Thus, I ask a 100-year-old Navajo found cultivating, why corn is still so important to him, and he replies: "You must understand that corn is like your wife, and the weeds are like another man who comes to steal your wife. You have to kill those weeds!" Unlike the pre-survivor aged men, this veteran does not dwell on the beauty or the taste of the corn; rather, he reverses the usual age priorities and turns a potentially oral experience into an occasion of rivalry and combat.

In sum, the normal aged seem to use magical mastery in the form of gross *denial* of reality in order to protect their passivity: "I do not have to act; someone up there loves me, and everything is for the best in the best of all possible worlds." By contrast, the old survivors use magical mastery in the form of *projective* distortions of reality in order to justify their continued action: "There is a sea of troubles, of enemies, and I must take arms up against them." They turn the death within their bodies into a thief or into an assassin "out there" who can be fought, and by thus externalizing and personalizing their enemy they preserve the active, fighting stance on which their continued life may partly depend.

Doctors with whom I have spoken to about such matters all concur: in the absence of "hard" clinical data, death can be predicted when the patient "stops fighting." Working from the other end of the life-cycle, the psychoanalyst Ernst Kris has shown that foundling infants under "adequate" though impersonal care will develop a depressive, apathetic "hospitalism" syndrome that is notably lethal to them. By the same token, longitudinal studies of our panel of traditional Navajo indicate that men who score high on the various indices of passive-dependency at time 1 are much more likely than men with low scores on this dimension to develop severe and/or terminal diseases by time 2, four years later. This effect is predictable, regardless of age, except for the very oldest men. All these convergent findings, from a wide range of populations, suggest that there may be something quite deadly about the passive-dependent conformation. Conversely, there may be something life-preserving about the stubborn, recalcitrant posture. Sweet, wise old men deserve better, but they seem to lose out. Perhaps the fighting, oppositional stance is the psychic counterpart of a generally more vital organism; or perhaps this oppositional stance itself keeps the immune system tuned up to such a pitch that it can better overcome disease effects. If so, then in later life the necessary mobilization is brought about by a kind of "adaptive paranoia" that provides the fighting survivor with the necessary but non-existent enemies that he requires to keep him on his toes.[5] The old curmudgeons do finally die, but it is usually under protest: they "do not go gentle into that good night."

Perhaps we can summarize the findings and speculations concerning longevity and survival with this observation: The men who die before age 70 in traditional societies go to death as to a mother; and those survivors who live beyond 70 fight it like a father.[6]

Pre-Senile Youth: The Counter-Culture

I have described two postures, two syndromes, found among aging men. One involves disavowal of aggression and competition, and their replacement by dependency, sensuality, and ego diffusion. It is associated with early death, or with a life span of less than 70 years. The contrast syndrome is centered mainly around aggression and resistance against passive-dependent wishes within the self, and against those outer agents that would force the self into a passive and dependent position. This active-assertive orientation is associated with temporal distance from death, and with survival, being mainly found among the younger men of our samples, those far from death, or among the very old men, who have outlived most of their fellows. Turning back to the topic of youthful involvement with death, we can see that the so-called counter-culture has amplified and made a politics out of the first complex of attitudes—those associated with normal aging, with closeness to death, and with low survival. In short, the counter-culture, its theorists, and PR men have co-opted, as the very badge of youth and renewal, those qualities which are the species insignia of aging and morbidity.[7]

Counter-Aggression and Counter-Productivity in the Counter-Culture

Consider for example the pivotal matter of aggression, which is repudiated both by aging men and by the "kids"—and for much the same reason, namely, that individual aggression is disruptive to community, to oneness with others. Thus, many young people now react to a competitive urge within themselves as their puritan ancestors might have fought an impulse towards illicit sex. And their major charge against the university, one most likely to fuel their rebellion, is that it forces them—through grading systems, exams, and other occasions of sin—to compete against each other.[8]

Perhaps as part of this turn away from competition, the counter-culture also sponsors the same rejection of the productive stance that we find among aging men of various cultures. Of course, certain forms of productivity are still extolled by the counter-culture: the production of handicrafts, or organic foods, etc. However, there is at the same time a rejection of *apprenticeship*. Thus, any production which reflects untutored spontaneous "creativity" is encouraged; but the process of education for production, which involves delaying the pleasure of self-expression, and the acceptance of standards which have not been devised by the self, is generally discredited.

The Sponsorship of Dependency in the Counter-Culture

The young men of the counter-culture manage their dependency much like aging men. True, the counter-culture does not espouse dependency as openly as it supports non-violence and counter-dominance. The dependent aged can plead a life of service to others, but the alienated young lack this justification, and so do not voice their succorant wishes as openly as their elders. However, such needs are central to both cohorts, and the dependent wishes are lived out by young men (and women) in explicit ways, particularly in regard to emotional needs. Twenty years ago David Riesman wrote of the other-directed quality of American youth, who rely on their peer groups and peer group leaders for legitimation, identity, and direction. The "lonely crowd" has become the lonely T-Group, and it is particularly in such quasi-communities of encounter and T-Groups that the demands for love and complete acceptance that Riesman could only infer twenty years ago are now directly voiced. Furthermore, the demands have escalated: words are not enough—now the demand is for the tangible, reassuring caress, the hug, whether it be given by man or woman, friend or stranger.

And, like the aged, who worship in some external form the power and resource that they can no longer feel within themselves, important segments of youth—whether the New Left, the Jesus freaks, or the addicts of rock—pay homage to their human icons: the "charismatic" rock stars, drug cult leaders, movement heavies, encounter group *papalois*, commune tyrants, or revolutionary *enragés*. Anybody who can speak with authority, who has some supplies of his own, who does not seem to care if he is loved, can quickly become a center of adoration by those sad, empty, strangely "uninflated" children who throng the urban world today. The politics of the hero do not really matter: Left or Right, racist or universalist, John Wayne and Eldridge Cleaver are both admired more than any well-meaning but undramatic liberal.

The Sponsorship of Sensuality in the Counter-Culture

But, as with the aged, the receptive orientation involves supplies from non-human as well as human sources. We have described the "post-genital" sensuality of the aging man, the mild pleasure that he takes in the rediscovered pleasures of mouth, sphincters, and eyes. Similar pleasure strivings mark the young food-faddists of the counter-culture, who share with the aged the interesting belief that they *are* what they *eat*. Thus, inner purity can be guaranteed by organically grown foods. Like the rock superstar, organic food is another "hero" of the counter-culture: it is an external source of strength and wholeness to be absorbed into the self, whether through identification, imitation, or mastication. Oral imagery is found everywhere in their "culture," from the names of rock groups (The Cream, The Lovin' Spoonful, The Carnal Kitchen), to the titles of favored books (*In Watermelon Sugar, Naked Lunch, The Strawberry Statement*). And as with the aged, what is taken in through the mouth becomes the core of conscience: good food means more than good flavor—it is the assurance of inner spiritual goodness, as well.

The visual interests that flourish among old men are also important to the young: light shows, posters, movies, hallucinations. And the addiction to flicks is so extreme that movie-makers now cater almost exclusively to the youth market. Similarly, photography has become a leading hobby for the green Americans: the most expensive Nikons and their armory of special lenses dangle and shine between scruffy beards and ragged jeans. By the same token, every rock group has its attendant *paparazzi,* whose hand-held cameras photograph the action generated in the swarm by the presence of a hand-held camera.

Regarding this matter of diffuse sensuality, the parallels between the aged and the counter-culturists could be drawn out indefinitely. To sum up, in both cohorts we see the withdrawal from genital sexuality towards a mild sensuality that is no longer restricted to a few erogenous zones, but is diffused over all sense organs, sphincters, and skin surfaces. In the aged the pleasures of the table tend to replace the sharper but briefer and often more troublesome ecstasies of the bed; and in the young cohort we also see that—despite all the public relations of the "sexual revolution"—there is a devaluation of genital sex in favor of diffuse pleasure experience. In the young this shift has some political and ideological back-up. For one thing, women's lib functions as an Orwellian Anti-Sex League: young men are instructed to feel guilty about the libidinous desires that presumably turn their girl friends into "sexual objects." Then too, the aging movement gurus, Norman O. Brown and Herbert Marcuse, have pushed the idea that polymorphous sensuality, normal in later life, represents "liberation" and "life-enhancement" for all ages. The libidinal position that old men must adopt is presented to young men as the one that they *should* prefer over the more vivid options that are available to them.

The Sponsorship of Unisex by the Counter-Culture

But the politics and rhetoric of unisex and polymorphous sexuality could only come along after the fact to legitimate the deep shifts away from the phallic orientation that had already taken place among the young. Thus, the anti-phallic emphasis is related to another point of resemblance between the aged and present-day youth: the loss of inter-sexual distinctions, and the merging of men and women towards *unisex.* As we have seen, this routinely comes about in later life, when each sex can afford to live out some of the potentials, passive or aggressive, that had been denied to them in the service of the parental role. Their previous self-denial has earned the aged the right to consume life-styles that were previously out of bounds to them. The young seem now to be demanding the same consumer's right, though without having first paid the usual dues: the right to be psychopathic and sensitive, active and passive, hard and soft, man and woman—all of the above, and all at once. In any event, it is clear that young men are busily exploring the hitherto closed-off possibilities of sensitivity, adornment, tenderness, and receptive sex; while girls, eschewing cosmetics, are everywhere hiking out on their various visionary quests, intent on proving their manhood. Thus, the usual pattern of late middle life, the tough, domineering wife linked to sweet but vague grandpa, has become the pattern of the young unisex couple. As James Thurber once described them, "She, bold as a hawk; he, soft as the doe."

The Religiosity of the Counter-Culture

We have mentioned the religiosity of the aged. The parallels with youth are again clear, and were evident even before the advent of the Jesus Freaks. Prior to them, the young had mainly gravitated to varieties of Eastern mysticism, laced with food-cultism; and these directions had been pioneered for them by dotty old ladies in California. As with the aged, the religiosity of the young has in it the desire to lose a weak self and to merge with some larger entity that betokens strength, wholeness, and productivity. The old turn to these sources because their own productive capacities are being demobilized, deprived of sustaining energy; but the counter-culture young turn towards divine representations of strength and life because (although they are bright and "creative") they rarely develop the sense of internal resource in the first place. Lacking this self-reliance they remain endlessly dependent on versions of the strong and reliable other: the group, the "people," the charismatic leader, or—like the aged—the omnipotent gods.

The Cult of Madness, and the Hatred of the Ego

Finally, the two cohorts, the normal aged and the counter-culture youth, have in common the rage against the ego. For the ego is both the creation of self-boundaries, and their creator; and ego boundaries stand in the way of the desired experience of merging, of union with something larger and more powerful than the self. The hatred of the ego is intense and explicit in the counter-culture, whether it is expressed as the distrust of rationality, the intolerance of delay, the impatience with linear thinking, or the reliance on boundary-busting drugs. The complaint among contemporary students—even graduate students—is that their acquired habits of rationality and categorical thinking cut them off from *union* with the phenomenon or group that they are asked to consider. As one student in my fieldwork class put it, "I don't want to *study* the community, I want to be *part* of it!" And this middle-class Jewish student went on to explain that only the exercise of his intellect put a boundary between himself and the "people" (in this case, Detroit inner-city blacks).

A more ominous symptom of the rage against the ego is the cult of madness, the contemporary adulation, *a la* R. D. Laing, of the psychotic. The current youthful sentimentality about madmen is based on a naive Rousseau-ism of the inner life, on the belief that there is within the deepest recesses of the self some inner strength, perfection, wholeness already formed and waiting for release. Inner resources are not *potentials* to be brought into being through hard work, they are *already there* waiting for the magic touchstone that will unlock the prison that the ego has set about them.

For the aged, the antagonism towards the ego, and the passage into magical mastery is enacted fairly easily: it is a side effect of the draining away of vital energy from the structures of the ego. But in youth the ego does not die easily. It has to be overcome by acts of "revolutionary" violence: drugs, particularly the hallucinogenics, are the Molotov cocktails which accomplish the internal revolution. They bring about the unboundaried state which is achieved naturally in later life. The counter-culture drugs are a kind of pre-senility equivalent; anybody who has seen a geriatric ward and a pot party can recognize their essential sameness. Thus, Woodstock was not peaceful because our youth has by some magic learned to love; it was peaceful because of marijuana, which turned the young participants into replicas of their grandparents in, say, St. Petersburg, Florida: nodding, dozing, and beaming in the sun.

Encounter groups, implosive therapy, group-grope, rock music, are also "plastiques" in the warfare against the ego. Where drugs are mainly levelled against the internal id-ego boundary, the various group techniques are designed to reduce the outer, self/other boundaries. They are in the service of a kind of "socialism of affluence" which aims to collectivize experience, rather than capital goods. In the group setting, for a while at least, the inner contents of the psyche and the flesh that covers it become pooled, defined as collective property. In the Esalen-style settings there is practiced a kind of id-communism where distinctions between inner and outer, between self and other, between group and individual are treated with the same disdain that traditional Marxists treat the distinction between state and private property. But this revolution is against the individual, not the state; and the goal is to bring about the dissolution of the self-boundary and the triumph of magical mastery that is the normal state of affairs at the end of life. For both cohorts, old and young, the ego is sacrificed in order to reinstate the early illusion of omnipotence, the consoling "oceanic" sense that one includes or is included in everything that is strong and whole in the universe.

Here again is the paradox of narcissism: we cannot make the self the center of and target of our love without also making it the center and target of our lethal hate; and we cannot exalt the self and restore its original infantile claims without destroying whatever is most distinctive and individual about the self. That the destruction of ego is touted to us by Charles Reich as Consciousness III, or the "discovery of self," does not change matters. The sentimental myth that drives such thinking is that loss or destruction of intra- and inter-individual boundaries is necessary for freedom and for the expansion of self-consciousness. In reality, at least in regard to aging, it is the condition that seems to precede somatic death. For other age-groups it may lead to morbid preoccupations with death, and to rather suicidal flirtations with death—as through hard drug use—of the sort that are becoming terribly popular now. And on the political level the dissolution of the ego is the precondition for the kind of social death that we call totalitarianism. Like the gods or like the charismatic cult-leaders, the totalitarian leader claims that perfection and wholeness reside only in him, and that followers can be included in his perfection and power if they will give up their *boundaries,* the prides and distinctions that go into defining their ego and their individuality. Like it or not, for all the isolations and alienations that it imposes, for all that it reminds us of the deaths and the obligations that we want to forget, the ego and its supporting institutions are the best guarantors of individual liberty that we have. In a real world there is nothing else.

Anti-Instrumentalism:
Causes and Consequences

My personal biases against the counter-culture, and against normal aging come through clearly in this paper. This is because I am afraid of both of them, and probably for much the same reasons. Both represent to me a kind of death: the death of the body in the one case, and the death of the ego in the other. And like the old traditional Navajo, I respond to the kind of passivity that the counter-culture publicizes and politicizes, as though it were a metaphor of death. But while my bias no doubt leads to various distortions, I do not think that it led me to see connections that were not there; rather, I think that it made me particularly sensitive to some more than superficial resemblance between "new" youth and the aged that have to do with their shared relationship to the productive life. Whether they are young or old, men who reject instrumentality may do so in the name of liberation, but they have bound themselves to consequences which are as predictable and as fixed as those which follow from the opposite choice, of a hard-working and competitive existence: namely, diffuse sensuality, unisex, reliance on illusion, vague religiosity, and all the rest of it.

Among men, psychological aging occurs whenever the productive, autonomous position is either abandoned or fails to develop. In this fundamental respect, the normal aged and the alienated young men are alike. What differentiates the old from the young are their reasons for turning away from instrumentality. The old man has outgrown the period of chronic emergency that required his focused instrumentality. Weakened by age and effort, his species and social dues paid, he can repossess some of the pleasures that he was once pressured—both internally and externally—into giving up. The productive life is difficult at best, most men do not really like it, they take it up grudgingly, and they only accept its burdens in exchange for much symbolic reward of status and prestige.

The aged of traditional societies drop out of the productive system when they have an organized moral system that they can at the same time drop *into*. The problem is different for alienated youth who refuse, even from the start, to affiliate with the technical/productive order of the secular society. Thus, the complex, sophisticated secular society does not have the power possessed by the simplest, most "backward" folk society to create legitimacy, or to endow sacrifice with high significance. In the secular urbanized society, the badge of rank, the medal for valor, the membership in the honorary society cease to be rewards that men are ready to fight, die, or sweat for.

Thus, strangely enough, as society becomes more complex, its component individuals tend to become—psychologically at least—more primitive. Unwilling to settle for more abstract and intangible rewards, for tokens of honor and prowess, they demand in exchange for their effort more immediate, tangible enjoyments: material goods, sex, drugs, sounds, textures, foods, *experiences*—and preferably all of them at once. The secular society becomes the consumer society, and finally for any chronological age, the *geriatric* society. Cut off from meaningful work by mass production, by the absence of clear necessities, and by the failure of symbolic incentives, the young men spiral slowly towards the psychological conditions normal for the aged: they become a premature gerontocracy.[9]

Perhaps that is why the young are fascinated with death; though chronologically they stand at the beginning of life, psychologically many of them live close, too close, to the end. And as we see from the rising number of stupid, useless deaths and cripplings from drugs, VD, and suicide, many are tempted—with all the impulsivity of youth—to hurry to that end.

Notes

1. Shortly before his death in 1965, the American poet Randall Jarrell wrote, "Thinking of the Lost World," in which there is clearly expressed the wish to relive

the beginning of life, with food being the touch-stone that calls up the climate of early life and mother's presence. "This spoonful of chocolate tapioca/Tastes like peanut butter, like the vanilla/Extract mama told me not to drink." (From *The Lost World,* by Randall Jarrell, New York: Collier, 1966.).

2. In this stage, real threats can be summarily defined as blessings; an old Mayan looks at TAT picture of malignant flying creatures hovering over a recumbent man, and declares that they are angels, come to bless and nourish a tired man. In his story the malignant birds that could stimulate his fear are transformed into "angels." The frightening beasts are, in effect, transformed into the comforting presence that an old man looks for when he is confronted by frightening beasts. This is magical mastery: the immediate, unboundaried, "umbilical" relationship between the stimulus, the subjective reaction that the stimulus provokes, and the final interpretation of the stimulus.

3. Thus, the survivor Navajo would typically tell us about their hardihood training in early life. When they were five or six years old, their father or uncle would drag them out of their warm sheepskin and toss them semi-naked into the snow outside of the hogan, saying, "Now you must run a foot-race in the snow, down to the spring. You must sing as you run. When you get back here you must go to that tree and shake the snow from the branches over yourself." We assumed that our subjects would retain some grievance over this treatment, but they claimed not to: "It was done in love. My uncle said to me, 'I ran like this all my life, starting from when I was real small. Now you see that I have lived a long time, but my hair is still black, and I do not have the old-age lines in my face. This is because of that running in the snow. It made me tough. If you do this, you will live to be as old as me.' And he was right; I did as he said, and I have lived a long time."

Through these reminiscences, the Navajo survivors were of course reminding themselves and us of their hardy youth. But these memories are *functional* as well as expressive: through them the Navajo survivors remind themselves that, as in the past, continued survival is still guaranteed by continued movement, by rejection of tempting beds, the warm sheepskin, the recumbent, passive position.

4. Along these lines, a crippled, 79-year-old Druze, whose wife has died recently, says that at the age of 80 he will "turn into a garden of flowers." I laugh with him about this, and suggest that he will become every kind of flower in the world; and fruits, as well. But this strong man will not finally permit the murder of his ego. He leaves off laughing, and says, "But this is not true. We do not become flowers. This is a penicillin to ease pain." (What pain?) "The pain of death."

5. Women are much more likely than men to rely on adaptive paranoia in later life. For them, this defense sponsors much intrusive and offensive behavior. It permits old women to interfere in the lives of others, "for their own good." Consequently, they remain fighters; and perhaps that is why old women typically outlive milder, gentler husbands.

6. The mountaineer tribesmen of the Caucasus are famous for their longevity. They are quite explicit about the "paternal" nature of the death that they fight.

Thus, a ninety-year-old horseman meeting his crony on the road will say, "I've beaten the old man for another year."

7. I cannot be very specific as to what I mean by the term "counter-culture." I am referring to that admittedly amorphous, always changing cohort, usually young, composed of all those who live in opposition to an official "establishment" culture which reputedly emphasizes the values of competition, industry, and the consumption of mass-produced goods. I exempt the activist radicals: these reject the official culture, but they also reject the more self-indulgent, pleasure-oriented aspects of the counter-culture—such as hard drugs.

8. I would have more sympathy for this position if it were really possible to leg-islate aggression out of existence by a kind of *fiat* of the liberal will. But aggression denied, or deprived of its usual occasions does not disappear; it only defines new goals. I once observed an encounter group where the participants were told to line up according to their importance in the group. Four young men—but no girls—shoved and contended against each other for five minutes for the last place in line; and they only left off when the dominance "lower-archy" had finally been estab-lished.

9. I am not the first observer to note the similarity between the post-pubescent and the pre-senescent. Saul Alinsky, the well-known community organizer, notes the anti-instrumentality of large segments of this generation, and likens it to old age: "I've run into more senility among the 19 to 20-year-olds than among the aged. . . . Life is too much for them, so they jump off into a mystical future. . . . These kids are not going for a revolution, they are going for a revelation." He advised a college audience to stop looking for somebody with charisma, and to get busy and start organizing. "Do you want to communicate, or sit there like God?" (*New York Times*, Jan. 5, 1971).

Dr. James Anthony, a psychoanalyst, draws the psychological parallels between youth and age in a more systematic way. He claims that present-day adolescents, far more often then their predecessors, show symptoms of aging even before they are out of their teens. He claims that oldsters' and adolescents' most commonly shared symptom is depression: "For both, the future looks black and unappealing. . . . *Preoccupation with death and nothingness is frequent.*" Besides, the two groups are alike in being "intensely self-absorbed: the narcissism of old age and the narcissism of adolescence are two peaks in the development of human egotism." (Reported in *Time*, May 1, 1972).

8 The Subjective Politics of Power: The Dilemma of Post-Superego Man

This study was and continues to be my favorite but least quoted paper. It holds a system of ideas that continues to shape my thinking about the sources of psychic power—the special energies that underwrite the sense of self and individuality across the lifespan. It was in part inspired by the example of the Druze elders, paradigm gerontocrats whose tremendous social power was based on a special charisma that had nothing to do with physical strength or economic clout.

Like most personally significant papers this one has its private history. I began putting it together after my return from the Golan Heights in 1969 and in the course of conducting an advanced seminar on methods and conceptions in the study of culture-personality relations. In those days I had begun to "find my voice" as a field worker and wanted to talk with clinical psychology students about the application of clinical methods and sensitivities to the field interview. Between us we began to put together a picture of the autocentric mind referred to in this paper.

In the more personal sense, I was also reacting against my own culture shock on re-entering Ann Arbor. Bear in mind that my field notes were filled with observations of tough, dignified Druze mountaineers, and my memory still held—as it does until today—the shining image of the Israeli nation in the Six-Day War, shocking the "four corners of the world in arms." I had been living among strong adults, but in Ann Arbor I mainly found petulant children who, on the grounds that they had experimented with hallucinogens, laid claim to the honorable title of "Revolutionary."

At first I buffered the shock of re-entry by sneering at countercultural pretensions but soon realized that name-calling was the New Left's game. I needed to step outside of the culture wars, into some overarching conceptual frame—a kind of unified field theory—that would make sense both of the Druze Aqil's dignity and the desperate power hunger of the Ann Arbor pseudorevolutionary or hippie.

In retrospect, I can see that this paper also represented an attempt to detoxify and master—intellectually, at least—my various encounters with the primitive mind: in the field with preliterate native informants; in clinical practice with borderline patients; in myself; and on the Michigan campus with bright and privileged students who believed that their own egos were foreign implants of the "life-hating establishment" within their heads. More recently, this same collection of ideas has helped me to understand—though not to sympathize with—the horde of pseudo-identities that march under the banners of various "victim" constituencies.

Regarding the study of aging psychology, the ideas set down in this paper helped me better understand the major paradox of gerontology, which is the ubiquity of gerontocracy: How is it that old men, who are physically weak, are routinely given dominion over young men, who are physically strong? This paper represents an attempt to identify the special, irrational sources of the gerontocrat's power and also to understand the decline of the gerontocrat in socio-political systems like ours, which conceive of power in more "rational" terms.

For this revision I did delete some dated attacks on the 1960s counterculture. Nevertheless, "Post-Superego Man" remains a rather long and prolix essay. However, dramatic anthropological vignettes take up some of the space, and these—despite the patches of barren text—may prove to be sustaining. In any event, this essay should provide the reader with a conceptual introduction to later papers in this collection.

This is an age which belittles the conventional holders of power, as well as the conventional routes for attaining power, but which at the same time eulogizes power itself. Indeed, a major impetus to group formation and cohesion in our time is the shared feeling of powerlessness among founding members and subsequent recruits. The complaints of these cohorts—migrant workers, Chicanos, American Indians, blacks—usually have to do with the outer, objective aspects of power: they insist that they cannot shape or alter the goals, the personnel, or the weaponry of the agencies which control the lives of these plaintiff groups against their best interests. The spokesmen for the oppressed may also complain of subjective trouble, of an inner feeling of self-hate or impotence, but they assert that the inner damage can be repaired only by outer success—it is a side effect of their real impotence in the real world, and can only be corrected out there.

However, the history of our time gives us ample reason to believe that there is a subjective face to power, and that the inner sense of vitality, of substance, is not completely tied to the individual's socio-economic situation, to his objective power base. The sense of inner malaise, of inner depletion, can occur at the highest levels of society, infecting precisely those groups who have the greatest leverage over their objective circumstances. This inner blight (recently given the name "alienation") has been throughout history the occupational hazard of aristocracy, the inner counterpart of royal decadence. Routinely, the aristocrat tries to ignite some sense of vividness and excitement within himself by courting danger, or by exploring the further reaches of sense experience—pain as well as pleasure.

Along these lines, we find that affluent middle-class students—heirs to a fair degree of social influence—also complain of their alienation and have rediscovered the remedies of the aristocrat. They hunger for sharp, vivid experience—the bad trip as well as the good trip—to temporarily allay some inner deadness. Often, the political activism of relatively advantaged groups serves the same purpose. The inner malaise is politicized, rephrased into a plausible attack against social injustice, but the ultimate complaint is against a self that seems devoid of substance rather than an establishment that withholds power. In fact, for the "lonely crowd" activism itself rather than any particular piece of social change becomes the real goal and the real remedy. A fullness of rage against the establishment and a sense of unity with other activists are partial substitutes for the absent morale, the missing core of self.

This paper will be devoted to a discussion of power and lack of power in this second, more subjective sense. We will not consider the organizational, political aspects of power—the ways in which the will of an individual or a group is imposed on nature or on other men. Instead, we will consider the internal counterpart of effective action: the *sense* of agency, the *appetite* for reality, the sustaining sense of rootedness and *thereness* as a self, by which the subjective realm acquires its own objectivity, its own solidity in the substantial world. There may be a dialectical relation between the inner and the outer faces of power; certainly in our time there is a chilling growth in the organizational and group aspects of power; and there is a perhaps correlative decline as regards its inner, individual face. In these terms there is in fact a pathology of subjective power, endemic in secular postindustrial society whether it is organized by capitalist entrepreneurs or by socialist visionaries. In our case, the American tragedy seems to be that democratic, egalitarian society, founded on the concept of the free individual, does not maintain the inner sense of vitality, the inner sense of power, that individualism requires. As a consequence, the forms of power awareness, acquisition, and maintenance that were the rule in preindustrial and autocratic societies are again making their appearance among us.

The Animistic Relation to Power

This argument requires a kind of natural history of power—a brief review of the ways in which the sources and routes to power have typically been conceived in the small, tradition-centered, and preliterate community which was the evolutionary habitat of man as a social being.[1] But first, in order to grasp the animistic relation to power, we have to consider the kind of mind that typically develops in the isolate, face-to-face community, the kind of mind that generates and is satisfied by animistic explanations.

The Autocentric Mind

Many anthropologists claim, and with justice, that the mind which develops in the preliterate folk society is far from primitive; it has its own subtleties, sophistications, and complexities which become apparent to those who deal with this mind in its own terms. I agree, but my own comparative work in Indian societies of Mexico and the American Southwest has convinced me that there are qualitative differences between the kind of mind that I met in these centers of folk life and the kinds of thinking that were familiar to me as an urbanized man. The work of comparative psychologists such as Heinz Werner (1957) convinced me that these mental qualities were not peculiar to the communities that I had studied but were distributed across the range of societies that shared the folk character. I proposed (Gutmann, 1970) that the folk mind was distinguished from the "urban" mind not by its primitiveness but by the tendency to experience self-dynamisms in the world, to confound outer stimuli with the reactions that they evoked in the interior self. Thus, whatever its particular skills and virtues, this *autocentric*[2] mind is notable for its disregard of boundaries: it does not experience and it does not create sharp boundaries between and within the objects and agencies of the world. In the autocentric mind, objects and actions are blended into a continuous world, where there is relatively little separation of the personal from the social, of the objective from the subjective, of the abstract from the concrete.

The autocentric mind, so conceived, is an inward translation, a kind of metaphor of its psychosocial ambiance, which is the small and isolated community. Thus the autocentric ego is a metaphor of the ways of relating that are found in the traditional isolate folk milieu, a setting which does not provide much experience of separation or distinction between fellow tribesmen, clansmen, or villagers. The world of the folk is redundant: ideally speaking, each man can see in every other man his own concerns, his own appetites, his own aspirations, his own past, his own present, and his own future. Where men extend their sense of "selfness" or "me-ness" to those others who are in many important respects much like themselves, the sharp sense of boundary between self and other does not develop as a fixed structure of the ego. Consequently, preliterate men discover in those agents that are emotionally relevant to them the feelings and sentiments that they themselves bear toward these agents. By the same token, they tend to experience in alien parts of the natural world those aspects of their own inner nature that they are alienated from. Autocentric reality is in part an extension of the geography of the self; and the various parts of what is, potentially, a coherent self are distributed into their exemplars in the world, and experienced most directly and concretely out there. As we shall see, this phenomenon, of the distributed self, dictates the usual animistic conceptions of the nature and sources of life-force, or power.

The Nature of Mana

The autocentric mind has trouble with abstractions; nevertheless, along with the idea of "soul" or "spirit," the idea of "power" represents one of the first true departures from concrete thinking and one of the universal inventions of the human mind. The ubiquity of the conception is indicated by the great number of disparate societies that have "power" terms: to name a few, the Melanesians knew it as "mana," the Sioux as "wakan," and the Iroquois as "orenda." Examination of the meanings that qualify these terms suggests that there is cross-cultural generality to the conception of power. Perhaps the experiences from which the conception of power was abstracted—whether it be the exposure to fire, to lightning, to orgasm, or to all of these—are so intense and unequivocal that they determine and standardize, across cultures, the ways in which the idea of power is developed and understood by primitive man.

Because the autocentric mind does not tease out the abstract from the concrete, the two dimensions are generally blended in the folk conception of power. Thus, like the primitive idea of "soul," the idea of "power" mingles the material and the insubstantial. "Mana" is an essence in nature that may only be manifested through tangible agencies while at the same time existing independently of them. Accordingly, though power exists prior to tangible events it still has "thingness" and limited quantity. It is stuff that can be sold, transferred, or captured. Again, the relevant model may be fire, which can be thought of as the by-product of a self-maintaining process of combustion, or as a *thing,* an organism that feeds, grows, and dies according to the laws of its own appetite. When power is viewed animistically, it is not impersonal but exists in a dynamic relationship to man: it has *intention* and meaning in regard to those human actions which have to do with the defense against, or the acquisition of, power.[3]

The autocentric mind does not discover much constancy in the forms of the world or in the self. The self does not persist as a stable entity across all the shifts of mood and excitation. Strong feelings, excitements, cannot be contained within some framework of self; rather they spill over into the world, blurring the distinction between inside and outside. Thus, for this osmotic, autocentric mind, dynamism or power is rarely experienced as an intrinsic, stable property of the self, but constantly presents itself as some motivated, dynamic quality of agents "out there," potential threats to the self.

As something real that is within events yet independent of them, power corresponds to and has its source in those beings—the spirits, gods, and demons—who influence ordinary events but who ultimately have their true ecology somewhere beyond the borders of the familiar human community. But it is not only the gods or the demons that have power. Power resides in *all* those agents which are not quite human, but which intrude into a human world. Animals have power and become totems, corpses have power, madmen have power, and strangers and enemies have power. For men, menstruating women can have an eerie *mana*. All these are sources of power that is not of this world but that is potentially useful or dangerous within it.

All primitive communities, while they have different ideas as to the particular sources of *mana*, exist as islands in a sea of power that beats up on the shores of the known, comprehensible world but that stretches into the disquieting reaches of the unknown. Power gets into the mundane world, to sustain the self and the forms of nature, but it does not originate there; and the major task of the community is to ensure—through all of its cultural activities—a constant supply of the vital essence.

Power is always sacred, and it is always double-faced: it can uplift, energize, vivify, but it can also blast and destroy its possessor, or those that its possessor turns it against. Power can be helpful, but the objects or persons who contain the power can be dangerous, *tabu* to those who do not have counterpower or ritual protection against it. Because of his high status, the tribal chief can be an adequate vessel for dangerous power. He can convert it and disperse it outward, with good results, into all the sectors of communal existence; but an ordinary man who touches the person of that same chief, or his paraphernalia, will be blasted by the *tabu* power that resides in them. In effect, one of the earliest meanings of status probably has to do with immunity from the power that comes with status.

The Primitive Intermediaries with Power

In the "Elementary Forms of the Religious Life," Durkheim (1947) holds that no abstraction, such as the conception of power, can come into being without the prior existence of community. However, the primitive human community can also be viewed as a system which brings in power, where power is animistically conceived, for individual and collective purposes, *via* intermediaries that the community maintains with surrounding forces. In the folk society, ordinary individuals do not by their own private efforts collect or generate the *quanta* of power necessary to secure themselves and their dependents against the threats of hunger, illness, accident, and failure in warfare. Power is collected by those *unordinary* representatives of the community who can live on the borderline of sacred power, contain this power, refine power, and disperse it into the community for collective purposes.

The power bringers are the first version of the *Hero*, they are the dominating figures who overlap the ultimate sources of power, suffer the unbearable contact, refine power, and neutralize it so that it will flow into and sustain the pragmatic world. Without this bridge, the pragmatic world would be without substance, a place of shadows. The hero is a converter of potentially bad power into good power or—in the priestly version—he is an *interceder* who persuades the gods to direct their bad power toward the enemies of the community and to send their good, life-sustaining power to his people.[4]

Generally, these heroes comprise within themselves the paradoxical aspects of the power that they manage. Those who traffic on the dangerous intersection between community and supernatural power have to be metaphors of the power that they would encompass—they have to be both destructive and benevolent, in some cases both male and female, or both humble and arrogant. But in all cases they have to be of this world and yet, like the power that they seek, living beyond it or transcending its pettiness and limitations.

Across cultures, the standard power brokers are the magician-chief, the warlock or sorcerer, the warrior who brings in the power of enemy dead, and the hunter who slays the totem animal. For some cultures, the interface is also the madman or the epileptic, both of whom live in this world but sometimes seem to speak out of another. And *within* the individual, the dream is sometimes taken as an intersection of the individual's life with the supernatural agencies. As such, it is a window through which power can move. We will discuss each of these power brokers and transformers at greater length.

The Magician-Chief

The magician-chief is a prime example of the hero who must combine and integrate the paradoxical aspects of the power that he attracts and contains. According to Frazer (1949) he was the major power bringer devised by primitive humanity, the first version of the king. Yet he combined power *and* weakness, sadism *and* masochism: he was the king who must die. He acquired power and lost power *via* regicidal murder, and both his triumph and his death were necessary to the health of the community.

In all cases, the magician-king must have uncompromising audacity: he must be beyond good and evil, narcissistic without guilt, and without regard for the opinion of others. He is uncompromisingly strong, invulnerable to the guilts and slights that would harm ordinary men. Clearly then, he has the stature to live on the god plane and to be continuous with god power. Within the community, the people's power is an extension of the leader's power: if the magician-chief appears strong and in good favor with the gods, then the people feel themselves, individually, to be strong and secure against the dangers which threaten human life. However, if the king appears to be weak, unlucky, or irresolute, if he cannot put down his rivals or satisfy his wives, if he shows signs of aging (hence mortality), then the community members feel themselves emptied of strength and powerless to resist evil influences. When the king shows his humanity, the community is no longer linked to sustaining extrahuman vitality. As Geza Roheim (1930) puts it, "the beginning of morality is the end of *mana*; the first parricide who felt compunction for his deed was the first hero-magician to lose his mana."

When he shows his mortality, the old king must be killed, replaced by a new power bringer, so that the sundered tie to sustaining power can be repaired. In the first true societies, the murder was probably carried out in a direct and literal fashion, and the first heroes were those who were strong enough, bold enough, and lucky enough to kill the king. They thereby demonstrated their own superhuman audacity, and their own capacity to live—as the old king had done—on the dangerous bridgehead to the gods and to be isomorphic with their awful power. Through the successful regicide, the lost link to god power was restored, vitality could again flow into the community and its natural domain. Through the murder of the old king and the accession of the new king, the community was in effect reborn.

This pattern survives in many fairy stories. The special child, foretold in augury to replace the king, is born. The evil king banishes him, or tries to kill him; but the child is lucky, favored by the gods, and so survives to kill the king and take his daughter. He reigns in his stead, and the whole kingdom flourishes again through the replacement of aging evil by vibrant youth.[5]

Power Through Suffering

The king who must die suffers and loses power when he ceases to maintain a magnificent scorn, when he ceases to pantomime the arrogance of power. But *mana* is double-faced, paradoxical in its nature, and just as the magician-chief moves to certain death because of his investiture with power, other candidates move to power *via* death and suffering. They aspire to the free, even sadistic use of power, but they first approach the gods in the masochistic mode, through demonstrations of suffering. These candidates do not show their superior scorn but rather their more than human capacity to endure and even relish pain and privation. They earn their power by suffering the exercise against them of the power that they will eventually claim. To the autocentric mind, power has substance, and the victim automatically comes to possess the power that is stabbed, beaten, or raped into him.

Shamanistic power is mainly acquired in the masochistic mode. Consider Roheim's (1953) description of the initiation of the magician in the Australian bush tribes. He goes to the place of the spirits; he lies down passively, facing toward their cave; he is taken into their cave, cut to pieces, eaten and put together again with a new set of organs by the same spirits that first destroyed him. He emerges from the cave imbued with the power of the dangerous spirits who now have become his sponsors. In effect, he has gone through a cycle of death and rebirth: having survived the fearful contact with the spirits, he has beaten death and has thereby transcended the final and greatest of human limitations. He has some of the omnipotence of the immortal gods.

Halfway around the world, the future medicine man of the Sioux moved, via the vision quest, through privation to power. The Sioux candidate went into the desert without food, clothing, or arms. He carried with him nothing of society's protection. He starved, he froze at night, he sang his death song. Finally, when he was delirious, his totem animal appeared to him in a vision and indicated to him the source of his future power. Returning to the tribe, the candidate knew his totem lodge and the appropriate rituals that would link him with the power of his totemic sponsor.

In the Siberian cultures, the theme of masochistic suffering as the route to power was made quite explicit. According to Roheim, the Chukchi shaman invoked the spirits in the guise of a woman; he wore a woman's cloak, parted his hair in woman's fashion, and wore two iron circlets, representing breasts, on his shirt. When possessed by the spirits, he would writhe on the ground, miming the motions of a woman in orgasm. However, at the height of his ecstasy, he would cry out in a deep, resonant voice that he was the mighty bull of the earth, set above all beings by his all-powerful master. By playing the woman before the gods, by being passively possessed by their power, he had acquired their power and had become mightier than any man. Apparently, the gods are more willing to give their potency to men who approach them as yearning women rather than as Promethean rivals, but the basic equation still holds: he who can endure the awful power without being destroyed by it will be the vessel of that power.

Across preliterate communities, old men are more likely than young men to live on the frontier between the community and the gods. Young men are bold; hence their task is to capture strength from enemy and from nature, while the task of the old man is to beseech it from the gods. The old man of traditional societies is a good example of the dual-natured power bringer. He usually has high prestige—even heroic stature—in the extended family and larger community; but at the same time, as an outcome of normal development, he has deep yearnings toward passivity and submission. In effect, he has entered into the bisexuality that characterizes later life for both men and women, and thus integrates within his nature the dual character of the power that his prayers make available to him. My older informants among the Galilean Druze would play the autocratic patriarch to their sons and wives, and they would at the same time play a yearning, self-effacing, stereotypically feminine role toward Allah. Clearly, their submissive face toward God is a precondition for their haughty face toward ordinary men.

The Warrior and Enemy Power

As societies develop and diversify, the functions of the magician-chief are split off and divided between a priesthood and the secular chieftain. The priests were told off to maintain the community's linkage with the gods; the chieftain's job was to lead the community in the task of beating back the attacks of enemy powers and in the task of taking power from the enemy. For while the enemy is not a god, neither is he completely human. Though he has human form, he is not of the people; he does not share in the feeling of "we-ness" that is the badge of humanity. Both human and strange, embracing two realms, he corresponds to the spirits, and therefore he has power. Animistically conceived, war is the set of practices whereby the community beats back "bad" enemy power, captures that power, and converts it to the collective store of "good" or community power. Considering the Papago Indians of Arizona, Redfield (1947) wrote: "All acts of the community at war—not just the war party—tended towards one goal: success of the war party and then the draining off of the supernatural power acquired through the slaying into a safe and useable form."[6]

Enemy power is by definition malignant; doubly so, because the spirit of the slain enemy will be vengeful to his slayer. Accordingly, the relics of the dead enemy as well as of the warrior who killed him become *tabu*, vessels of bad power. Like any other form of power, enemy power must be transformed and neutralized before it can enter the community in a constructive form.[7] Accordingly, among headhunters of New Guinea the successful warrior was for a time shut out of the community, confined to a hut beyond its borders where he lived alone in a special, dyadic relationship with the head of his slain enemy. There he would propitiate the trophy; he would make it gifts of food and pray to it. After this required term of peace-making between the slayer and the slain, the successful warrior would reenter the community, and the trophy would be adopted into his clan. The once destructive power embedded in the trophy had become an integral part of the clan's power. Through the practices of peace-making and adoption it had been converted into the community's store of courage and warlike spirit. Along these lines, Wallace (1960) tells us that any scalp taken by the Iroquois would be put through an adoption ceremony and would become in effect, with its power, part of the Iroquois nation. Here again the trophy of the dead enemy is treated by the Indian as the Siberians treat their gods: the slayer submits to the trophy, humbles himself before it, and thereby claims its power.

In an interesting variant of these practices, the Iroquois would subject their captives to vicious tortures for twenty-four hours during which period the enemy was expected to retain his humor and his scorn and to entertain his captives with jokes and stories. If he broke under the torture, he was summarily killed; but if he remained humorous and aloof, he was praised by his captors, inducted into the Iroquois nation, and then killed and eaten. Thus the enemy was made to demonstrate his own "good" power, his own calm courage in the face of sadistic bad power, and that courage, in the person of the enemy, was inducted into the tribe and built into the very flesh of the Iroquois warriors. The Iroquois were perhaps the most sophisticated North American Indians, so developed that they had begun to recognize that trouble could come from within, from an unruly inner life, as well as from outer enemies. In this case, it appears that they used the captive as a converter of the bad, sadistic aspect of the inner life into good power: courage and grace in the face of death.[8]

The Dream Connection

Sacred and *tabu* power penetrates the mundane community through the person of the priest or the chief. But it can also penetrate and find lodgement in the average individual through the agency of the dream. From the autocentric viewpoint, the dream is a real experience that blends routine and bizarre events: figures speak words that have the tonus of sense but yet do not make sense; long dead kinsmen appear and behave in their accustomed ways; familiar persons change their form into something strange. Clearly, the dream can be another corridor linking the prosaic to the transhuman domains and their powers.

Except in the practice of psychotherapy, our society tends to ignore the dream; but preliterates tend to take dreams very seriously. They approach them with the concrete attitude and do not regard dream events as figments of the inward imagination. Rather, the dream image is confounded, autocentrically, with the reality that it presents. The dreamer assumes that the dream-being is actually present within his own self-space. Thus dreams of gods, totem animals, or dead kinsmen are power dreams: these agencies have moved into the body of the dreamer, and have brought their *tabu* power with them. If such power is not dealt with carefully, it will destroy its temporary vessel. Thus, the Iroquois believed that power dreams represented the wishes of a god, and if the wish was not met, the dreamer would be destroyed. Similarly, my traditional Navajo subjects believe that dreams of the dead are unlucky: these indicate that the spirit "wind" of the dead person is now concretely lodged within the head of the dreamer and can do him harm. Likewise, the dream can represent a power that is looking for a victim; if a Navajo dreams of a death he will not feel at ease until he hears that someone outside his own circle of kinsmen or friends has died. Then he knows that the power that moved within his dream has found its target away from him and his intimates.

The Connection to Bad Power

We have briefly reviewed the ways in which good power is brought into the community through the person of the magician-chief or the priest, and the ways in which bad power is fended off from the community and converted to good power through the actions of the warrior. But there are also primary sources of bad or *tabu* power of the sort which cannot easily be converted to good and productive purposes. Almost universally, corpses have such power, as do menstruating women: across cultures, men tend to avoid their wives during their courses, and it is particularly common for warriors to avoid them prior to battle.

But the most important interface for malignant power is always the sorcerer. Where the magician-chief—however arrogant he may be—turns the power that he has acquired to the uses of the community, the sorcerer is the *entrepreneur* of power. He makes his own deals with the evil spirits, and he does not convert the bad power that he collects into good power that can vivify the community. Rather, sorcerers use such power in its original, malignant form: to increase their wealth at the expense of others, to blast their enemies, or to overcome the resistance of the women they desire. They may—in the forms of spells, potions, and curses— market their power to private individuals in the community, but they do not refine power and deploy it to the service of the community as a whole. The sorcerer is the entering wedge of destructive or unneutralized power within the community.[9]

Like anyone who would live on the interface with supernatural power, the sorcerer has to first demonstrate that he is of more than human stature. The magician-chief is a hero because he excels in those pursuits—hunting, warfare, rhetoric— that are valued by all proper persons; but sorcerers establish their superhuman stature precisely by violating the community's firmest *tabus*. For example, the Wimbaio sorcerer of Australia reputedly digs up a corpse and eats its bones. In the Western Sudan, sorcerers are reputed to eat their own children. In the Banks Islands, the sorcerer eats a morsel of corpse flesh, so that the ghost will join in alliance with him and direct his destructive power against any target indicated by the sorcerer. Kluckhohn (1962) reports (and my native informants confirm) that Navajo witches gain entry into the witchcraft society by committing incest or by murdering a close relative, even their child.[10]

The sorcerer is in effect telling the community, within the setting of its most cherished values and beliefs, that he fears nothing, not even the gods. By violating the great *tabu* with impunity, he demonstrates his superhuman courage and—if he escapes unscathed—his invulnerability. He can provoke the gods in the grossest manner and they will not punish him; clearly, he is more than ordinary men—he dwells on the spirit plane.

In summary, while there are many interfaces to power, the net result of their operation is in all cases the same: to fill the individual with the sense of energy, of resource, of sheer existence. Indeed, at the preliterate stage of development, the member of the community does not usually feel himself to be a *self,* a center of being, except at those times when the power brokers delegated by the community publicly and successfully perform their task of bringing in and refining power. The unordinary chief, king, or magician blends with the gods and is continuous with or identical with their power; but the subjects share identities—of common belief, place, and birth—with the king and so are blended with him. He has accepted the power, survived it, and so made it safe for its passage into the general, communal domain. The common individual feels strong to the degree that the leader and the community are strong and prosperous, its flocks extensive, and its warriors brave. If his ties to the community and hence to the leader are ruptured, the lone individual feels isolated and without substance. Once the protective shield of good power is removed, he will feel empty and terrified, exposed to the withering influence of bad power.

The Development of the Allocentric Self

The self-construction is an abstraction, produced by the mind out of the various instances that it has known of being a center of others' regard, or of being a center of its own sensations. Given the capacity to create and to cathect abstractions, the sense of a constant self can come to exist independently of the vital, focusing experiences that initially give rise to it. But the autocentric mind of the folk society does not easily move from concreteness to abstraction; in the folk society the elements potential to a coherent self are distributed, *experienced,* and lived through their external exemplars. Thus, regarding the matter of power, the people of the folk society will find the different faces of what are potentially their own powers in those interface agents whose task it is to deal with and master these powers externally. They will find their own courage in the chief; they will discover their own vindictiveness in the sorcerer; and they will meet their own rage at the dead who have abandoned them in the dead person's vengeful ghost. The sense of vital strength gets inside the individual and temporarily refreshes his sense of vital personhood; but in the experience of the individual, that strength is not ultimately generated within himself, and is only secured if he remains within the precincts wherein his particular gods hold sway, and if he maintains his active, ritualized contact with the power bringers—the chiefs, priests, or magicians. Again, power is *substance;* it is concrete stuff, and its maintenance within the individual requires the continuation of the concrete circumstances, in all their detail of place, person, and ritual through which the power was acquired. If the man of the folk society debases his ritual, if he leaves the sacred precincts of his people, if he loses touch with his chief or his priests, then his strength will depart from him—as Samson's strength departed with his hair—and he will feel empty, terrified, on the very edge of death.

Let us briefly consider the changes in psychosocial ecology that led to the advent of the objectified, allocentric self as an established human institution, and that brought about the "modern" conceptions of and routes to power. As communities grow and diversify toward urban and commercial forms, they undo the bases for the mechanical solidarity and for the sense of umbilical connection between man and man or man and nature that is the hallmark of the isolate folk society. As societies develop toward new technologies, new commerce, and new exchanges with hitherto alien peoples, they in effect lose control of experience. In the relatively closed and redundant world of the folk, society's predictions as to what can happen and should happen roughly match actual events; but this guaranteed congruence between the prediction and the actual event tends to break down as society diversifies, creates the marketplace, and brings about contact with strange peoples whose acts and schedules have a different social base.

This influx of new experience eventually brings about a profound revolution in social life and, by extension, in the psychic structures that develop out of social interaction. The diversification of social contacts means that a significant portion of the individual's life is spent in dealings with relative strangers. The "umbilical" connection between man and man that is the rule in folk societies breaks down in the emerging city: the actions and sentiments of the other can no longer be predicted from one's own sentiments and expectations toward that other. The other is no longer an isomorph or extension of the self; motives and sentiments that are potential within the self cannot be experienced "out there," in the other. The outer world does not confirm or extend the self, and the sense of familiarity and selfness retracts toward the physical boundaries of the individual. The cold winds of reality remind us that we have a skin; and a constant sense of self-other or ego boundary comes about. Thus when circumstances are in flux, when outer events no longer predict each other, there is laid down an important basis of the distinctive self experience.

The development of the boundaried self construct is also predicated on another major outcome of the "urbanization" and randomization of experience. This is the replacement of the autocentric, concrete attitude by the abstract attitude. Animism dies with the archaic connection between man and community. The abstract attitude grows out of the same unstable psychosocial circumstances that give rise to the sense of a distinct self. Men develop a sense of self constancy when they no longer feel intrinsically linked to their fellows; by the same token, they develop the capacity to build categories and abstractions when they are no longer tied to redundant happenings in some reactive and habituated manner. When they no longer find their own reactions within the sponsoring event they can stand outside that same event, make data out of it, and find structural similarities from one event to another across different times and places. This same capacity to categorize is turned toward the person's various experiences of distinctness and centrality; and it constructs out of these a generality, an abstraction: the concept of a discrete and separate self. The supply of libido that invests everything that is familiar is turned also toward this self-abstraction, and gives to it the tonus of permanence and reality. The allocentric self becomes a thing, or a location, independent of the tides of strength that might flow in or out of it.[11]

This shift, from a self predicated on community to a self predicated on its own distinctness and separateness, is a continuous process. It comes about whenever peoples move from the folk to the more urbanized condition, or from a condition of peasantry to some more sophisticated life. To some degree, it probably takes place as slum dwellers within the city move toward middle class status. It is clearly a reversible process: since every individual in the course of his own mental evolution passes in childhood through an autocentric period, then every individual has in him the memory of that mode of thought, and is tempted to regress to it under conditions of personal emergency (as in neurosis or psychosis), or under conditions of social emergency and pressure (as under totalitarianism, or under the condition of mob rule).

But while we are describing a continuous evolution of the human ego, there are times when this shift has had particularly dramatic consequences, and has been thoroughly documented and reviewed. The Renaissance was characterized by the emergence of the modern self, and Erik Erikson (1958) has documented and discussed this transition, from medieval to Renaissance man: the evolution was from medieval concreteness, where the individual's relations to powerful gods and demons were mediated by the church and its priests, to the Renaissance discovery of the abstract self as a power that could range over and dominate its concrete circumstances. Thus Erikson quotes Huizinga (1954) on the mind of the Middle Ages:

> The church, it is true, has always explicitly taught that sin is not a thing or an entity. But how could it have prevented the error, when everything concurred to insinuate it into men's minds? A primitive instinct which sees sin as stuff that soils or corrupts, which one should, therefore, wash away or destroy, was strengthened by the extreme systematizing of sins, by their figurative representation and even by the penitentiary technique of the church itself.

Erikson then asks:

In contrast to these medieval trends of thought, what did the Renaissance man think of his relative reality on this planet? First of all, he recovered man's identity from the periphery in the eleventh heaven, he refused to exist on the periphery of the world theater of borrowed substance, subject to God's whims. He was anthropocentric, and existed out of his own substance; created, as he somewhat mechanically adds, by God. This substance was his executive center. His geographic center because of his own efforts turned out to be peripheral to the solar system: but did lack of cosmic symmetry matter, when man had regained the sense of his own center?

Erikson goes on to cite a statement by Ficino, one of the prime movers of the Platonic academy of Florence, that is vibrant with the sense of the discovered self: "The soul of man carries in itself all the reasons and models of the lower things that it recreates, as it were, as its own. It is the center of all and possesses the forces of all. It can turn to and penetrate this without leaving that, for it is the true connection of things. Thus it can rightly be called the center of nature."

In these excerpts the Renaissance advance to the internalized sense of self and ego primacy is striking. The self is no satellite to draw its strength from vital centers; rather, it becomes the center that gives connection and vitality to the things of the world.

The Superego as Power Bringer

But what is the source of this renewed power of the self, this sense that the self dominates and orders the sensible world? By itself, the boundaried, allocentric self contains no power; and by virtue of its boundaries it is no longer bonded to the usual intermediaries that the community maintains with external and supernatural sources of power. In the course of its evolution, as the self separates itself from the web of community, it also takes into itself the functions of community; it becomes a community unto itself. But if the mundane community is empty of power, and must maintain interfaces to vital power, then the same must be true of the mundane and isolated self. Its autonomy does not rest on its boundaries: these define the self, but also isolate it. The *autonomy* of the allocentric self, its ability to tolerate the alienated condition, must be fueled by independent sources of vitality. The argument of this paper is that the superego, the dynamic aspect of conscience, plays this interface function within the isolated self, and so acts to remedy the alienation that is the price of individuation and selfhood.

The superego is not a new institution; it has always been a by-product of the tensions and inequalities that are inherent in the relation between parents and children. But prior to the "invention" of the coherent self, the superego was an aspect of the distributed self. Its strictures and mandates were experienced externally and concretely, in the shape of particular moral and legal authorities, and in the arbitrary rules of behavior that they laid down. Prior to the establishment of the "modern" individual, the moral enforcer is not part of the stable furnishing of the self. When the enforcer is out of sight he is also out of mind, and when his particular requirements have been met, one is at least temporarily quit of the demands of conscience. Hence the pre-Reformation man could alternate between saturnalia and repentance. He could glut himself one day, confess and repent the next; his acts of contrition paid for the last sins and were a down payment for the next orgy. The new superego moved the enforcer "inside," to become an unremitting, chiding eminence in the head, and its strictures were now couched in more abstract terms: they had more to do with obedience to principles than to particular rulers or to particular rules.

But this new internal autocracy also promised a new freedom. Conscience supposedly makes cowards of us all, but it must be remembered that the modern, autonomous conscience was in itself the product of bold social and psychosocial revolutions. The new conscience that created and respected *principles* above received rules required the ability to abstract these out of the blur of events that have moral relevance; but in addition to the cognitive advance, a social advance was called for: *Power itself* had to be redistributed. Erikson has discussed the Protestant Reformation, launched by Martin Luther, as a revolution in which the power to judge right and wrong was taken away from the priests and the church that had misused it, and conceded to the individual. The power of the priestly rulers became, in its inward translation, both the internal persecutor—the nagging voice of conscience—and the internal route to power. Prior to the Reformation, submission to priests and princes earned for the individual access to the grace of God; their former social powers, now diminished, reappeared as the power of the principled superego, which maintained, internally, the power-transforming function of the semi-sacred ruler. The old drama between the hero and the mana-bearers is now acted out internally, as a dialogue between the ego and the superego. As Freud saw it, the ego is humble and propitiatory toward the superego; and through this posture of submission toward the internal moral authority, the ego as it were "earns" the right to the good power which it can then deploy for active, constructive purposes. Much like the shaman, passive and suffering under the weight of the god, the ego earns its right to productive power by submitting to the punitive moral strictures laid down by the superego.[12]

In recent times, in a revolution led by psychoanalysis, modern man has turned against the superego on the grounds of its repressive cruelty. But the ideologues of this revolution overlooked the connection between internal harshness and internal security. Quite rightly, it has been pointed out that the superego involves the submission and even the enslavement to arbitrary and irrational standards. It is seen to cut men off from much of their inner potential for freedom. But this analysis points only to the submissive and restrictive aspects of the superego, and leaves out the fact that submission is one of the guaranteed routes to power. By submitting to his superego, the righteous man earned the right to his own strength—so long as he devoted that strength to the service of his own principles or against their enemies. The autocentric statement "If I do what the gods require they will assert their strength in my behalf" becomes, through the superego, "If I live up to my moral principles, I will have strength sufficient to my purpose." Thus, Erich Fromm (1955) has noted that "external power is transformed through the super-ego into internal power." Roy Schafer (1960), in his paper on the "loving" super-ego, has noted its usually overlooked power to commend and dignify the self.

In sum, for all that it put limits on sensuality and sadism, the superego freed modern man in another sense: it gave him physical and social autonomy—from the tyranny of his immediate community, from idols, from temples and sacred precincts, and from charismatic priests or sorcerers. The Sioux youth who had finished his vision quest could reach the source of his totem power, but only if he stayed close to his medicine lodge, and within the sacred lands wherein the totem deity held sway. But modern "superego" man could carry the totem and the lodge within him. Given the superego, he carried his strength and the means of reaching that strength within his own head, and to all parts of the world. Strength was seemingly limitless, could be generated out of oneself at the price of effort, of de-privation, of decent restraint. Western man conquered and colonized much of the known world not only because of his superior technology, but because of his superego. Through the superego he had an internal sense of what was good, excel-lent, and central in the universe. He was not free of the need for myth, for the as-surance of a numinous world that he could in some manner touch; but he was free of the *concrete,* physical version of the sacred, the mediator defined as some holy place or sacred person. The certainties, the mediators, traveled with him, and all he needed by way of concrete token was the Bible to remind him of the word of God. He maintained his linkage to central and excellent verities through the en-actment of *principles,* redefined anew for each situation, rather than rituals which required some particular fetish, temple, priest, or congregation. The rituals of superego man were not aimed at coercing the will of some deity, but at coercing and curbing his own will and appetites, when these were unduly or destructively aroused. Fixed ritual was translated to flexible self-discipline.

Western man could dominate the known world not because his courage was in-trinsically superior to that of the "natives," but because his courage, his morale, his sense of luck was internally based, therefore less vulnerable to the ebb and flow of circumstance. The tribesmen he faced on the frontiers of empire felt strong so long as the chief lived, slew his enemies, and flew his banner; but let the chief die in battle, let the banner fall, and the tribal warrior felt emptied of his strength, deprived of his luck, bereft of his "medicine." By contrast, the European trooper could see his captains fall, take up their duties, and continue to fight.

In sum, it can be said that modern or post-Renaissance man developed—perhaps to its highest degree ever—the boundaried, individuated self. The price for this development was deracination, alienation from the sense of unboundaried unity with external centers of strength and wholeness in the community, in its rulers, and in its natural and supernatural surround. The gain was in physical and cognitive mobility—"superego" man could range above and below the surface of the earth, and he could push ahead on all the cognitive frontiers. The alliance of the allocentric ego and the superego sponsored the rise of a scientific man who would incidentally demythify the world, turn icons and totems into the subjects of natural science, and in effect take their power into himself. The modern individual could withstand and even enjoy his alienation from the compact community so long as he had the superego to play the power-bringer role that was once played by kings and heroes, shamans and sorcerers.

Power and Psychopathology

The pivotal role of the superego in maintaining self-esteem is made clear when we consider some features of modern neurosis, perversion, and addiction. In normal development, the installation of the superego in males marks the phasing out of the period of oedipal conflict and rivalry with the father. Developmental failures in these terms occur when the oedipal struggle cannot be successfully foreclosed—for example, when the father takes up and escalates rather than cools out the son's oedipal challenge. The father in such cases has regarded the son as a real threat, has confirmed the son's bloody-minded fantasy, and has threatened or symbolically played out a real castration. The "father as enemy" remains "out there" as a counterplayer in a life-or-death drama. The father jealously keeps his power; and the son retains the fantasy that all significant power is outside of the self and can be garnered only through some primitive act of violence or propitiation. Power can be brought into the self only through magical and symbolic practices equivalent to the ritual of the compliant priest or the corrupt but daring sorcerer.

Perversion and Power

For all that they appear to underline and flaunt their "castration," homosexuals are often involved in a power quest. Thus the homosexual who takes the passive role toward stronger men seemingly plays out a woman's role in intercourse, but depth analysis of these individuals often reveals a restatement of the ancient shamanistic myth in which one becomes a man by playing a woman's part toward the potent gods. In his inner fantasy the feminized homosexual has stolen the phallic power of the penis that he has received into himself. He stoops to conquer: the father has been symbolically castrated and his strength co-opted through the very postures which denied the castrating wish. Concurrently, the homosexual violates profound *tabus,* bridges culturally incompatible worlds, and thus achieves some of the eerie *panache* of the sorcerer.

Alcoholism and Power

The conventional wisdom concerning alcoholism is that the heavy drinker is either orally deprived or fixated, and looking for an anodyne against anxiety. Liquor is for him an equivalent of the breast. However, cross-cultural work by McLelland and his associates (1972) as well as my own clinical and cross-cultural observations suggest that liquor is another interface to power and that masculine drinking particularly is often a means of power acquisition.[13] In addition, McLelland reports that, transculturally, drinking is most likely to occur in hunting societies where men are clearly active rather than passive, but also feel that they need some extra "charge" when they go out to face a chancy environment.

We see the same merging of drinking with power concerns in the dedicated alcoholic. For him alcohol is two-faced power: it can elevate man's spirits and give him courage, or it can bring him down—castrated, bereft of his faculties—to his ruin. The heavy drinker uses alcohol in both these senses: he drinks to replenish his self-esteem when he has been humiliated; and the same drinker may use liquor destructively, to humiliate himself following some unacceptable triumph. By the same token, the drink that elevates a man's spirits and sharpens his wits at the outset of the evening reduces him to helplessness and vulnerability by the end of it. Thus, as well as giving them power, alcohol externalizes for these men the punitive functions of the superego: let a man rise too far and it will bring him down.

By the same token, many alcoholic men have had some history of overt homosexual behavior, and for them the taking in of alcohol often serves as a fellatio equivalent. In effect, the drinker downs the "shot," the "slug"—the potent, fiery "male" liquid. Like the Siberian shaman in the grip of the gods, he shudders masochistically under the lash of this power, but then transforms his suffering into strength: "I can lick anybody in the house."

Psychosis and Power

With regard to certain psychotic syndromes, the paranoid insists that the world is charged with bad power that menaces him, the vessel of good power. Alternatively, he is constantly vigilant against those who would deprive him of power and render him passive. The manic-depressive psychoses are less obviously tied to power themes, but there is a connection in that, within this syndrome, there is a clear enactment of the death and rebirth theme, much like that played out before the gods by the archaic magician. Like the candidate for magical power who was first killed by the gods and then reborn into their ranks, the manic-depressive dies a symbolic death in depression, transcends death through that dying, and is finally "reborn" again with a hectic conviction of high purpose and superhuman capacities.

For psychopaths, whose affective and superego development has been aborted, there is a clear recapitulation of the "sorcerer" theme. The psychopath is truly an empty vessel; he can feel alive only when he is causing or receiving the sharpest sensations—and there are none sharper than pain. Thus the psychopath willingly and even gleefully violates the inviolate: the firmest *tabus* and conventions of his society. His resulting feeling of omnipotence is partly validated by the response that more orderly people have always given the sorcerer: a mixture of shock, fear, and covert admiration.

The Psychiatrist as Interface

As the self system individuates and diversifies, it develops a varied and complex sense of its own terrain. Freud had said, "Where there was id, there let ego be," and thereby defined the ego as a kind of tame suburbia, with the id as a savage jungle growth, full of danger and ominous vitality, beyond its fences. To the expanded modern "scientific" self, the outer world, to the further reaches of space, becomes tame, empty of essential menace; but the inner life, the id, takes on the countenance that once belonged to the land of the stranger, beyond the borders of the known community: "here be beasts and monsters." The physical world becomes tame, but inner unconscious becomes converted into the unknown realm, the dwelling place of angels and devils, of good power and bad power.

The problem for modern man remains what it was for his archaic ancestor: "Who shall live on the interface with dangerous power, neutralize it, and convert it into restoring vitality?" We have described how—given normal development—the ego itself can play this mediating role *vis-à-vis* the superego: the ego plays the part of the ancient hero who abased himself before the gods to receive their power. When superego or ego development is lacking or faulty, other intermediaries must rise up to do the ego's work on the inward frontier of power. For example, the psychiatrist or the psychoanalyst. In classic practice, the patient merely provides the occasion for the analyst to deal with what Freud called the eternal adversaries—*Eros* and *Thanatos*. In effect, the analyst invites and even relishes the patient's ego-alien appetites and sadism. Exposed to the full blast of the id, he meets it with calmness, assurance, and even zest. He redefines the sadism and rage of the id into energy and vigor. The patient can identify with the good power that the analyst displays in the face of the patient's own bad power; and in this identification, through taking the good analyst into his own ego, the patient effects the necessary transformation of power. In effect, the analyst is the modern equivalent of the captive who was used to transform the Iroquois warrior's burden of sadism into the tribe's store of courage.

In sum, certain psychopathologies can be seen as desperate attempts—based on primordial human schemas—to contact the external sources of power when the superego has either failed to develop or when it can no longer function as an internal regulator of self-esteem.

Postsuperego Man and the Crisis of Selfhood

Individual failures in superego formation lead inevitably to driven, regressive, and magical attempts to eat up or blend into the outer sources of power. But what are the consequences for the masses in what might be called the "postsuperego" era—when the cultural perspectives, continuities, and consensus which sponsor the superego as an individual and social institution are undermined?

When the linked "psychoecological" chain that stretches from myth and sanctity through parental authority to the inner constellations of identity and superego breaks down, we move toward "postsuperego" man and, by the same token, toward empty or alienated man. The diverse "urban" experience which results in the individual's sense of boundary and separateness persists; it continues to produce the isolated, self-aware individual. But without the superego as the internal converter and reservoir of strength, that same allocentric self is experienced as an empty shell rather than as a center, the "cause of all causes," the connection of all connections. Without the superego to detoxify aggression and turn it into good power, aggression *per se* becomes frightening, coded in all its manifestations as "violence," and is forsworn. And when aggression is compromised, a central source of energy—for construction as well as for destruction—is also lost. In effect, without the superego, cut off from both communal and intrapsychic sources of self-esteem, selfhood becomes an intolerable burden, to the point where the modern, individuated self is hardly viable. Accordingly, we see in our times many feverish attempts to reestablish the lost, archaic connections with external as well as internal power centers through dismantling the allocentric self and its boundaries.

I am suggesting then that much of what we call the new politics, the new life styles, and the new religions represent attempts to get back to the forms of community, the practices, and the world views which maintained those archaic connections to power through which preliterate man felt replenished. In the next section we shall examine some of these.

The Return of the Power Bringers

With the breakdown of the internal energizer, individuality becomes a burden rather than a blessing, a seeming enslavement rather than a liberation. And there is a growing tendency—not only restricted to youthful cohorts—to throw away individuality, self boundaries, and that set of integrated functions known as the ego whereby selfhood is maintained. This is done in the name of "liberation," and it is seen as a route to power where power is animistically conceived and represented.

As a consequence, ideas of the "thingness" and externality of power have returned. Members of encounter groups are now instructed to throw away or burn some token of whatever troubles them, as if bad power is a substance that is contained in objects, to be tossed away with them. Power again becomes something that has quantity and location "out there" beyond the boundaries of either the mundane self or the bourgeois existence. Accordingly, it exists in some pristine state in the untamed "exurban" unconscious, in the colonialized but not yet tamed "third world," and in what Riesman has called the "urban pastorale"—those who live in the city but are not urbanized: ghetto blacks, Puerto Ricans, drug pushers, pimps, and prostitutes. Again, power is seen to be vested in those who have human form but who live beyond the humdrum, ordinary community in some mythic, dangerous urban jungle where life and death eternally contend.[14]

As the materialistic conception of power is revived, and when resource is no longer felt in the very fabric of the self, then men will attempt to reduce their intolerable alienation in predictable ways. They will become catholic in their quest for certainty; anything that works, anything that seems to promise resource and integrity, will be uncritically taken up and just as uncritically abandoned. Men become magpies of power, forever looking for the stuff that promises trustworthy sustenance. Furthermore, they will look for interface agents or "allies" to connect them to whatever new version of power fashion or appetite might dictate. Finally, having found the ally, the interface, they will seek to reduce the personal boundaries that are responsible for the tragic sense of separation from that longed-for center. The intermediaries to power—both human and inhuman—proliferate in our time.

Food, Drugs, and Divination: The Nonhuman Interfaces

We see a revival of magical divinatory practices—astrology, tarot, and I Ching—all based on the idea that the self is not *alone,* that it is resonant, in some truly personal way, with the elemental forces of the universe.

Foodstuffs, particularly organically grown, are also seen as magical linkages to power and as manifestations of power in its concrete, thinglike aspects; and so food has become a kind of hero of the counterculture. Through organic foods, the concrete and abstract ideas of good power are condensed. The idea of being without taint, of being *pure* in the moral sense, is confounded with the idea of being without additives in the culinary sense. "Wholeness" is not an abstract, moral property; it becomes a concrete property of grains that have not lost their hulls. One takes in the moral quality, integrity, by eating whole grains.

Drugs—particularly the hallucinogenics—are the major substances for achieving oneness with the outer centers of vitality. The mind-expanding drug is doubly valuable: itself a representation of the cosmic powers, it also reduces the intolerable boundaries of the self which prevent the sought-after experience of fusion with these great universals. Certainly, the philosophers and PR men of the drug culture have touted the mind-altering drugs as being both the doorway to and also the very source of new lives. Because they nullify the experience of self boundary, drugs have become the chief weapons in the new revolution against the individuated self. By reducing the nagging sense of self-other distinctions, the drugs allow the user to feel that he is bonded to whatever arouses his emotions—he is part of the music or, more importantly, he is one with the charisma of the musician. Such drugs also reduce the inner boundaries of the ego and make available, sometimes in the form of hallucinations, the fantasies and motives which—since the ego has no conventional language to bind them—are normally unavailable to consciousness. As noted earlier, the unconscious also exists outside the mundane routines of life and so is visualized as another potential storehouse of wholeness, of vital sustenance. Drugs become sacred because they relate these hidden bays and reaches of the mind to consciousness.

Thus, the drug taker's directive myth is a restatement of the myth that drives the political activist. The revolutionaries storm across social boundaries seeking confrontations with establishment power so they can degrade this power and take it for their own; and the drug magicians raid across their internal frontiers to find the center and source of "Godly" power within themselves. In their cosmology the psychedelic drugs are the "sacrament" which dissolves the internal ego barrier and opens up the internal treasure house.[15]

Besides interfacing with the unconscious, drugs provide analogues of other classic power-acquiring experiences, notably the sequence of death and rebirth. At one time I conducted intensive interviews with heavy users of LSD. For them the acquisition of power, of omnipotent status, was a central theme. They reported vivid, drug-induced experiences of disintegration, of dying as a self, and then of coming together again as a new and stronger person armed with a superior insight. As one put it, "acid is an instant Ph.D. in psychology." From the Olympian heights of the drug experience they had seen through the social games that ordinary mortals feel obliged to play and through which they gain a false security. The acid heads now felt that they could play all the games or none of them as they chose.

Through experiencing psychic "death" and surviving it, they felt that they had transcended the limits of ordinary human existence and were thereby endowed with true power. Even the bad trip—the catastrophic loss of self—has its value: the self dies in order to be reborn; it finds within some core that persists, that gropes back toward coherence even from disintegration and death. Having conquered death, one has presumably assimilated and turned into good personal power the bad power that brought one close to death. Like the Sioux vision quest, the bad trip reminds the drug taker of some hitherto unrecognized resource that only makes its appearance when all other supports have disappeared.

Saints and Psychopaths, Madmen and Superstars: The Quasi-Human Power Bringers

The human versions of interface are also proliferating—the gurus, the charismatic rock superstars, the Maharishis, and the *gruppenfuhrers* of encounter. These capture the imagination either because of their "cool" or because of their ebullience. "Cool" charisma signals that the leader has his own supplies and that he needs nothing from anybody else. Such figures are immensely appealing to the members of the "lonely crowd," who are humiliated by their own desperate hunger for response and support from others. The schizoid detachment, the *cool* of the leader, seems to them a form of omnipotence. By the same token, the manic, "overflowing" leader suggests to his empty followers that he is a fountain of the vitality they cannot find within themselves. If they lose their boundaries, if they forget their selves, if they *merge* with him, he will fill them up. Often these authoritative and paternalistic leaders derive their legitimacy as the spokesmen of a god: Krishna or Jesus. In these cases the follower scraps the tokens of individuality and in return is filled with "Krishna consciousness" or the tangible, immediate "presence of the living Jesus." But whatever God these "masters" claim to represent, they all sound the same essential message: "Abandon your own burdensome self, allow the essence of individual selfhood to become concentrated in a few heads, give your adoration to them, take your direction from them, and you will be re-plenished." In effect, die and you will be reborn.

Becoming the Enemy

We noted earlier that, for primitive man, the enemy was a potential totem: he could be loved and absorbed once you had defeated him and subsequently allowed him, in some symbolic manner, to defeat you. In our time we see that the class enemy of the parents has become the hero of the alienated child. The world of the parents appears barren, a metaphor of the death and emptiness that the alienated child feels within himself. The enemy—whether it be the Vietcong, the ghetto dweller, the prostitute, the pimp, the drug pusher—is seen to contain some primitive aggressive or sexual vitality. In the small community, the power of the enemy is also recognized, but it is the community rather than the stranger that is identified with. The individual warrior stays loyal to his own community even as he goes out on the risky mission of capturing enemy power. But the alienated youth reverse these priorities and redraw the boundaries between enemy and community. They acquire enemy power passively, by "becoming" the enemy—usually in the token, cosmetic sense. They turn enemy into ally, and the previous ally—the parent—into enemy. By becoming "enemy," the alienated child gains—at least in his own eyes, and in the eyes of his parents, teachers, and administrators—the aura of enemy power. As one hippie informant, quoted by Nicholas Von Hoffman (1968), put it, "We are the people our parents warned us against."

But not all the enemies of America have become the enemies of its more favored children. The Soviet commissar is a political rather than a cultural enemy of America and is therefore not identified with. The true, the *valued* enemy violates the *tabus* that our children were taught to respect and fear. By becoming this "fearful" enemy, the young rebel is in effect claiming the status and power of the sorcerer. Like the archaic sorcerer, those who publicly violate important *tabus* acquire the sense of, and the appearance of, power. Their message to others is: "I do the things that fear of social disapproval would prevent you from doing. Therefore I am not dominated by the fear and the need for love, for approval, that guides your actions. By contrast to you, I am without fear and without need. I am elevated above your human limitations." Modern examples of the sorcerer are those who dramatize themselves by becoming avowed Satanists and black magicians, the Hell's Angels who sport the swastika of the enemy, and all those who parade perversions as though they were virtues. Those who live by the principle of "eviler than thou" have ushered in the age of *psychopath as hero*. Their Faustian spirit is well expressed in some excerpts from the White Panther statement of purpose, written by John Sinclair:

We are free mother country madmen in charge of our own lives and we are taking these freedoms to the people of America. . . . We Are Free, we are a bunch of arrogant mother-fuckers and we don't give a damn for any cop or any phony-ass authority, control addict creep who wants to put us down . . . for the first time in America there are a generation of visionary maniac white mother country dope fiend rock 'n roll freaks who are ready to get down and kick out the jams . . . and we will not be stopped. We are bad. WE ARE THE SOLUTION. We have no "problems." Everything is free for everybody. Money sucks, leaders suck. Underwear sucks. School sucks. The white honkie culture that has been handed to us on a silver plastic platter is meaningless to us! We don't want it! Fuck God in the ass. Fuck everybody you can get your hands on. . . . We are LSD driven total maniacs in the universe.

All the new power themes are concentrated in this manic statement: the legitimacy, indeed the holiness of the madman, the psychopath, LSD, and the enemy. To be bad is the precondition for being good. This is the consumership of experience, the modern version of gluttony: one can be saint and psychopath, motherfucker and Godfucker, and all at once. No possibility for pleasure or expression rules out any other. Anything that might temporarily fill the void of self is snatched at and devoured: the self can be finally liberated from the humiliating bondage to things only after it has sucked the marrow from every object. But also, in this strange mingling of opposites, the purity of evil and the morality of badness, we hear the last mutterings of the dying superego.

The Totalitarian Connection

But no final and absolute freedom is gained when the tyrant superego dies. Rather, this death is likely to usher in a political fascism in place of the subjective master. We forget this, but it was the superego that sponsored democratic man: the judgmental and punitive powers of the prince—whether prince of the blood or prince of the church—were, through the agency of the superego, abstracted, and so could be partialled out among all men rather than concentrated in a few. Without doubt, democratic man had all the faults that his zealous accusers have documented: he could be sanctimonious, hypocritical, rapacious toward nature and exploitative of the "lesser breeds without the law." His great virtue was that he had little need for princes. He was often a prig; but he was not likely either to become or to accept a tyrant. He feared little but his own conscience, and he pursued the good conscience with the same fervor that his successor, post-superego man, pursues the "Good Relationship."

We still live by the old law of the King Must Die—in order to be born again. And when the internal autocrat of the superego disappears, it is reborn externally, along with all the other devices and mediators that animistic man devised for dealing with external frontiers of vital and *tabu* power. The superego, which was the internal judge, the internal ruler, is distributed back into its outward antecedents: it becomes the coercive power of the priest, the prince, the sorcerer—and the "group." Already, many intellectuals have turned the word "individual" into a sneer, and many are busily celebrating the felicities of Red China, where the superego takes an outward form—the identical book in every hand. They call for the charismatic leader—for Fidel, for Uncle Ho, for Mao—but perhaps their real wish is for Big Brother to kick them full of his strength.[16]

When the superego is degraded, when the individual is dismantled in the quest for certainty, then conscience and individuality do not finally disappear from social existence; rather, they become concentrated in the hands of a few powerful moralists and arrogant individualists who will be only too happy to let others participate passively in their power at the price of freedom. The prince has always let others live in his reflected glory; all he asks in return is eternal submission and mindless adoration. Charles Manson, surrounded by his pack of mind-blown worshippers, may be more than a passing fever out of California. If we continue to undercut the foundations of ego, superego, and individuality, then he is the shape of our future. He is the new totalitarian leader foretold to us by Golding in *The Lord of the Flies* and by Orwell in *1984:* "The boot forever in the face."

Notes

1. Cultural anthropologists might argue against this comparative approach on the grounds that cultural ideas of power can be understood only in their own terms, relative to the particular symbolic system of a particular society. "Power" is not a constant, to be compared across societies; once abstracted from its own semantic surround, the term is emptied of the meanings that should be brought to such a comparison. This argument may be true, but it may also be a gambit of academic politics. It has the effect of leaving the cultural anthropologists in charge of all the sociocultural data from human communities.

2. The terms "allocentric" and "autocentric" were introduced by Ernest Schachtel (1959). For him, these terms referred to distinct modes of relating to objects: the autocentric mode being a self-serving use of the object, the allocentric being a mode in which the properties and needs of the object *per se* are recognized. As used here, these terms refer to the personal implications of social organization. That is to say, the autocentric social organization gives each individual recurrent experiences of being a focus, the center of communal events and ties. The allocentric order conveys to the individual the sense that the centers and sources of orga-

nization, social bonds, and initiatives are extraneous to him—or that his alignment with such centers is not final and secure.

3. When power is perceived both concretely and animistically, it leads to the calculus of envy, which is pervasive in the typical folk society: "If he has the good stuff and I do not, then (in some manner) it was gotten from me." Conversely: "If I have the good stuff and he does not, then he will envy me and do me harm." This calculus of envy gives rise to the witchcraft practices and fears which haunt the life of many small preliterate communities. The envious man feels justified in retaliating against those who have emptied him of his substance; and the envied man feels justified in protecting himself against the malice of others.

4. An eighty-three-year-old Navajo medicine man first introduced me to the inner life of the power bringer. He felt that he was close to death, and was concerned because young Navajo did not try to learn the "rain songs, the livestock songs, the grass songs" that he knew. His songs literally brought in the power that sustained these forms in nature. If they were not sung, sheep, rain, and grass would disappear, and the people would starve. In effect, the world would end with his death. There is probably a note here of "*Après moi, le déluge*," but his was a cultural idea rather than personal megalomania. He and his medicine songs were not in themselves the ultimate sources of vital power, but only the incidental bridgeheads through which it moved to revitalize the daily world. In his view, any man who knew the chants could restore the crucial connection to supernatural power.

5. An equivalent myth propels many revolutionary undergrounds of our time. Across such movements, revolutionary imagery opposes bad power in the hands of old men to good power that will be brought in by young men. When the old men are killed, when the revolution succeeds, the whole society is presumably quickened and vitalized by the good power that the young revolutionaries bring with them. John Kennedy knew how to live this myth: the country felt a new endowment of energy when the youthful-seeming Kennedy replaced the sick and elderly Eisenhower. The mythic sequence was reversed when Kennedy was killed and the young "king" was replaced by an old one. The people mourned for Kennedy, but they also mourned for the vital sense that had come with him and that disappeared from our national life following his assassination and his replacement by Lyndon Johnson.

6. The Navajo maintain to this day, in their traditional camps, the ritual of "Enemy Way" for protection of those who have been in contact with non-Navajo populations or corpses. The Navajo veterans who have presumably killed enemy soldiers, and even Navajo nurses who have been in contact with "enemy" (white man) dead, are still subjected to the Enemy Way ritual on their return to the reservation. The Navajo believe that it is the unharmonious relationship between the subject and the enemy dead that makes the power of the enemy malignant. The ritual, which has the aim of restoring the lost harmony, consists of the ceremonial reenactment of a battle in which both sides fight over some ceremonial token, achieve possession of it in turn, and finally make peace, celebrated by a dance (the

Squaw Dance). The peace established between the warring factions is supposed to bring harmony between the Navajo patient and whatever piece of enemy power he has been at odds with.

7. Indeed, many of the seemingly reckless acts of young men are not based on male chauvinism; they are based on a need to demonstrate male strength and the capacity to withstand enemy power prior to the confrontation with the strange power of the female. By enduring privation in the vision quest, by counting coup and conquering his fear in battle, by enduring token castrations, the young man demonstrates to himself that he has the strength and resource sufficient to see him through the coming sexual trip into another homeland of stranger power, the interior of the female. It is only when he has some conviction of his own luck, and of his own power to survive and overcome danger, that the young man can make—and truly enjoy—that trip.

8. Like the Iroquois captive, Jesus Christ is also a converter of bad inner power into goodness. He is exposed to the blind storm of human sadism; he meets it with courage and forbearance, forgives it, and defines it as a human trait. He transforms evil into grace. By eating his flesh in the form of the Eucharist, Catholics make the transforming figure of Christ part of themselves.

9. Actually, the entrepreneurial sorcerer may be the precursor of individualistic, alienated modern man. The primitive community sets very great store by conformity, and in many cases the men named as sorcerers may have been nothing more than premature bohemians. These men may have been strong individualists who would not subject themselves completely to the conventions of their folk. Such non-conformity could easily lead to a reputation for heresy and evil. Once excluded from the compact majority, some of these men may have turned to actual witchcraft, both for purposes of revenge and for purposes of self-aggrandizement. Certainly, the reputed sorcerers of my acquaintance—like Carlos Castaneda's (1968) Don Juan—have been flamboyant, strong-willed men of large sexual appetite. Their success with women is viewed by their fellows from the autocentric perspective: these men are not seen to be personally "sexy," but as the possessors of borrowed supernatural powers to attract women.

10. The myth of Oedipus is in effect the story of a *de facto* sorcerer posing as a king. Unknowingly, he had violated the ultimate *tabus*: he had killed his father and lain with his mother, and he had thereby become the entering wedge of bad influences—manifested in plagues and famine—within his kingdom. True, Oedipus does not have the sorcerer's zest for evil and he is overwhelmed by Tiresias's revelation. But the bold act itself, regardless of its intention, has removed him beyond the realm of the ordinary and into the realm of dark forces.

11. The idea that the free-standing individual is a product of urban experience has been criticized on the grounds that city dwellers typically deal with each other in fragmented ways. By contrast, it is only in the small face-to-face society that we supposedly deal with others more wholly, in their full humanity. But this very tendency to constrain our dealings with others within a limited range determined by

prior role conceptions is vital to individuality. Role conceptions are, after all, abstractions, generalizations that we carry about in our heads and that we map onto unpredicted experience. These cognitive inventions, these internalizations, have permanence despite the flux of events. Particular individuals—clerks, drivers, policemen—may exit from their proper roles, but while such deviance may surprise us, it does not destroy our internalized conception of the role itself. Our general expectations do not have to be revised with each piece of idiosyncrasy that we encounter. Accordingly, while our role definitions limit the potential richness of our human contacts, they also give us the autonomy from immediate experience that is necessary for the development of self-awareness and individuality.

12. As Otto Fenichel (1942) described it, the superego corresponds to the trophy of the archaic warrior: it is the prize of power taken into the self from the enemy. But, like the severed head, scalp, or heart of the enemy, its power—though potentially sustaining—is clearly dangerous. Such power must be placated and neutralized. The internal relation to power still has about it the magical and animistic tone that once characterized the relationship between primitive man and external power: the internal power is concrete, having quantity, and it is double-edged. As Fenichel notes, the achieved identification with power is equivalent to the seizure by force. He adds that the stolen power is viewed from the concrete perspective: having stolen it, one must guard it (and like a stolen dog it may turn on its new master). Before the "stolen" power can be made part of the assured resources of the self, it must be neutralized. Peace must be made with the superego, and the internal reconciliation follows the lines laid down by the ancient hero on the interface with the dangerous and powerful gods. The superego must be placated, submitted to: it must be approached humbly and even masochistically. In turn, the superego rewards the ego for its submission with the sense of rectitude and self-esteem.

13. The Maya Indians of Chiapas that I studied are ferocious drinkers, believing that alcohol brings men close to divinity. They say: "Liquor [in their language *pox* or 'medicine'] makes men like the gods." But again, the power that conveys godhead can also bring men down; these same informants will complain: "Liquor makes our heads go mad, we fight and kill each other."

14. The sense that power has both dimensions and location "out there" is captured in this excerpt from the *Ann Arbor Sun*, an "underground" newspaper whose masthead reads "Free newspaper of rock n' roll, dope, and fucking in the streets": "Martin Luther King just got killed. Inevitable. I used to want to die from natural causes until I realized that murder is the most natural cause of all. War, assassination, murder. The stupid killer shot him in the throat, we heard, and probably figures he cut off King's balls. That's not what happens: they get transferred. Kennedy's got transferred to American students. Malcolm X's to Black people, King's to me a bit, perhaps. If I die by any method other than assassination, I haven't lived as boldly as I intend to."

Here the sense of trophy is clear: power is *stuff*, it has a testicular locus, and such stuff is not created anew by each man out of his own potentials, but can be inherited from a fallen chief or, by the same token, snatched from an enemy. Similar ideas were expressed during the 1967 "attack" on the Pentagon. Then, demonstrators urinated on the walls of the building to show their contempt for the power of the building itself. In effect, they announced, "I can defile this building, and it will not kill me." Along with the defiance there is also the covert belief that if the *mana* of the fortress did not kill the defiler it would come into his possession. Power would travel into the penis *via* the same stream that washed it off the Pentagon.

15. Allen Ginsberg says it more dramatically in his poem "Howl": "I saw the best minds of my generation destroyed by madness, starving hysterical naked, dragging themselves through the negro streets at dawn looking for an angry fix, angel-headed hipsters burning for the ancient heavenly connection to the starry dynamo in the machinery of night . . ." In these lines, Ginsberg moves from the vision of starved emptiness and frantic hunger, to the idea of a healing connection, established through the drug fix, to the "starry dynamo," the external center of mythic power.

16. At rock concerts, I notice that couples no longer dance together; rather, single dancers, male and female, face the lead singer, the "superstar," and pantomime a dance with him. It is quite chilling to see these human particles of the dance completely ignoring each other and all magnetized toward the leader.

References

1. Castaneda, C. (1968). *The Teachings of Don Juan: A Yaqui Way of Knowledge.* Berkeley: University of California Press.
2. Durkheim, E. (1947). *The Elementary Forms of Religious Life: A Study in Religious Sociology.* Glencoe, Ill.: Free Press.
3. Erikson, E. (1958). *Young Man Luther.* New York: Norton.
4. Frazer, J. G. (1949). *The Golden Bough: A Study in Magic and Religion*, abr. ed. New York: Macmillan.
5. Fenichel, O. (1942). *The Psychoanalytic Theory of Neurosis.* New York: W. W. Norton.
6. Fromm, E. (1955). *The Sane Society.* New York: Rinehart.
7. Gutmann, D. (1970). "Female Ego Styles and Generational Conflict," in Bardwick, J.M., *et al.* (Eds.), *Feminine Personality and Conflict.* Belmont: Brooks/Cole.
8. Huizinga, J. (1954). *The Waning of the Middle Ages.* New York: Doubleday Anchor.
9. Kluckhohn, C. (1962). *Navaho Witchcraft.* Boston: Beacon Press.
10. McLelland, D.C., *et al.* (1972). *The Drinking Man.* New York: Free Press.
11. Redfield, R. (1947). "The Folk Society," *American Journal of Sociology,* Vol. 11, No. 4.

12. Roheim, G. (1930). *Animism, Magic, and the Divine King.* New York: Knopf.
13. Roheim, G. (1953). "The Superego as Trophy," in *Collected Papers.* New York: Norton.
14. Schachtel, G. (1959). *Metamorphosis.* New York: Basic Books.
15. Schafer, R. (1960). "The Loving and Beloved Superego," in Eiss, R.S., *et al.* (Eds.), *The Psychoanalytic Study of the Child*, Vol. XV. New York: International Universities Press.
16. Von Hoffman, N. (1968). *We Are the People Our Parents Warned Us Against.* New York: Quadrangle Books
17. Wallace, A.F.C. (1960). "The Institutionalization of Cathartic and Control Strategies in Iroquois Religious Psychotherapy," in Opler, M.K. (Ed.), *Culture and Mental Health.* New York: Macmillan.
18. Werner, H. (1957). *The Comparative Psychology of Mental Development*, Rev. ed. New York: International Universities Press.

9 Oedipus and the Aging Male: A Comparative Perspective

The following paper is one of the spin-offs from my earlier essay on the sources and varieties of psychological power, "The Dilemma of Post-Superego Man." In that piece, I described the various "collectors" of totemic power, those interposed by traditional cultures between the community and its gods. I noted that these intermediaries, these "strangers," generally came from the ranks of those who reside in this world—but only in the physical and not in the social sense. They suggest nonhuman origins, other places of the heart. Madmen are of this stranger breed, as are the totem animal, the enemy dead—and the aged. Like these other strangers, the aged carry the taint of "eeriness": Within life, they remind us of a far land, of death. As such, they are destined to act as the community's representatives before the ultimate strangers, the gods. Building on that original formulation, in the following paper I consider the special factors that underwrite gerontocracy—the rule of the elder (usually, the elder male)—in the traditional human community. I focus particularly on the incest tabu, *which protects the old man from his competitive sons, as well as on later life androgyny, the senescent mildness that removes him from the masculine killing-ground and renders his prayers acceptable to the gods.*

In this piece, I am still drawing on my experience among the traditionalists of the Druze and the Navajo and on the theoretical ideas put forward in the earlier paper on "Post-Superego Man." The focus is still on the strong face of aging, on the sources—cultural and psychological—of that strength, and on the contributions that strong elders make to the cultures that sustain them and their people.

A major but neglected question in the study of human aging does not have to do with the special weaknesses of our elders, but with the blunt, inescapable fact of their survival—particularly the longevity of elderly males—as a common human event. If we could find reasonable answers to the question, "Why Elders?" (or, alternatively, "*How* Elders?") then other concerns, having to do with their nurture, their proper claim on national resources, and their function in society, might either fall into place or become irrelevant.

The "Why Elders?" question becomes more manageable when we limit its scope to this particular concern: "Why Male Elders, e.g., Why Male Gerontocracy?" We are, after all, the only primate species that has maintained, across history and across cultures, a population of powerful male elders who routinely survive as leaders for many years beyond their reproductive and muscular peak. The same question could also be a starting point for psychoanalytic inquiry, since the structures and mechanisms that contribute to the survival of a post-reproductive male cohort may be, as we shall see, those that have been studied almost exclusively by psychoanalysis.

For the sake of contrast, I will introduce some evidence from physical anthropology concerning the fate of elderly apes, both male and female, from the most advanced and socially organized pongid species. I will then sketch out the situation of the older man, at the simpler, more primitive levels of human social organization: hunter-gatherers, as well as the preliterate folk-traditional societies. Next, I will speculate about the generic human practices and institutions that may be instrumental in bringing about some crucial man-ape differences in the psychology of the aged, and in the social treatment of senior males.

Turning first to the lower primates, we find that certain physical anthropologists have already done pioneering studies at this level. Thus, Hrdy (1981), a Harvard anthropologist, has recently demonstrated the importance and the vital social functions of post-reproductive female apes. She finds that, even among the lower primates, older females already play a significant role in the tending and physical protection of their grandchildren at crucial points in early development. They even take over some "masculine" responsibilities, for defending the troop as a whole on its outer defense line. Much as in human affairs, the female ape has two quite distinct lives, one lived out in her young adulthood, as a mother, and the other lived out in her seniority, as an active grandmother—even a matriarch—of her extended three generation family. But there is little precedent among the same lower pongids for male elders and particularly for male gerontocracy. It is only when we cross the ape-human barrier that the elderly male clearly appears, standing out as a significant and even dominant force in human affairs.

By contrast to their twice-born mates, male apes have one life: an existence centered on their muscular strength and on their capacity to command sexual favors by virtue of their successful aggression against other males. They may, in the course of adult life, store up practical lore but their accrued wisdom does not compensate in the later years for the loss of physical strength and ferocity. However smart or experienced they may still be, they drop out of the male dominance hierarchy, losing sexual privileges as their fighting qualities wane. Without sexual access to females, older primate males appear to become listless, even depressed, and they soon disappear from the primate band. Since physical anthropologists cannot simultaneously observe all troops of a given species in the same general area, we do not know the fate of these male, elderly drop-outs. They may wander off in search of a band whose dominance hierarchy still holds a niche for themselves; or they may disappear from society to suffer lonely, unrecorded deaths.

Scattered reports mention aging males who do remain with the primate troop even though they no longer hold a dominant position vis-à-vis other males. However, these survivors are not tolerated by virtue of their superior experience, but mainly because, in the symbolic sense, they have ceased to be males. Thus, they may become satellites of a dominant younger male who uses them sexually. They are apt to take on clear feminine mannerisms: for example, the female "squeal" vocalization. On the one hand, these aging male survivors lose their access to females, but they become, in themselves, token females. If these were elderly humans instead of apes, psychoanalysts might remark that they had reconstituted the sundered tie to females by introjecting and even becoming the lost object.

This then is the usual state of affairs in the most advanced and socially organized primate troops, whether composed of baboons, rhesus monkeys, or macaques: among them, we do find precursors of senior matriarchy, but very little evidence of patriarchal gerontocracy. However, when we move up one notch on the evolutionary scale, to no more than the most primitively organized human hunting and gathering bands, the situation in this respect is reversed, and for the first time the older male appears as a significant, established actor on the social scene. True enough, hunter-gatherers sometimes abandon their aged when they are too weak to follow the band's migrations, but in most recorded cases this is not an uncaring act on the part of the young. Rather, it is an event of profound spiritual meaning, and usually takes place at a time of the elder's choosing.

But certainly, as we move away from the migratory condition toward stable communities, those based on sedentary agriculture, then the evidence for universal male gerontocracy is clear and indisputable. At this level of human organization, the positive primate correlation between muscle mass and leadership is reversed: now it is precisely the male who is too old to fight who is most likely to exercise ultimate leadership. In some cases, he may rule by virtue of powers, in accumulated wealth and experience, that he has stored up in his younger, more active years. (Indeed, in our own American gerontocracy we are governed by leaders who perch on a base of powers that they have already amassed in their youth.) But in the pre-literate, tradition-directed sedentary community, the rules for the most part support *participatory gerontocracy*: rich or poor, the old man leads by virtue of being old, and by virtue of the privileged access to supernatural power sources that is the automatic endowment of advanced age. Thus, an old man's curse, a father's curse, can be more feared and more psychologically damaging than any sword thrust. In effect, the traditional elder maintains his place in the status ladder by finding new sources of strength, of the sort that are unavailable to younger men (or to male apes at any age). Such power is not located in the muscle, but is borrowed, *via* ritual and through the sufferings that attend long life, from supernatural, totemic sponsors. Old men are not in themselves power sources but bridgeheads to dangerous supernatural power; and the face of the magician is always the face of an older man.

But this equation that we discover, between advanced age and totemic power, does not in itself answer our opening question, "Why Male Elders?" Their seeming supernatural sponsorship only underwrites the generic power of older men in a social atmosphere that has itself been brought about by a prior condition of male gerontocracy. By and large, because of the social leverage that they already command, older men can elevate their special priorities—supernatural over muscular power, wisdom over impulsive action—to the point where these become the general law for men and women of all ages. That is, once they have achieved their social power, older men are no doubt instrumental in creating the projective ecologies, particularly the religions, that compensate them for their failing physical powers; but we have to look beyond organized religions to discover the ultimate sources of elder power in human affairs.

Freud addresses the question of the organic linkage between old men and the gods in "Totem and Taboo" (1913). He proposes that in human pre-history old men kept title to all sexually available females. However, the price of their selfishness was revealed when the rebellious sons banded together, killed the father, ate him and deified him, thus bringing about the intrinsic connection between senescence and godhead. Once cannibalized, the father's stolen powers become a hostile, retributive object within the son's mental constitution. Guilt therefore emerged as a personal experience and as a social institution to protect future generations of fathers against the crime of parricide.

While Freud's fable represents a creatively imaginative attempt to deal with the question, "Why Male Elders?," his interesting myth is not supported by sophisticated anthropological observations of the primate band. Thus, as we have seen, under proto-human and pre-superego conditions, males do not gain sexual access to females by virtue of their seniority, but by virtue of their physical strength and ferocity. This being the case, then how could the primal fathers of Freud's story manage to accumulate and hold on to their harems during their season of declining vigor? And how did the prohibitions against parricide become fixed, a genetic feature of the human psyche, and a universal institution of human society? To argue that the prohibition was first learned in the course of a parricidal act and subsequently genetically transmitted through the germ plasm is to take an unacceptable Lamarckian position.

True enough, just as our species is unique in its tolerance for elderly males, it is also relatively unique in its adherence to a great and universal prohibition: the incest taboo. Thus, although some ethologists claim that prototypes of the taboo are found at pre-human levels, such that male Hamadryas baboons have an inhibition against taking any females who are paired with other males of their troop, we do not know if this inhibition would extend to their un-paired biological mothers, daughters, or sisters. In any event, the inhibition noted among apes is raised to the level of an explicit and universal prohibition among humans: men and women should not mate with their parents, their children, or their siblings. And while Freud created an origin myth for the incest taboo, it can only be correctly understood as an outcome of evolutionary selection (rather than collective neurosis): the uniquely vulnerable human infant requires a stable family; and that stability is preserved in part by the incest taboo, which converts the family into a demilitarized or neutral zone, in regard to sexual competition.

To repeat, however it came about, there is a specifically human, explicit prohibition against incest, one that is found at all levels of human social organization. Often enough, that prohibition is not honored (and it is less likely to be observed by fathers with daughters than by mothers with sons), but such violations are always fraught with danger, even when—as in the case of Oedipus—they are inadvertently committed. In Sophocles' play, the depth and force of the prohibition is revealed by the drastic consequences of the transgression against it: learning of his "sin," Oedipus blinds himself.

Whether this great prohibition is lodged in the human gene pool, or whether it has its ultimate origin in a mythic murder that converted parricide into deicide, the incest taboo that distinguishes us from the apes also plays a vital part in bringing about a further (and equally crucial) man-ape distinction: the human institution of male gerontocracy. The incest taboo does not only protect children: in human societies we see a clear linkage between the social fate of children and the social fate of elders. Thus, the incest taboo also underwrites the emotional security and the physical existence of the older male: it guarantees his sexual and emotional access to at least one female, even during his season of declining physical strength. Unlike the elderly ape, he can enjoy his mate without having to fight his sons (or younger males generally) for the connubial rights. He does not—as would be true among the apes—lose his access to women in step with his loss of physical strength. Thus, retaining touch with a major wellhead of physical and emotional comfort, he is not inevitably fated to become depressed, or to drop untimely out of the human band. With reasonable assurance of at least one more or less nurturing female companion, he can remain in the community, which then becomes the beneficiary of his accumulated experience and wisdom.

While social evolution has brought about one great protection of the older human male in the form of the incest taboo, the psychological evolution of later life brings a second great protection: the normal androgyny of later life. This latter development seems to predate the human species in that we find its tracings even in the sub-human bands. As noted earlier, the older primate female becomes, in her postreproductive years, something of a "masculinized" warrior in defense of her own blood-kin and of the troop as a whole. Conversely, we also saw that the weakened older male can only survive unmolested in the primate troop by displaying stereotypically feminine characteristics. Carl Jung was the first psychoanalyst to note this great sex-role reversal of later life in human clinical samples, and I have traced it as a universal human phenomenon across a range of disparate cultures: specifically, the urban United States, the Navajo, the Maya, and the Druze. This androgyny of later life is clearly developmental in nature (see Gutmann, 1969), and like other universal features of the human life cycle, it is tied to the special needs and potentials of the human child. Thus, current research finds that, while infants are adept at provoking socioemotional support from caretakers, they are almost completely lacking in the skills required for physical survival. But there is a trade-off in human affairs between the infant's neediness and human potential. The human infant is relatively free of pre-programmed, instinctual learning— hence its remarkable vulnerability—but, by the same token, it is uniquely ready to acquire new learning for itself and for our species as a whole. However, the child's freedom from inflexible, instinctual patterns also binds the human adult to a long parental service. The human child requires from its parents the assurance of two kinds of security: emotional and physical. Under the usual human conditions of danger and scarcity, these distinct forms of nurture cannot easily be provided by the same parent. Accordingly, across cultures the tendency is to sort out, by gender, the responsibility for supplying these two basic securities: Men are generally held responsible for the provision of physical security, while women are generally held responsible for the provision of emotional security.

The parental investment in this service entails time, work, and worry. It also entails the sacrifice of personal potential. Thus, in order to provide physical security, parental men routinely move to the boundaries of the community. In so doing, they give up some of the warm, affiliative yearnings that would bind them close to the domestic center, but would keep them from the vital task of securing the periphery.

However, as children develop the capacity to supply their own needs for physical and emotional security, the sense of chronic parental emergency phases out, and mothers and fathers begin to take back into themselves, and to live out directly instead of vicariously the contra-parental and contra-sexual aspects of their own natures. Cultivating hitherto untended self-potentials, the father reclaims the softer, more nurturant and more affiliative qualities that he had put aside in order to provide physical security to his offspring. Women, normally responsible for the provision of emotional security, can reclaim the more aggressive potential that would have put their vulnerable children at risk in the psychic and even in the physical sense.

However, such advances carry price tags that are particularly evident in the case of older women: armed with her new found aggression, in many societies the "phallic" older woman earns the title of "witch." As a Moroccan proverb puts it, "When a girl is born she is surrounded by a hundred angels, and when a boy is born, he is surrounded by a hundred devils, but with each passing year an angel is exchanged for a devil, so that by the time a woman reaches a hundred, she is surrounded by a hundred devils and a man by a hundred angels."

Thus, while older men may pay an internal psychological price, in the form of shame, for their pacification and "feminization," they do make clear and corresponding gains at the more overt, social level. This androgynous, gentle older man is exempted from the sweat and burden of male competition. Just as the incest taboo preserves his sexual rights, the androgyny of later life protects his social rights. Because of his milder nature, he can move on to new attainments, new social ranks without fighting bruising battles to get there. Like the elderly president Ronald Reagan (or like Eisenhower before him), he is somehow above the fray, protected by young spearbearers rather than attacked by them. Freed from the pressure to live by his wits and ferocity, he can cultivate the "softer" qualities of wisdom, sensitivity, and objectivity; and he can move up the status ladders, unique to human society, that are reserved for attainment in the less bruising meritocracies of art, religion, academia, and statesmanship.

We have seen that the feminization of the older male ape restricts him to a subservient place in the retinue of a younger dominant male, but in the human case the same androgynous nature frees the older man for attainment in conservative fields—such as religion, or the tending of great traditions—that are relatively closed off (and usually uninteresting) to younger men. Accordingly, protected by an incest taboo that guarantees their emotional security, and by the mildness that guarantees their physical security, older men can stay within the human band, add their accrued wisdom to the common knowledge pool, and sustain the cultural traditions that are the bedrock of decent social life.

The interweaving of these late-life protections can be seen as they affect the manifestations of the Oedipus complex in the later stages of the extended family. Thus, a number of ethnographic observers, working across a wide range of traditional village societies, have independently noted a standard pattern of family relations that comes into play when the older son attains his majority as a married man, and his aging parents ease out of their parenting responsibilities. These observations focus on the renewal of a highly charged, ambivalent, and covertly erotic arrangement between the aging wife and her older son in the patrifocal family. In these arrangements, after the son marries he typically brings his wife home to the parental compound, and his wife takes on the status of handmaiden to the matriarch, his mother. Thus, when older men relinquish the active householder stage, aging wives will still maintain power in the family compound in concert with their married sons (their husbands having moved on to more "spiritual" stages).

The following citation from Sudanese Africa captures all the recurrent, generic features of this universal pattern. Hayes (1975) observes: "The older woman achieves a status more closely resembling that of men. They have influence and authority over the daughters-in-law of the compound, as well as their own daughters still living at home. Mothers are greatly respected by their sons, and sons often have closer emotional ties to their mothers than to their patriarchal fathers. Grandmothers are respected as fathers."

The Oedipal character of this reversal, involving as it does a removal of the father from secular affairs, and a strong alliance between the mother and her oldest son, is revealed in this account by the anthropologist Robert Pehrson (personal communication) from the warlike, patriarchal Baluchi of the Afghan Highlands. Among them, the aging father, though nominally still in charge of his clan, will lose interest in secular affairs and spend his time talking to the priests. Meanwhile, the control of daily affairs is taken over by a *Junta* made up of the aging wife and her oldest son.

Reports from the observers mentioned above come from a variety of distinct and independent cultures—Africa, China, and India. They all converge toward a strikingly similar picture of the role reversals in the three-generation extended family. Typically these follow on two pivotal, developmental transitions: the eldest son's attainment of sexual and social maturity through his marriage, and the older woman's attainment of a "masculine" virility at the end of her procreative period. Both advances are in phase with and perhaps require a third critical event: the voluntary abdication of patriarchal secular power by the aging father in favor of patriarchal, totemic power.

It is as though the Oedipal strivings that existed only in fantasy in the early years of the family finally (except for their specifically murderous and sexual goals) reach fruition in the adulthood of the son and in the postadulthood of the aging mother. In keeping with the terms of the Oedipal fantasy, the father abdicates (though without having to be killed) and the son inherits (though in acceptable form) the available women. Under the sway of the incest taboo he splits his affects, reserving sexual passion for his wife and the more reverent feelings for his mother, as whose consort he rules the family. Here we see that the father enacts his androgyny by leaving secular power to his son while he moves on to reach for totemic, spiritual power through ritual and religion. Unlike the aging male ape, the male elder brings his supplicant needs to God, rather than to a younger Alpha male. Thus deployed, his androgyny earns the older man not social disparagement, but a protective mantle of supernatural power.

In sum, the liberated postparental energies of men and women seek out and flesh out new roles. In order to understand their generic functions we again refer to the parental imperative model alluded to earlier, but now we consider the needs of the parents, as well as the needs of their offspring. The model reminds us that the uniquely needful child requires caretakers beyond the nuclear family and its limited panel of biological parents. In order to nurture sturdy children, who will in turn be adequate parents, the biological parents require two great pivots of support. The first is the extended family, which distributes the burden of child care among a pool of obligated relatives, and which provides emotional nurture, particularly to young mothers. The second great social support to parenthood comes from the cultural system, viewed here as a set of idealized rules or norms that relate the conforming encultured individual to the founding myths of his society. As such, culture compensates parents—particularly fathers—with a sense of significance and meaning in exchange for the masculine freedoms that are given up in response to the parental emergency. It should not surprise us to find that older, postparental individuals man the executive positions in these two great support systems: typically, across the human scene, older women move from hands-on care to administration and become the tough, matriarchal executives of extended families, while older men, having abandoned their position on the physical perimeter of the community, move out to the spiritual perimeter. As masters of ritual, as culture tenders, they mediate between the community and its gods. Older male apes may wander off in search of some illusory comfort, but older men stay close to home in the physical sense, even as their minds and imaginations rove out, to meet the supernatural sponsors of their society. By refreshing the society's link to its special protectors, older men keep alive the sense of unique mythic origins on which the culture as a whole depends.

We are already well aware that parents tend needful children; but in their two roles, as kin tenders and as culture tenders, strong postparental elders take care of needful parents. Without executive elders, young mothers could not easily tolerate the physical and emotional burdens of direct child rearing; while men would always long for the condition of unfettered barbarism, and would quickly defect, as too many already do, from prolonged domesticity.

Erik Erikson (personal communication) once remarked that deprivation *per se* was not psychologically destructive; that only deprivation without meaning was psycho-toxic. Through their myth-tending efforts, elder men help to provide, especially to younger individuals, the sense of meanings and significance to compensate for the sacrifices required by orderly civil and parental life.

The cognitive developments of later life act to endow older men with the requisite "culture tending" capabilities. Dealing constantly with routine "real world" emergencies, young men do not see the forest for the trees; more removed from the battlefield, older men can see and make real for others the larger context of action—the forest. Older individuals in effect create, out of the blur of daily social events, the larger contexts of social action: *the objects of culture*. They remind the young of the great though intangible traditions—the special significance, the moral meanings—that should guide daily performance in social roles. In effect then, under optimal circumstances, the aged may mature a special capacity that could be called the "cathexis of otherness."[1]

If older men provide the cultural realities that compensate for deprivation, they may also create those psychic structures that enforce the sacrifice of personal claims. Thus, in "Civilization and Its Discontents," Freud (1930) showed us that the pan-individual social order requires an intraindividual institution, the superego, to convert antisocial into prosocial aggression. But if the superego is to find secure lodgment within young men, then it requires outer supports and models. These too are routinely provided by senior men.

Contrary to traditional psychoanalytic doctrine, masculine psychic development does not end with the installation of the superego in adolescence. Having endured the burden of the superego during his early years, under properly facilitating circumstances, the older man—protected by the incest taboo and by his privileged association with the gods—*becomes* the outward face of the superego, for society as a whole, and particularly for young men. Thus, just as the extended family as an institution ultimately rests on the administrative efforts of elder women, the common culture ultimately depends on the superego-tending and myth-invoking efforts of older men.

Societies and subsocieties make full use of these special capacities of the aged. The only orderly revolution in American history was accomplished not long ago, in the "Watergate" affair, by elderly lawyers, most of them in their 70s, opposing a powerful president who had dared to tamper with our sacred document, the Constitution. Like the artist playing with the appearance of light, elderly lawyers and legislators had taken the Constitution, an insubstantial tissue of words, and by an act of love and idealization, made it *real* for themselves and for the nation as a whole. In their minds, in their words, and in their actions, the democratic principles that lie behind daily political life were manifested and made real for the nation. The combination of indignation and political energy mustered in defense of that reality was enough to bring down a powerful, unscrupulous president.

Returning to our opening question, "Why Male Elders?" it appears that those developments and protections that have the special effect of preserving old men as a distinctive feature of human life may ultimately protect us all. As we have seen, when the older man appears as a permanent fixture of social life, culture in its more mythic, ritualized, and enduring aspects appears with him. As his stature is undercut, the cultural regulation of social life is correspondingly weakened. We have compelling evidence for this last assertion: As we in this society move away from participatory gerontocracy, as we undo the role of male elders as superego and culture tenders, we also move into the condition of deculturation. When culture and the extended family are no longer tended by strong elders, then the unsupported, isolated nuclear family becomes the staging ground for various forms of child abuse. Thus, while the crisis of meaning and stability that comes with deculturation has special consequences for the aged and perhaps touches them first, it is finally revealed as a shared affliction that ends by destroying the children. Finally, the question "Why Male Elders?" might be answered for us were we to enlist them in the vital task of *reculturation* that faces us now.

Notes

1. Older artists, for example, give substance and reality, for all of us, to those matters which are insubstantial but also fundamental. In the work of the older painter, we can see tracings of a development event, the late maturing capacity to cathect and to make real those agencies which do not in any direct way bear on the security and priorities of the self. Thus, when we review the work of the leading impressionists, Monet (a Frenchman of the 19th and 20th centuries) and Turner (an Englishman of the 18th and 19th centuries), across the span of their creative life, we note some striking and parallel changes in the later years. Their early paintings are naturalistic, devoted to capturing the "trees"—the immediacy of the social world: human forms are central, in action, sharply defined, and carefully detailed. But around age 50, both make a sharp break from literal representation, and become confidently impressionistic: boundaries become indistinct; "social scapes" give way to landscapes in which sea, sky, and earth are fused; paint is no longer purely in the service of representation but becomes a textured element of the work in its own right; and human figures either lose their distinctness and centrality, or fade entirely from the scene. The artist is no longer captured by the immediacy of things, but seems to be looking beyond them, trying to picture the primary armatures of reality, *light* for example, that are prior to mere surfaces and appearances. Light is no longer used to distinguish objects; instead objects are used to demonstrate the play of light and its changing values.

References

1. Freud, S. (1930). *Civilization and Its Discontents. Standard Edition* 21:59–145.
2. Freud, S. (1913). *Totem and Taboo. Standard Edition* 13:1–161.
3. Gutmann, D.L. (1969). "The Country of Old Men: Cross-Cultural Studies in the Psychology of Later Life." In Levine, R. (Ed.): *Culture and Personality: Selected Readings.* New York: Aldine.
4. Hayes, R.O. (1975). "Female Genital Mutilation, Fertility Control, Women's Roles, and Patrilineage in Modern Sudan: A Functional Analysis." *American Ethnologist*, Vol. 2.
5. Hrdy, S.B. (1981). "Nepotists and Altruists: The Behavior of Old Females among Macaques and Langur Monkeys." In Amos, P.T., and Harrel, S. (Eds.): *Other Ways of Growing Old: Anthropological Perspectives.* Palo Alto: Stanford University Press.

10 Culture and Mental Health in Later Life, Revisited

As I write these prefaces and reread the pieces that they introduce, an age-related trend is beginning to show itself. Thus, in the later years, my interests shifted to the study and treatment of the psychological disorders of aging. The young Gutmann took time off from the clinic to study, as a natural scientist, the normal and developmental psychology of aging. Then, in the later years, I turned back to my roots in clinical psychology and began applying to the older mental patient the insights that had been developed in the field.

As a younger investigator, I had detailed the strong face of aging, the unique powers of the elders, particularly in traditional settings. But such triumphant reports from the younger Gutmann have begun to give way, as in the following piece, to a more somber note. Here I dwell more on the elder's weaker face, the transformation of "elder" into "aged." In this particular work, the clinician is indeed reappearing, but the voice of the anthropologist is still strong. In later articles I do go more fully into the disorders of aging individuals, but in this piece I am still working on a broader canvas: I try to define culture as it relates to individual psychology, and I try to specify the social pathologies—such as the slide towards deculturation—that set the stage for individual psychopathology in later life.

I. Introduction: A Field Without a Literature

In 1980, while writing an earlier essay on culture, mental health, and aging (Gutmann, 1980), I found very little written work on this topic; clearly, back then the psychological status of elders under varying cultural conditions was not a hot topic in gerontology. Now, ten years later, a definitive literature on the geropsychology of culture-personality relations is still not much in evidence.

However, in the interim, the cultural if not the personality variables have in fact gotten some coverage. In large part stimulated by the recently formed Association for Anthropology and Gerontology, a long overdue ethnogerontology literature is now showing up: *Culture* and particularly *cohort* have become buzz-words in gerontology. Predictably, these ethnographic reports do not address the question of mental health; instead, they quite properly report on matters that interest anthropologists: the social roles of elders; the rituals through which they enter and exit from age-graded statuses; the characteristics of their social relationships, both formal and informal; the systems and quality of elder-care in various societies, etc. While carefully wrought descriptions of this sort are immensely useful in breaking down culture-bound stereotypes about the aging process, and in establishing social gerontology as a natural science, such accounts—which record the normative consequences of social adaptation—cannot tell us much about adaptation or psychopathology. In short, an anthropologist can tell us interesting things about the cultural antecedents of a psychiatric patient, but he cannot, on that basis alone, make the clinical diagnosis. By the same token, social status does not reliably predict mental health or illness; madness occurs in the best of families (and, as the playwright Philip Barry reminds us, "especially the best").

Indeed, the elevated status of the aged can even put them at risk. Thus, Opler (1959) found that young Tonga (Africa) tribesmen revere their elders, but also believe that they achieve longevity through human sacrifice. Vampirelike, they presumably steal the life-force of their youthful victims, and so are blamed for the death of young people. In my own field work among the Highland Maya (1968), I saw that elders were treated with great deference, but that same respect was mingled with fear: these same venerated elders were suspected of demonic practices. Village lore had it that the *Naguales* (the animal familiars) of elderly Highland Maya men would meet on mountain tops, and these covens would decide the fate of individual villagers. Accordingly, deaths caused by epidemics were sometimes blamed on the *Naguales* of powerful elders; and these unfortunates were occasionally shot from ambush by vengeful survivors. However we choose to define this construct, the mental health of Highland Maya elders did not match their elevated social position. Summing up his fearful, frozen posture, an elderly informant told me, "I keep quiet" ("quedo callado").

Clearly then, ethnographic accounts bearing on the social status and roles of human elders—and that is about all that we have—can give us, at best, very imprecise and even misleading information about their psychological status.

II. Fieldwork and the Limitations of Academic Geropsychology

But neither do we get much help from psychology. A minority of ethnopsychologists do report on the feelings, attitudes, self-conceptions, and mental symptoms of elders in various societies; but while they claim to study aging psychology, their work, like that of the ethnogerontologists, does not really tell us much about the mental health of elders or its mediation by culture. My major objection is that only a few of the relevant studies utilize the depth-psychological instruments that were specifically crafted to probe the unconscious dynamisms underlying mental health, or psychopathology. Instead, the usual study is based on *standard* instruments—often standardly administered pencil and paper tests—which purport to measure the life satisfaction, stress, mental symptoms, etc., of elders in various societies. But standardization is a subjective rather than an objective condition; it is not reached *via* precoded instruments or standard instructions given by examiners whose behavior is invariant from subject to subject. Such procedures give the illusion of standardization; they reassure investigators as to their "scientific" credentials; but they do not reassure unsophisticated, often preliterate subjects, who routinely suspect that the foreign investigator could be a witch, or a government spy. Indeed, these essentially bureaucratic research procedures fuel such suspicions. Despite its cross-cultural pretensions, the field methods (and as a consequence, the findings) of academic geropsychology—with a few notable exceptions (Cohler & Lieberman, 1979; LeVine, 1978a, 1978b; Shanan, 1985)—remain steadfastly culture-bound.

Psychologists could break out of their self-imposed constraints by adopting less concretely behavioral guidelines for our field methods. The standard condition that we should aim for with naive or preliterate subjects is best covered by the term *rapport*—that special state wherein the subject *wants* to explore matters that are of importance to him, and of scientific interest to the investigator. Rapport is in all cases achieved by nonstandard, *ad hoc* methods, by procedures that are responsive to the fears and idiosyncratic concerns of the naive respondent confronted by a strange examiner, strange instruments, and strange demands. But when the real goal is methodological purity rather than illumination, we do not get rapport; instead, we get expressions of test anxiety, social desirability, and the naive subject's fear of a foreign investigator. What we do *not* get is an accurate reading of the subject's psychological strengths, vulnerabilities, and possible pathologies. We do not learn much that would be of any use to a clinician concerning our subject's true mental status.

III. Culture and the Elder

A. The Need for a Psychosocial Definition

In sum, the developing science of comparative geropsychology is in part retarded by the methodological orthodoxies of academic psychology, but also by the conceptual biases of the cultural anthropologists. The latter group presume to *own* the definitions of culture that are applied to culture-personality studies, but these have the unfortunate result of bending both domains—psychology *and* culture—out of shape. Thus, despite substantial disagreements among cultural anthropologists, the majority join in treating culture as an independent variable, and in asserting that all expressive behavior is dependent: a socially patterned outcome. The proponents of this externalized view—many psychologists among them—hold that nurture in the form of cultural indoctrination is supreme, and that there are no *natural,* organismic sources of coherent, organized behavior. In effect, the culture-centric view establishes, at the very heart of the social sciences, a mind-body dichotomy: the body, its imperatives, rhythms, and appetites, is a source of anarchy, not order; and in later life, of debility and decay.

These definitions that make culture primary serve the academic imperialism of anthropologists, but they retard our understanding of psychological adaptation or breakdown at any age. Such a view of personality as the dependent, unmediated product of culture is particularly misleading in gerontology, and does violence to the observed facts. It does not, for example, help us to understand—without forcing the data into a procrustean bed—the finding (see Gutmann, 1987) of universal, culture-free personality change in later life.

At worst, such externalized understandings of human psychology lead to a simpleminded *Lumpen-Marxism:* Motives, attitudes, and their attendant behaviors are ascribed to economic conditions, to social class, or to "the later stages of capitalism." More commonly, given the exaggerated scientism of American psychologists and anthropologists, the search for quantifiable dependent (psychological) and independent (cultural) variables does violence to the natural systems being studied. The complex, intertwined systems of *culture* and *personality* are not easily assimilated to glib independent-dependent variable sequences or designs.

Christine Fry (1985) is one of the few ethnogerontologists who resists the conceptual colonialism of her discipline: She proposes a partnership, an implicit equality between culture and those aspects of personality that mature in encultured frameworks. Thus, Professor Fry:

> Individuals are not the passive recipients of knowledge, rules and standards from enculturators who are older, bigger, stronger, or more important than they are. Knowledge, rules, and standards are not learned to be blindly followed in motivating action or determining responses. . . . Culture is a model each individual has formed of what others know, believe, and mean. . . . People use their models to generate the actions they think will lead *others to validate a certain identity.* People conform to rules to demonstrate to themselves and to others that they are a particular kind of person (p. 217) (Italics mine).

Fry speaks out of the psychoethological position first enunciated by Erik Erikson (1959). In his view, the universal or structural aspects of culture have co-evolved with the deep structures of the mind—the ego executive capacities that, while they develop under conditions of sociality, also function so as to maintain the nurturing conditions that sponsored them. Thus, culture and individual personality are equal partners, metaphors of each other, entwined in a dialectic exchange. Culture is not individual personality writ large, nor is personality only a print-out of local norms, cohort influences, and belief systems: It is not culture writ small. Clearly, investigations devoted to the linkage between culture and elderly mental health should attend to those aspects of culture that extend and sponsor psychological capacities, particularly those that underwrite a culturally regulated social life.

In the balance of this essay I will put forward some conceptions of culture that take into account its functions *vis-à-vis* the social collectivity as well as its functions *vis-à-vis* individual personality. This discussion will focus on two related phenomena: the special role that older individuals play in maintaining the ritual aspects of culture; and the special bonus of mental health that elders may possibly receive in exchange for this service. I will also discuss the pathogenic consequences for elders when, under conditions of deculturation, they lose their special, privileged relationship to culture.

The gerontological literature is burdened with references to "culture"; absent are any clear understandings of the meanings that may be packed into that overused term, or its relation to individual psychology, particularly in later life. In the following section I will try to put forward some psychological content to challenge the anthropologist's ownership of "culture."

IV. Culture: In Relation to Social and Psychic Structure

While culture requires the human mind as a precondition for its own continuity, it is also a *social* reality, existing apart from particular brains. Like language, it outlasts its founders, it is transmitted in recognizable form from generation to generation, and it is based in those parts of the mental apparatus that (like the deep structures of language) are common to all socialized adults. Possessing in these senses an objective reality, culture is a guarantor of individual as well as social continuity. Social scientists emphasize mainly the part played by culture in bringing about the continuity of trustworthy communities rather than trustworthy individuals. Culture is invoked by them as the proper context for understanding social conformity, social continuity, and social change in any organized, corporate body. In their designs, individuals are only the *genes* of culture. Thus, cultural anthropologists generally use individuals as informants not on their own lives, but on the beliefs and customs of their local culture. In their view culture is mapped into the *tabula rasa* of the individual gene through formal and informal learning; and while psychological conflict may trouble the mind, it originates externally in discrepant social norms, rather than in inevitable conflict between competing needs or appetites. But a truly psychological conception treats culture not as prior to the psyche, but as the counterpart and sponsor, on the collective scale, of the mental processes that underwrite the psychological traits of delay, rationality, and control—the capacities that are necessary to the individual's participation in society and culture.

A. The Stimulus Barrier

The psychosocial role of culture is clarified when we consider an overriding need of the human psyche: to establish autonomy from stimulus overload, the blur and buzz of immediate experience. The mental apparatus has preformed, deep structures to match that need: inbuilt potentials to abstract, to symbolize, to *name*. The ego generalizes: it abstracts categories out of the regularities that it discovers in the wash of events, it *names* these categories, and it endows them with the tonus, the solidity of reality. Having constructed these constancies, these *objects,* the psyche has established the structural base of its autonomy, its freedom from the tyranny of the immediate. Rather than endure the shock of unbuffered experience, the ego can fix attention on its own constructions *about* reality; in so doing, it gains the capacity for delay of impulse and gratification that is fundamental to rationality and mastery.

Redfield (1947) held that any proper culture is a coherent system of *shared understandings* as to what is good and bad, possible and impossible, thinkable and unthinkable. So construed, culture facilitates the psyche's *conquest of experience:* it restricts in advance the range of permissible mental and physical activity, and it provides already established *names*—as well as the precedents and pre-ordained meanings that names call up—to neutralize the individual encounter with the new and the strange. *Via* language, culture speeds the process of bringing order, predictability, and significance to new experience.

B. Narcissism

But culture is the counterpart and reciprocal of the irrational as well as the rational, order-seeking side of the psyche; more than a collection of shared and shareable understandings, culture is reciprocal to the narcissistic tendencies studied by psychoanalysts such as Kohut (1978) and Kernberg (1975). By restoring the individual's conviction of centrality, and by supplying emergency rations of self-esteem, narcissism buffers the vulnerable individual against the "slings and arrows of outrageous fortune." Thus, narcissism fosters the illusion of security, either by elevating the self, or by endowing those parts of the world related to the self with unordinary stature, power, and grace.

In particular, culture sponsors a central aspect of narcissism: the plasticity of this powerful tendency. Narcissism can lead to an excessive glorification of the isolate individual self, or it can lead to the idealization of the social objects that condense out of collective experience. Under the sway of culture, the balance tilts toward society: the narcissistic investment is shifted away from the self, away from personal grandiosity toward idealization of the cultural icons, traditions, and institutions.

The great power that culture wields in this regard derives from its critical relationship to the founding myth, the legend that is graven in the annals of all vital societies. The cultural mystery is typically a drama of redemption. It tells how a special people were, in dire straits, rescued by the intervention of unordinary beings—whether gods (Yahweh at the Red Sea Crossing) or human though legendary heroes (George Washington at Valley Forge). The founding myth is the power-shed of the encultured society: it lends special significance to shared values, for these express the nature of the gods; and it lends dignity to conforming behavior, for such discipline is required by the gods and pleases them.

In effect, the myth is a narcissistic dream on the collective scale: the vulnerability of the people countered by the *Deus ex machina,* the omnipotent, rescuing deity or hero. Thus, culture meets the human need to create illusory security by encumbering parts of the world with more than ordinary stature or power; in short, culture offers *objects of veneration.* These attract individual narcissism, and bind it to the communal service. Culture's great achievement is to transform potentially asocial narcissism into prosocial idealization of venerated gods, the traditions that reflect their nature, and the institutions that, through ritual, uphold these founding traditions. Culture is not—as some anthropologists would hold—the sum of distinctive group habits (in that limited sense, baboon bands could be said to have culture); culture is the system of idealized objects, including the institutions that service and defend them. Culture is what you will die for, or send your sons to die for.

C. The Cultural Uses of Splitting and Projection

But power—particularly the *tabu* power of the venerated gods—is always ambivalent, double-edged: like fire, it can warm your house, or burn it down. Likewise, the empowered, venerated gods, because they are vessels of might, may destroy their followers. Children deal with this dilemma, the essential unreliability of powerful providers, *via* the psychic mechanisms of *splitting* and *projection.* Malign aspects of the parent, those that detract from the ideal image, are deleted, and projected on some alternate—a step-parent, a strict teacher, or the "Bogey-Man." As a consequence, parts of the child's world may become frightening, but the Good Parent, the reassuring rescuer, is preserved. Culture uses these primitive defenses, whose first goal is to protect the immature self, for its own higher purpose: the protection of the idealized icons, and by extension, the social order.

Thus, as they impanel demonic representations of bad power, cultures provide a *projective ecology* to accommodate the dark side of ambivalence. The world fills with devils, witches, or traitors, but the venerated objects remain uncorrupted. In adult life, splitting and projection can fuel individual paranoia, but culture is the talisman that converts these defenses to prosocial uses: the preservation of the collective icons. Culture uses evil, the names of the Devil, to protect the good.

D. Inner Control

Erik Erikson once pointed out (personal communication, 1961) that deprivation *per se* is not psychologically destructive; it is only deprivation without meaning that is psychologically destructive. In this succinct thought, the great psychologist summed up the essential contribution of culture to the integrity of the psyche, and to its vital system of inner controls. By satisfying the hunger for the ideal, culture supplies encultured individuals with the sense of *meaning* that makes possible—even palatable—the conformities, disciplines, and sacrifices that are required by decent social life and by adequate parenting. In the encultured society, such conformity is not a mark of shameful passivity. Instead, it becomes an aspect of ritual, a link to the founding mystery. To conform, to act in a seemly way, is to garner—better, to recapture—for the self, some of the ideal qualities that have been conceded to the cultural icons. Thus laundered or neutralized, narcissism reverts to the self, in the form of self-esteem rather than megalomania. In effect, culture functions as the immune system of the social body: by providing individuals with meaning in exchange for their controlled, conforming behavior, it protects the social order against anarchy and unbridled, asocial narcissism.

E. Self-Continuity

Strong cultures provide the ecology not only for inner controls, but also for a secure sense of selfhood. In particular, culture provides the conditions for an assured sense of rootedness and inclusion. As Sigmund Freud (1922) pointed out in *Group Psychology and the Analysis of the Ego,* individuals who idealize the same leader automatically come together as a community. But even in the absence of a charismatic leader, culture brings about social bonding: culture-mates recognize in each other a portion of themselves—the shared identification with the cultural icons, and the values that these represent. Through self-examination, through knowing themselves, encultured individuals are familiar to each other without prior acquaintance. In this manner, culture performs the great work of transforming potential strangers into familiars, and asocial narcissism into social bonds. The encultured individual has an automatic sense of recognition and inclusion, of being folded into a larger social body composed of those others who are, in important ways, extensions of self. The tie to leaders, those who best exemplify the virtues of ancestors and sponsoring gods, gives to the encultured individual the sense of being in touch with the redeeming powers who once rescued his people and who will now succor him; through the offices of culture, he discovers an echo of the founding mystery at the very core of self. A strong culture—an expression of society—sponsors a strong sense of identity at the individual level.

F. The Components of Culture

Summing up, the particular aspects of culture that co-act with individual needs for community, security, and self-continuity are these:

A founding myth: The legend of special beginnings of a special people, favored by special gods.

Traditions: Formats of collective ritual, belief, and social action that reflect the ways of the founders, and partake of their sacred nature.

Institutions: Organized bodies, persisting across generations, that represent, guard, and enact the myths and traditions. In general, religious institutions are wardens of the founding myth, while secular institutions are wardens of tradition.

Rituals: Patterns of stylized action choreographed by religious institutions to be metaphors, enactments of the founding myth. Ritual practices provide encultured individuals with some sense of participation in the mystery, and its powers.

Age grade systems: Status elevators that reliably move accredited individuals, in their seniority, to the seats of institutional power, and to the gates of the mystery.

Whatever values they embody, strong cultures meet these criteria. When culture is in these terms strong, then its adherents will be encultured, the culture will be a daily reality in the life of the people, and its values will be securely lodged in the mental life of the typical citizen. These internal certainties will constrain individual behavior, and lead to the perpetuation of culture by the next generation.

When culture is in this sense perceivable, rooted, and transmissible, then the society is in a condition of *culturation:* whatever its ethnicity, whatever its particular values, whatever its economics, whatever its terrain, then there are predictable consequences, arising from the condition of culturation alone, for the collective and individual life. Whether pacific or war-like, the culturated society will almost certainly maintain strong families, trustworthy parents, emotionally sturdy children, and—however much it may trouble the peace of other societies—a relatively orderly, usually productive civil life. Finally, the vulnerable pre- or post-productive members of a culturated society—children, the infirm, and the old—are likely to be protected rather than grossly exploited by the strong.

V. Elders: The Wardens of Culture

Thus, the aged are major beneficiaries of an enculturated society; but those who review the status and functions of the elders across cultures will find that the elders are also the most vital supporters of a strong culture, particularly in its mythic or *numinous* aspects.

The elder's special relation to culture helps us to understand male gerontocracy, another unique feature of human social organization. Leo Simmons' (1945) review of ethnographic studies shows that older men were chiefs in 56 of the sample societies, that they could choose to hold office in eight more, and that in no case were they deposed on account of age. Humans then are the only primate species in which the older male, despite his loss of physical strength, his warrior's edge, can find alternate sources of spiritual strength to sustain and even increase his status. The special strength, even *charisma,* of the older traditional male comes not from his physical dominance, but from a resource that hairier apes do not have: his special, privileged access to *culture,* and to the power inherent in the cultural myths.

Older traditionals, because of their special access to the gods, to the myth-embracing past, and to the spiritualized ancestors, become the living exemplars of the founding legend. It is they, the elders, who bypass the time gap between then and now, bringing the two into conjunction. *Via* the elders the mythic past and the mundane present are interpenetrated, and the climate of mythic origins is brought forward, into the here and now. Through the rituals managed by the older men, the power-shed of the past is tapped, and the same *mana* that once rescued a desperate people reenters the world to heal the ill, to bring reviving rain down to a wasted land, or to move puny boys into strong manhood.

A substantial number of ethnographers report (and their accounts accord with my observations of the Navajo, Highland Maya, and Druze) that when society maintains a traditional consensus, older men lead the congregation. Thus, the correlational study by Timothy Sheehan (1976) of the relationship between societal type and senior prestige reveals that, for a sample of 47 preliterate groups, a settled, non-nomadic, relatively isolated and traditional society provides the best communal ecology for the aged and cultural life. There is folklore to be guarded and handed down by seniors, there is religious thought, cosmic ceremony and *rites de passage* through which they gain special access to the empowering gods.

Individual ethnographic accounts from a broad range of traditional societies bear out Sheehan's generalizations. Thus, from the Orient, Kalab (1990) reports on the ascension of Khmer elders, as they acquire new learning, to high rank in the Buddhist religion. Cowgill (1972) found that Thai elders withdraw gracefully from formal roles in society, but show marked increase in religious observance.

Shelton (1972) observed that Igbo (Africa) elders were thought to be exemplars of the life force, and were "most like a spirit." According to Biesele and Howell (1981), the title "big" is respectfully added to Kalahari Bushman seniors. Fuller (1972), who worked among the African Bantu, discovered their elders to be wardens of the land. They come to personify their clan lineage, and they are regarded as the living link to the ancestors. Similarly in Samoa, Holmes (1972) observed that older men have special access to the spirit world.

In the course of my own field work among the Druze, I found that these Middle Easterners were no exception to the general rule. At around age 55, postparental Druze men, those who have lived an exemplary life and raised exemplary children, are invited to join the ranks of the *Aqil,* the accredited elders who guard the secret religion that defines their sect.

Coming full circle, back to our continent, we find that older American Indians "return to the blanket" and take up the traditional religion, even in the face of rapid modernization and deculturation. Thus, Fowler (1990) notes that Arapaho elders will maintain high social standing, despite loss of economic security, so long as they can enhance their ritual role in the native religion. Amoss and Harrell (1981) assert that, paradoxically, the prestige of the Indian elder in North America has risen, owing to a modern development: the return to nativistic roots on the part of young, relatively deculturated Indians. The revival of interest in tradition and ritual has brought with it a special advantage to those remaining elders who still remember—or can claim to remember—the old ways.

Summing up, we find a general rule that drives gerontocracy, across cultures: Older persons are less apt to control resources that have to do with pragmatic, economic production, but by the same token, their grip over the ritual sources of sacred power increases with age. Thus Lucien Levy-Bruhl (1928) observed that, in the preliterate folk society, the old man is possessed by an essence so pervasive that his body parts and even his excrement can become the residence of *tabu* power.

Claude Levi-Strauss (1983) perhaps says it best: For him, the old are to the young as culture is to nature. The young are naturally social, but without culture. Their groups are like the packs of animals: either anarchic or subject to the harsh rule of the strongest, most ferocious leaders. It is only under the sway of culture—the human reinterpretation of the social—that living becomes orderly and predictably calm. It is the aged who represent the specifically human creation of culture. They know its ways, they have lived under its discipline, and they have become part of the mystique from which the society derives its traditions, its rituals, and its enduring strength. In traditional societies, the aged are seen to be isomorphic with culture; they are its human face.

VI. Elder Passivity and Elder Power

The older traditional's special access to spiritual power rests on a number of bases, including the endowment of wisdom, which is most evident under the redundant, relatively predictable circumstances of the small, isolated society. In addition, those hardy individuals who survive to old age under the stringent circumstances of the preliterate society are quite naturally regarded as special, unordinary. They have a special edge, which—since it does not come from their depleted bodies—must be the gift of the favoring gods. Their wrinkles do not betoken weakness, but dueling scars from god.

Wisdom and longevity should bring prestige in any social setting; but I have speculated elsewhere (Gutmann, 1987) that the aged are additionally favored, under traditional culture, by qualities that can lead to their stigmatization, and social disadvantage under modern conditions. For example, as noted by Simone de Beauvoir (1972), the aged are always in danger of becoming the *stranger,* the *other.* The stranger is eerie, not quite human, even revolting, but also strong. And in the traditional assemblage, the aging strangers are told off to deal with the ultimate aliens, the gods. Owing to their dramatic contact with the gods, revulsion is checked, while the aspect of strength is amplified.

The passive traits that emerge in older men (see Gutmann, 1987) can lead to stigma and shame in our society, but under the conditions of traditional culture, this same dangerous quality fits the older male for his special, power-collecting relationship to the gods. In the traditional society, the pacified older man acts as the intermediary between the society and its nurturing but also potentially dangerous, easily offended gods.

There, accumulating the gods' *tabu* power for social purposes is not a task for Promethean young men. The necessary passivity is alien to them; their boldness would insult the gods, and—like Oedipus—bring disaster on the community and on themselves. To avoid this fate, the power brokers who man the sacred perimeter of the community must, in their own nature, be metaphors of the benign power that they would attract. Accordingly, in the traditional and religious community, it is the postparental older men, cleansed of sex and aggression, humble in bearing, who can beseech the nurturing influences of the gods, without offending the divinity.

What we activist Americans might think of as shameful passivity becomes, under encultured conditions, the essential requirement for the strong traditional elder. Older men discover in the supernaturals the strength that they no longer find within themselves; they use prayer, *au fond* a passive-dependent modality, to beseech, for themselves and for the people, their fire from the gods.

VII. Mental Health and the Traditional Elder

The older traditional revives himself through ritual, but he is also the power broker for society, the splice between the folk and its gods. The *mana* imported by the elder power-bringer revives the natural environment and social organs of his community. He becomes, for his people, the prime source of luck, of success in battle, of ripe crops, of fat herds, of healthy children.

Returning to our subject, mental health and the elder, our model allows us to make a prediction which cannot—in the absence of appropriate cross-cultural data—be adequately tested: namely, that under conditions of gerontocracy and strong culture, even economic hardship will not detract from the psychological resilience of traditional elders. They are buffered, *immunized*, by their special relationship to those cultural institutions that convert narcissism to social bonds, that support inner controls, and that counteract existential terror. In addition, through his special linkage to the gods, the older traditional makes the sense of divinity manifest to the community as a whole. In their turn, owing to their social and psychological bonds with their elders, individuals of all ages can feel connected to the vital center; and they can discover echoes of that vital center within themselves. *Via* the intercessions of the traditional elder, encultured people of any age receive the sense of grace that is vital to their self-esteem and the sense of significance that underpins their self-control. The same sacred connection supports the psychological health of older traditionals: they gain social status; respect verging on fear and awe; the assurance of support from obligated kinfolk; and the sense of personal connection to a benevolent supernatural order.

I am not proposing a comprehensive theory of later life mental health or pathogenesis; this passage is limited to specific features of the mental life that normally become critical in the later years: inner controls, narcissistic fixations, self-continuity. I will briefly consider the prophylactic influence of a strong culture against those narcissistic disorders that result in weakened controls, impulse disorders, depressions, and disruptions in the experience of self.

Developmental as well as sociocultural forces act to bring about salutary transformations of narcissism. Particularly during the years of active parenthood, idealization of the self and its goals is, if things go as they should, supplanted by the condition of *generativity* (Erikson, 1963) wherein parental narcissism is conceded to the now idealized offspring: the child should live forever, should not experience grief or want, should inherit the promise of the future, etc. This generational transfer of narcissism is vital to the child's development during its years of early vulnerability, before it has formed its own capacities, or found its own allies. But as children grow up, and as the sense of *parental emergency* (Gutmann, 1987) phases out, they do not need, nor do they justify, massive transfusions of parental narcissism.

As a consequence, in the postparental years (as in the preparental years), narcissism in its unbuffered—hence pathogenic—form, may revert the self. Hypochondria, egocentricity, fussily obsessive rituals, hypersensitivity to minor slights, and depression in reaction to the normal losses of aging can result. But despite the emptied nest, a strong culture can provide new catalysts for healthy, phase-specific transformations of narcissism. In their seniority, traditional elders do not—as claimed by Cummings and Henry (1961)—disengage from social interaction into self-absorption (in actuality, disengagement is much more likely to occur under conditions of modernity and secularization). Instead, the traditional elder typically becomes the *warden* of the cultural myths and becomes merged, identified with the representations of that mystery: he blends with the venerated cultural objects. In short, through the intervention of culture, traditional elders can shift self-concern away from themselves to transcendent icons, thereby converting pathogenic narcissism into idealism, into the *cathexis of otherness*. Thus, instead of fussing over his private obsessions, the older traditional can choreograph the details of shared ritual: the ballet of seemly behavior that ties the people to their gods. His own fate becomes incidental; what counts is not the persistence of the individual self, but of the people and the ways in which they serve their god.

In sum, a strong culture, by buffering and neutralizing narcissism, deflects one of the leading *specific* threats to mental health in later life. By the same token, as elders themselves approach the iconic status, their sense of personal significance, the meaning of their service to the venerated objects, increases. In their adult years their self-control was validated by the imperatives of parenthood; in their postparental years, their self-control finds new justification, and now derives from their *filial* connection to the parental gods.

The vital sense of self-continuity is normally at risk in later life, eroded by critical changes in the inner and outer *ecologies of the self*. Most geropsychologists (see Atchley, 1989) hold that self-continuity later in life is threatened by expectable changes in familiar social domains: retirement, losses of spouse, kin, friends, etc. However, our studies of late-onset psychopathology at Northwestern Medical School have shown that *tectonic* inner shocks, having to do with important shifts in basic appetites, sexual identifications, and associated fantasies can also bring about profound revisions in the experience of self. Intrapsychic changes powerful enough to alter self-continuity can result from developmental transitions of the postparental period, and also from the weakening of inner controls. Despite their different origins, all such eruptive changes have similar effects: the older individual may feel that an alien, uninvited presence has taken over some part of the personal space, leaving him estranged from himself.

In short, the integrity of the self is intimately linked to the integrity of inner controls; and, as we have already observed, these require endowments of cultural meaning to compensate for the deprivations imposed by such controls. In later life particularly, inner controls are threatened by the narcissistic wish for omniconsumption and omnigratification; strong cultures provide the intrapsychic controls with new anchors against the undertow of regressive appetites. Culture functions as the immune system of society, and it also braces the psychological immune system of the traditional elder.

VIII. Deculturation and the Elders

Culture has both structural and content features. The structural aspect refers to the *density* and *interiority* of a cultural regime—the degree to which its guiding voice is a constant *presence* in the life of encultured individuals. The usual assumption in geropsychology is that the mental health of elders in a given society varies according to the *content* features of the ambient culture, particularly, its stance towards aging. In this calculus, the mental health of older Americans is at risk because they live in a society that values youth and denigrates aging, etc. But the argument of this essay is that *deculturation*—the loss of cultural density and interiority—has the most profound consequences for the elder's mental health. As long as culture is intact in the structural sense, as long as it is pervasive in the society and insistent in the mind, then fluctuations in the value consensus will have little effect on the psychic constitution of traditional elders.

Thus, as we have recently seen in Iran, a holy Imam in his ninth decade, allied to the icons of Islam, could send revolutionary youth frenzied into the streets. Khomeini had a special *charisma* for Iranian youth because he was *opposed* to the "modern" values infiltrating from the West. The Shah, who represented the cultural values of progress and modernity, was overthrown by the youthful followers of Khomeini, who personified for them the timeless purity of Islam: through him, the Prophet was reborn.

As the Iranian example shows, traditional cultures can be very durable; many influences must combine to set in train the processes of social entropy that lead ultimately to deculturation, and to the psychosocial deracination of the elders. The usual assumption is that the influences of modernization or urbanization, particularly in combination, act so as to degrade culture and gerontocracy.

Briefly, modernity refers to influences that, while they usually originate in cities, are not exclusive to them: literacy, electrification, advanced modes of technology and manufacture, as well as rationalized uses of labor. Urbanization refers to the forms of association that typically occur in the city—with or without electricity or trams—but rarely in the village: the mingling of foreigners, the mixing of social classes and their contrasting manners, the open clash of philosophies—the city as market place of lifeways, ideas, and material goods.

Stable, insular, usually rural societies are the best setting for strong cultures. So long as traditional beliefs and values can flourish in their own niche, uncontested by alternate world views (particularly those emanating from more developed societies), they avoid the fate of being relativized and called into question. An inevitable consequence of modernity is loss of physical distance between hitherto isolate societies; and when a modernizing society moves out of its isolation—or is moved out of it, by conquest or colonization—the people are automatically brought into contact with contrasting, even conflicting conceptions as to what is good and bad, possible and impossible, holy and impure. Despite this disorienting and relativizing contact, the emerging society may retain much of the ideological content of its culture; but the usual relationship between the people and their special beliefs must change as a result. The shock is most severe when the emerging society makes contact with the beliefs and practices of one more technologically advanced, whose engineering and medical skills bring about immediate, tangible "miracles"—wonders that cannot be matched by prayer and ritual.

As an example, I witnessed the power of the Navajo medicine man being broken, not by white missionaries, but by Anglo medical interns working out of the Public Health Service hospitals scattered across the reservation. Despite his awesome dignity, despite being crusted with silver and turquoise, the medicine man's prayers cannot save a child with intestinal infections. The singer will chant powerfully for nine nights, while the feverish child dehydrates and dies. Devoted Navajo parents have learned that a callow white intern, who commands penicillin, can save the child that the magnificent medicine man will lose. Accordingly, at-risk children survive, but the mythic basis of Navajo culture is at the same time called into question, and Navajo lifeways lose their power to provide individuals with sacred sentiments, self-esteem, and discipline.

Under such conditions, the cultural conceptions may still be widely distributed, familiar to most affiliates of the society; but now they are known to be no more than symbols, rather than substance. Lacking *density,* they are no longer the basic, power-compelling axioms of the universe. And as the sacred ideas become relativized, as symbol is split from substance, the elders who represent and manage the symbolic systems are likewise split from their special powers. The elder loses the special cachet of "wise man" or "wise woman."

A. Economic Power and Elder Power

The economic changes that come with modernity are mainly important insofar as they degrade traditional ideas of sacred power, and the access to such power. *Wealth* in the folk mind is important only to the degree that it links up with traditional ideas about *tabu* power, to the degree that it represents favor from the gods (or the power of witchcraft used in the service of material gain). As *objective* economics intrudes into the folk world, the traditional conception of sacred power loses its commanding position within a special preserve, while the *modern* versions of wealth take on some of the vibrancy that the traditional forms have lost. Power becomes secularized, represented by cash, by machines, by the products of machines, by weapons, and even by beverage alcohol. In effect, under the dominion of the new economics, the distinction between totemic and secular power phases out, and the power boundary is reset. It no longer divides the sacred from the ordinary world, but stands instead between the underdeveloped community and the modern or Western world.

The effect on elders is profound: the aged are the monitors and heroes of the old power frontier that faces gods and demons; but it is the modernizing young who cross the new frontier between societies to bring back alien power, in the form of cash, weapons, and technology, for themselves and their community. This is a role for the Promethean young and not for the cautious elders. If anything, the role of the elders on the new frontier is a reactionary and even destructive one. They tend to distrust the new, deritualized sources of power; and they impede the flow of modern forms of power, from the developed world into the still relatively powerless, emerging community.

The sons of the old traditionals are also caught up in the economics of modernity, in ways that endow them not only with the new financial coinage of power, but also with the *mana* that their fathers are losing. The modernizing society typically provides a labor pool for the developed world; and the young men, instead of staying home to work their father's fields, leave the traditional village to find wage employment in the plantations, mines, mills, and armies of the more developed sectors. There, the young discover an economic base of power to which they have privileged access, resources not under the control of their fathers. They no longer have to ask him for the bride price that will accelerate their change from boys into men. The confirmatory power now comes from outside the community, rather than from within it. Thus, Rowe (1961) finds that Indian village gerontocracy has eroded as a direct result of changing employment. The young men find wage work in the cities and return home impatient with tradition, with the rule of the father, and with the slow-paced village life. And the wealth that they bring back undercuts the traditional association between affluence and advanced age, further corroding the status of the aged.

Press and McKool (1972) find that when they shift from agricultural to wage work, young village Maya can buy their own land long before their father is ready to surrender the family holdings in their favor. In his dotage, the father now comes to live in the son's house, rather than granting the son's family a place in the patriarchal compound. The once mighty leading men of the Maya, the *principals,* are degraded, and aging fathers who hold on to their land, refusing to recognize this shift in power, are sometimes murdered by their own sons. West and south of the Yucatan, among the Zapotec Indians, Adams (1972) found that the elder man's importance declines in step with the weakening of the *cargo* system, the age-graded regulator of responsibilities for church and ritual.

A number of African studies bear out these Mexican reports. Thus, Cattell (1989) notes that, in Western Kenya, elder knowledge is exclusively *local* in its scope. Modernization brings about the *delocalization* of knowledge, and the aged lose their special edge, their reputation for wisdom. For similar reasons, social change toward modernity induces doubt of their elders among young men of the Ethiopian Sidamo (Hamer, 1972). Fuller (1972) tells us that nowadays young Bantu find brides and "become men" without economic assistance from their fathers, or even in defiance of them. Consequently, his sons feel little obligation toward their father in his needful old age.

B. Deculturation and the Druze

Such observations, in settings as diverse as village India and rural Mexico, are confirmed by my own among the Druze sect of the Golan Heights. There, I learned that the various consequences of modernization are synergistic, mutually supporting. While carrying out a longitudinal study of aging psychology among the Golan Druze, I noted the ways in which economic, cognitive, and ritual changes bear on the fortunes of the elders in a traditional, classically gerontocratic village.

Clearly, in the Druze community, the generational transfer of sacred power does at least begin in the pocketbook. During these years of Israeli hegemony, the young Golan Druze, who used to work their fathers' land while waiting to inherit, now find wage work in the *kibbutzim* and industries across the Jordan, in the Jewish sector. Again, they become less dependent for resource on their fathers' whim or generosity, and their exposure to modern people who do not respect or fear their fathers gives them further reason to doubt their hitherto-unquestioned power. Furthermore, affluence and modernization mean machinery. In Majd-Al-Shams, the donkey has largely been replaced by the tractor, and while the old men might understand donkeys, it is the young men, with their trade school and Syrian Army experience, who understand tractors. They can command the exotic power of the machine and make it available for the general purposes of the Druze. They play the interceding role in regard to machine power, that of harnessing it for their under-powered community, that their fathers play in regard to the powers of Allah. As a consequence, there is notably less deference toward the aged on the part of the Golan young, who begin to resemble the young men of the less-traditional (Israeli or Galilean Druze) sectors of the extended Druze society. A generation gap has opened, such that their manner toward older traditional relatives begins to be pa-tronizing, and even insulting.

It is evident then, that as the traditional young discover an economic base out-side of their village and family, they acquire more than bank accounts: they begin to inherit the *mana* that was once exclusive to their fathers and grandfathers. As the society opens up to alien influences, new images, and new myths, based on the power of aliens and of contemporary heroes who stole alien power (and got away with it), fill the cultural space. The young can interpret and fit into these myths, for they have been to the place of the aliens; they have endured strange power, and they have—like Prometheus—captured some small part of it in the form of wages, technical knowledge, and even weapons. The young begin to take on some of the glamour of those who have danced before the gods and have survived the awesome contact with strange power.

Inevitably, as the young take on the bridgehead functions *vis-à-vis* alien power that the aged once performed, the prestige of the young is elevated, and the prestige of the traditional aged declines. Tectonic changes of this sort can take place in the cultural structure long before there is any evident change in its *official* values: The disrespectful modernized young of the Golan are still very aware of the Druze norm of cowed respect for the old. The cultural contents still persist, and are given fine lip service, but the *density* and *interiority* of the venerated ideas and objects are reduced, as is their power over behavior and the mental life. Now there is crime, neighbor against neighbor, in the Golan villages.

C. Deculturation and the High Culture

As we have seen, modernization, whether it takes place in the village or in the city, undercuts the elders' monopoly on *tabu* power by creating alternate power bases, rooted in the new economies and the miraculous products of technology to which the young have privileged access. The contra-gerontic influences of the city act to degrade the sources of *tabu* power by attacking the symbolic bases—the spe-cific icons and totems—on which gerontocracy is based. Furthermore, while mod-ernization and urbanization can proceed independently, in the growing city these tendencies are most likely to potentiate, to amplify each other's deculturating effects. In the city, the traditional culture is not only weakened by the fallout from contrasting values and lifeways; it is also actively opposed by the society of critical elites that forms naturally on the nutriments provided by the liberal metropolis.

The high culture of creative literature, experimental theater, academic criticism, and free inquiry, etc., gains its particular morale and vitality precisely by attacking—even symbolically murdering—the traditional, myth-centered culture. Thus, the high culture makes its agenda and its living out of questioning certainties, of exploding hallowed myths, of ridiculing conformity, and exposing the frailties, physical and moral, of commonly revered figures: George Washington had wooden teeth; Thomas Jefferson kept slaves; Abe Lincoln was a manic-depressive, etc. The activists of high culture kill off the traditional culture for the same reasons that young men attack gerontocracy: in order to remove the dead hand of the past, the established precedents that block curiosity, creativity, and the experimentation with new, undreamed-of pleasures. Unfortunately though, while the high culture makes the urban scene more vivid and amusing, it has no capacity whatever to generate the values that justify sacrifice, or that underwrite social security, domestic security, and sturdy children.

D. The Aging Strangers

Furthermore, in U.S. urban settings, we threaten the integrity of the founding culture in particularly American ways. Thus, the American impulse toward equality, which first struggles against the restrictions on ordinary civil rights, ends by politicizing the chronic complaint against existential restrictions. Individual Americans were long ago granted the right to choose their own leaders, careers, and political parties; but in recent times the principle of equality attacks a core cultural assumption, of commonly held, unquestioned values. Until recently, these were regarded as objective: fixed social realities to be internalized by the individual, but to be created and maintained apart from that same individual, by idealized cultural institutions and their leaders. But in recent times, the high culture has succeeded in democratizing the process of value formation to the point where it has been taken out of the institutional province and given over to the private individual. Moving thus, from the social to the personal sphere, values lose their shared and objective character, to become idiosyncratic and subjective. In effect, we have democratized and relativized the process of value formation to the point where each citizen is conceded the right to decide personally the standards against which he should be measured.

Thus, in the city the common culture is weakened by a dual assault: from the high culture; and, paradoxically, from the operation of a principle—equality—that is fundamental to our common culture. But whatever the causes of the decay, a depleted common culture loses the power to convert strangers into familiars, and narcissistic potentials into enduring social bonds. The consequent deculturation soon leads to social crisis.

The attack by the high culture on sacrosanct myths is particularly damaging to the elders. So long as the founding legends go unchallenged, their special tie to the mystery gives elders the charisma of the awesome rather than the repulsive stranger; and the culture's all-including *we* overrides the alienating effects of age, cohort, and cosmetic differences between the young and the old. Again, the encultured know themselves and their fellows through their association with transcending, idealized collectivities. But, much like the processes of aging, deculturation undercuts the institutions that direct the transformations of narcissism, from its raw asocial to its sculpted, prosocial state. Under the conditions of deculturation, narcissistic preference dictates the lines of affiliation. Decultured persons only extend the tonus of familiarity and *we*-ness to those who resemble them in the most concrete, immediately sensible respects: those who share the same skin color, the same body conformation, the same genitalia, the same sexual appetites, and the same age group. With deculturation, the principles of association are no longer based on shared standards but become instead the politics of narcissism: racist, sexist, homoerotic, and ageist. When the deculturating society fragments along the natural cleavage lines of race, gender, dominant erotic appetite, and generation, then the *stranger* potential of the aged is underscored rather than overridden. A strong culture underwrites the strong face of aging; but deculturation brings forth its weak face. The decultured society is automatically gerophobic.

Under conditions of deculturation, the gender and age distinctions that divide the larger society penetrate to the heart of the modern family. To the degree that family solidarity still persists across the generations in urban societies, it is mainly between the grandmothers, daughters, and granddaughters of the female line, more and more excluding of men. And by the same token, the mistrust between generations that is often a feature of the general social life under deculturation has also invaded the domestic life. The family, whether nuclear or extended, is usually the one enclave in which generational distinctions are overlooked, in favor of some higher principle of kinship solidarity. But the generation gap that is strikingly absent in the traditional village family bisects the heart of the nuclear and modified extended family in the city. The urban aged begin to know alienation even within their own primary groups.

E. Some Geropsychological Consequences

The fate of elders and children is everywhere linked, such that the condition of one group, whether good or bad, predicts directly the condition of the other. Encultured societies extend protection, automatically, to preproductive children, and to postproductive elders. But as the society decultures, as it loses idealized icons, the individual self becomes its own venerated object, and narcissism—as we have seen—becomes increasingly the coinage of social relationships. Under these conditions the pre- and postproductive cohorts are at risk, on the grounds that children and elders both require inordinate amounts of unreciprocated care. Thus, while child abuse is a major topic of contemporary congresses on family dynamics, papers on elder abuse now dominate the proceedings of the Gerontological Society.

I have argued that the encultured society provides a developmental milieu, one in which the nascent potentials of later life are encouraged, to become the special capacities of the traditional elder. Thus, deculturation not only deprives the aged of facilitating social circumstances; it also depletes their mental life. As a consequence, important developmental transitions of later life—particularly, the transformations of narcissism into idealization—are less likely to come about. These derailments are likely to leave decultured elders vulnerable not only to the narcissism of the young, but to their own, as well. Aged Druze, who have converted narcissism into worship of Allah, can look with equanimity on the prospect of their death, saying to me only, "This is Allah's will; to complain about my sickness or death would be to dispute his will." These aged Druze, because they feel identified with their changeless god, are able to accommodate—without much sense of shock or insult—catastrophic change, including the final transition into death.

However, the changes affecting the density and interiority of culture that arrive with modernity seem to release a more narcissistic, greedy nature, even in ostensibly traditional elders. This effect was revealed through a study on the oral dimension of aging personality (Gutmann, 1971) carried out among traditional Navajo and Druze. Having found strong correlations between passive-dependency and the degree of specifically oral concerns in Druze and Navajo subjects, I went on to examine the effects of age, culture, and modernity, as these affected the orality variable. Two statistically significant main effects were found. Orality increased with age, and with urban-proximal residence, regardless of age. Thus, as predicted, narcissistic self-concerns—as measured by the orality (or "feed me!") variable—go up with age. But while oral narcissism is not affected by differences in the value consensus between two very different cultures, it is strongly affected by the structural aspects of culture, as these weaken along the folk-urban axis of two traditional societies.

To repeat, the value content of Druze and Navajo culture does not change significantly in the transition from isolate-traditional to near-urban settings; the real change is in the structural features of culture, and these do affect the expression—if not the intensity—of individual oral appetites. The personality differences between the rural isolate and urban-proximal traditionals are not trivial: the traditional elders bring their neediness to God; but the high-orality, urbanized Navajo express their neediness and dependency through alcoholism, psychosomatic illness, and even criminality.

F. Deculturation and Geriatric Psychopathology

The decultured elder is at risk: his late-life narcissism peaks at about the time when he is most prone to suffer narcissistic wounds, in the form of physical, cognitive, cosmetic, social, and existential losses. Given the intense focus on self, the normal losses and changes of aging become insults, outrages, and terrors. Depression and hypochondriasis, as well as delusional attempts to deny depletion and imperfection, can be the too-frequent result. In our clinical studies of late-onset disorders at Northwestern University Medical School (see Gutmann, 1988), we note that many emotional disorders of later life represent frantic attempts to overcome the sense of insult and depression on the part of older individuals who have not relinquished their personal myth of centrality and perfection. In them, psychiatric breakdown occurs when the need to deny loss and insult, or to project onto others the responsibility for imperfection, is so strong that reality is abandoned in favor of the defense. Thus, *denial* of loss and threat, sometimes taking the form of manic psychosis, is one major defense of the older patient. A paranoid state, in which the sense of blemish or the responsibility for the blemish, is projected onto others, is an alternate but equally strong possibility. Severe depression and even lethal illness can result when these primitive defenses fail. In a real sense, later-life psychosis represents a hectic attempt to supply, for the self, the bonuses of self-esteem that are routinely donated to elders by an encultured society.

In sum, deculturation and the weakening of the extended family have major effects that particularly disadvantage older individuals. Wrenched away from culture, they lose their special developmental milieux, they lose their special bases for self-esteem, and they are transformed from *elders* into *the aging*. Losing their traditional character as hero, they take on their modern character, as victim. The weak face of aging appears; and this debility can be expressed in the form of individual psychopathology.

A *caveat* is in order: lacking reliable comparative mental health data from traditional societies, we cannot confidently assert that geriatric psychopathology increases under conditions of modernity, secularization, or deculturation. It may be, though it is not likely, that the rates of elderly depression and psychosis in more folk-like societies match those of the "first" world. But if this were the case, then ethnographers who study the condition of traditional elders in naturalistic ways would report at least anecdotal evidence of such trouble. Usually living among their subjects, not buffered from them by standard instruments and methods, these qualitative investigators develop the heightened sensitivities, the early warning systems, that would pick up the signs of emotional distress among their elderly informants. But, as we have seen, these dedicated ethnogerontologists are much more apt to report the high status, the powers, and the seeming contentment of traditional elders. Save for the Highland Maya of Chiapas, whose elders had high status and were hated for it, I came back from the field with similar impressions and with interview data to back them up. Accordingly, until we get trustworthy reports to the contrary, I will stick with this possibly shaky assumption: Modernity and urbanism, if they lead to deculturation, are not good for elderly mental health. In addition, I have tried to show that the pathogenic causes lie not in changing cultural content, or *cohort influences,* but in a much more ominous development: the degradation of culture, the loss of the social immune system itself.

Organized gerontology avoids this grim truth. For one thing, our sterile methods, driven by the need for invulnerability rather than enlightenment, are themselves a symptom of deculturation. Additionally, while dimly recognizing the trouble, we try to confine it to the aged: *They* will suffer the consequences of deculturation; it is our job as gerontologists to study them while it happens. But just as the study of aging does not stop gerontologists from getting old, the study of elder abuse will not protect us from the general decay of decency in our society. It is a common tragedy; and by not acknowledging it we accelerate the process of social entropy.

But we should remember that our elders, though they have lost their traditional link to culture in its external institutional form, still preserve culture in its internalized form: during a time of rapid deculturation, the American elders are still the most encultured minority among us. Contrary to the impression propagated by mass media and congresses of gerontology, the great majority of our elderly—even when enfeebled—are *not* candidates for long-term care. Quite the contrary: as inheritors of the now deconstructed American culture that suckled their characters, they still live by the *ethos* of rugged independence and self-sufficiency. They avoid long-term care up to the last moment of possibility. Our elders do have their psychic vulnerabilities and pathologies, and some of these are based on their unrelinquished pride; but they are still the wardens of what was once our common culture. Instead of devoting the bulk of our energy and concern to the elderly candidates for long-term care, we should think about the proper therapy for the silent majority, of stubbornly autonomous, still encultured elders. Perhaps the best therapy for these counterdependent cohorts is to let *them* help us. Perhaps they can counsel us concerning the maintenance of culture, and the proper steps towards its restoration.

References

Adams, F. (1972). The role of old people in Santo Tomas Mazaltepec. In D. Cowgill & L. Holmes. (Eds.), *Aging and modernization* (pp. 103–126). New York: Appleton-Century-Crofts.

Amoss, P. T., & Harrell, S. (Eds.). (1981). Introduction. In *Other ways of growing old: Anthropological perspectives* (pp. 1–24). Stanford: Stanford University Press.

Atchley, R. C. (1989). A continuity theory of normal aging. *The Gerontologist, 29,* 183–190.

Biesele, M., & Howell, N. (1981). "The old people give you life": Aging among !Kung hunter-gatherers. In P. T. Amoss & S. Harrell (Eds.), *Other ways of growing old: Anthropological perspectives.* Stanford: Stanford University Press.

Cattell, M. (1989). Knowledge and social change in Samia, Western Kenya. *Journal of Cross-Cultural Gerontology, 4,* 225–244.

Cohler, B. J., & Lieberman, M. A. (1979). Personality change across the second half of life: Findings from a study of Irish, Italian, and Polish-American men and women. In D. E. Gelfand & A. J. Kutzik (Eds.), *Ethnicity and aging* (pp. 227–245). New York: Springer.

Cowgill, D. (1968). The social life of the aging in Thailand. *The Gerontologist, 8,* 159–163.

Cowgill, D., & Holmes, L. (Eds.). (1972). *Aging and modernization.* New York: Appleton-Century-Crofts.

Cummings, E., & Henry, W. (1961). *Growing old: The process of disengagement.* New York: Basic Books.

de Beauvoir, S. (1972). *The coming of age.* New York: Putnam.

Erikson, E. (1959). Identity and the life cycle. *Psychological Issues.* 1, (Monograph 1). New York: International University Press.

Erikson, E. (1963). *Childhood and society* (2nd ed.). New York: Norton.

Fowler, L. (1990). Colonial context and age group relations among plains Indians. *Journal of Cross-Cultural Gerontology, 5,* 149–168.

Freud, S. (1922). *Group psychology and the analysis of the ego* (No. 6). London: International Psychoanalytic Library.

Fry, C. (1985). Culture, behavior and aging in the comparative perspective. In J. Birren & K. Schaie (Eds.), *Handbook of the psychology of aging* (2nd ed., pp. 216–244). New York: Van Nostrand Reinhold.

Fuller, C. (1972). Aging among the Southern African Bantu. In D. Cowgill & L. Holmes (Eds.), *Aging and modernization* (pp. 51–72). New York: Appleton-Century-Crofts.

Gutmann, D. (1968). Aging among the Highland Maya: A comparative study. *Journal of Personality and Social Psychology, 7,* 28–35.

Gutmann, D. (1971). Navajo dependency and illness. In E. Palmore (Ed.), *Prediction of life span* (pp. 181–198). Lexington, MA: D. C. Heath.

Gutmann, D. (1980). Observations on culture and mental health in later life. In J. Birren & R. Bruce Sloan (Eds.), *Handbook of Mental Health and Aging* (pp. 429–447). Englewood Cliffs, NJ: Prentice-Hall.

Gutmann, D. (1987). *Reclaimed powers: Toward a new psychology of men and women in later life.* New York: Basic Books.

Gutmann, D. (1988). Late-onset pathogenesis: Dynamic models. *Topics in Geriatric Rehabilitation, 3,* 1–8.

Hamer, J. (1972). Aging in a gerontocratic society: The Sidarno of Southwest Ethiopia. In D. Cowgill & L. Holmes (Eds.), *Aging and modernization* (pp. 15–30). New York: Appleton-Century-Crofts.

Holmes, L. (1972). The role and status of the aged in a changing Samoa. In D. Cowgill & L. Holmes (Eds.), *Aging and modernization* (pp. 73–90). New York: Appleton-Century-Crofts.

Kalab, M. (1990). Buddhism and emotional support for elderly people. *Journal of Cross-Cultural Gerontology, 5,* 7–19.

Kernberg, O. (1975). *Borderline conditions and pathological narcissism.* New York: Jason Aronson.

Kohut, H. (1978). *The restoration of the self.* New York: International University Press.

LeVine, R. (1978a). Adulthood and aging in cross-cultural perspective. *Items, 31/32,* 1–5.

LeVine, R. (1978b). Comparative notes on the life course. In T. K. Hareven (Ed.), *Transitions: The family and the life course in historical perspective* (pp. 282–297). New York: Academic Press.

Levi-Strauss, C. (1983). *The raw and the cooked.* Chicago: University of Chicago Press.

Levy-Bruhl, L. (1928). *The "soul" of the primitive.* London: Allen and Unwin.

Opler, M. E. (1959). *Culture and mental health: Cross-cultural studies.* New York: Macmillan.

Press, I., & McKool, M. (1972). Social structure and status of the aged: Toward some valid cross-cultural generalizations. *Aging and Human Development, 3,* 297–308.

Redfield, R. (1947). The folk society. *American Journal of Sociology, 2,* 293–308.

Rowe, W. (1961). The middle and later years in Indian society. In R. Kleemeier (Ed.), *Aging and leisure* (pp. 104–112). New York: Oxford University Press.

Shanan, J. (1985). Personality types and culture in late adulthood. In J. Meacham (Ed.), *Contributions to human development* (Vol. 12, pp. 1–144). Basel: S. Karger.

Sheehan, T. (1976). Senior esteem as a factor of socio-economic complexity. *Gerontologist, 16,* 433–440.

Shelton, A. (1965). Ibo aging and eldership: Notes for gerontologists and others. *Gerontologist, 5,* 20–23.

Shelton, A. (1972) The aged and eldership among the Igbo. In D. Cowgill & L. Holmes (Eds.), *Aging and modernization* (pp. 31–50). New York: Appleton-Century-Crofts.

Simmons, L. (1945). *The role of the aged in primitive society.* New Haven: Yale University Press.

Syryani, L., Kamar, T., Andjana, A., Thong, D., Manik, I., Putra, D., Widjaja, W., Tama, D., & Jensen, G. (1988). The physical and mental health of elderly in a Balinese village. *Journal of Cross-Cultural Gerontology*, 3, 105–120.

11 The Human Father and the Masculine Life Cycle

This paper continues the argument of the previous paper on "Culture and Mental Health."
In that paper I dealt with the older man's relation to culture: He sustains it; he is sustained
by it. In addition, that powerful connection between culture and the elder contributes, I con-
tend, to the vitality of families and the general health of the social order. Deculturation puts
the elders at social and psychological risk and leads eventually to the degeneration of the so-
cial order.

Written when I was older, the paper that follows is more chauvinistic but also more precise
concerning the role of elders in preparing men for fatherhood. I stress the vital role played by
fathers—themselves backed up by the elders—in helping sons separate from mothers, and—
as a consequence of that crucial separation—eventually join themselves to wives.

Again, time has passed, and so I can with greater specificity spell out, in this paper, the so-
cial and individual disorders that follow when young men defect from fatherhood and old
men defect from culture-tending.

This book is not only about aging but also about the species narrative, the human life-
cycle. Again, I am forced to admit that I am not exempt from that narrative. As a younger
writer, male envy drove my pen: I fulminated against the countercultural indulgences of my
male colleagues and younger brothers—the hippies and their faculty sponsors. As an older
writer, powerful women become my targets: This paper was meant to refute the contrapatriar-
chal rhetoric of the gender feminists. Young men fight other men; old men protect themselves
against ascendant women. I am reaching the point where I can only advance my theory by be-
coming its poster person.

Three Approaches to Understanding Fatherhood

The great anthropologist Ralph Linton once remarked (Kardiner and Linton, 1945), "In some ways, each man is like all other men; in some ways, each man is like some other men; and in some ways, each man is like no other man." (Nowadays, Linton's language has a sexist ring, but that's how the man said it.) Linton was referring to the major orders of human experience. His first level—each man like all men—refers to our common, universal ways of underwriting individual and species survival. Linton's second level—each man like some others—refers to the fact that we share common language, common culture, and common ways of achieving language and culture with a few socially selected members of our species. This level refers also to the ways in which we act so as to preserve society, and to maintain ourselves as social beings in the eyes of our fellows. Linton's Level Three—each man like no others—refers to the ways in which we experience ourselves and maintain ourselves as unique and special, different even from those with whom we share a common culture.

To be fully appreciated, the father's crucial functions must be studied *via* the methods and instruments that are fitted to the universals, to Level One. However, Level One perspectives are currently out of fashion: They remind us of forces that operate outside of conscious control, even as they influence the direction and content of conscious thinking. The tectonic forces that drive Level One experience tell us that—as Bruno Bettelheim once observed—"We are not the masters even in our own mental house." To consider Level One phenomena is to receive a narcissistic wound; and so in our narcissistic age these levels of experience are avoided, and left out of our p.c. behavioral science. Instead, the father's role is critiqued from the discipline and methods of Level Two, which is sociology, or from the ideology (or theology) of Level Three, which is humanistic psychology. According to the sociologists of the family, fathers who insist on playing a special, authoritative role, distinct from mothers, are not serving their children, they are oppressing their women. And humanistic psychologists also deplore the authoritative father: He is, they fear, expressing masculine needs to be dominant and "phallocentric" at the expense of his wife's individuality and "self actualization."

Thus, on the best campuses (and especially the best) biological paternity—the special role of the father in procreation—has been split off in theory from the social condition of fatherhood. Biological paternity is admittedly a fact of nature; but fatherhood, as a special condition with its own scope, powers, and responsibilities, is regarded by mainstream social scientists as a corruption of nature.

And now we find that too many men, happy to be let off the hook, have heard the liberating message from academia: They are helping to conceive more babies and more candidates for abortion than ever before, but they are too often refusing to be trustworthy, strong, and responsible fathers. According to the new dispensation, this liberation of men from bondage to the patriarchal ideal should lead to the liberation of women. It has not: For as men defect from traditional versions of fatherhood, they also defect from the traditional arrangements of marriage—and from marriage as well. As a consequence, too many women are left alone with the kids in single-parent families. Women are more oppressed than ever: The Patriarch has gone, but so are the special rations of security and companionship that he provided. Clearly then, the sociological and humanistic revisions of fatherhood are not working. Instead, it seems that the traditional phrasings of fatherhood were more than expressions of oppressive male politics; it appears that they too were an expression, an extension rather than a refutation of the kinds of natural law that also governed biological paternity.

Clearly, if we are going to develop some real answers, beyond political correctitude, to the important questions raised at this conference—what is the father's special contribution to parenting; and what do men get out of being fathers?—we will have to forage through the data of Level One, the language of human universals.

Fatherhood: Closeness Through Distance

Species survival—the major issue of the first level—is underwritten by the kinds of adequate parenting that raises children to be good parents in their turn, down the generations. Erik Erikson once remarked that the long dependency of the human child is the crucial agenda in human development at all ages. The unique features of human parenthood, including the distinctive features of paternal and maternal roles, are also shaped by that same great fact—the unique vulnerability of our children. A guiding idea of this paper is that the forms of paternity and maternity are not expressions of power politics between the sexes, but are evolved adaptations to the special requirements of the weak and needy human child. Appropriately then, before we address the matter of fatherhood, we should first address its context: the special needs, universal across our species, of our at-risk offspring.

Consequently, while societies have different child rearing goals, they nevertheless maintain common understandings about the basic needs that must be addressed by any acceptable child-care regime. Thus, if it is to thrive by any reasonable criteria, the vulnerable child must be assured of two kinds of parental nurturance: It must be given some assurance of physical security, and of emotional security.

There is also a general recognition, across our species, that the same parent cannot provide both kinds of security. The child's physical security ultimately depends on activities carried out far from home: Warfare, hunting (including the hunt for business and clients), and the cultivation of distant tillage. Men are generally assigned the task of providing physical security on the perimeter, not because they are more privileged, but because they are expendable. Thus, in the hard calculus of species survival, there is typically an oversupply of males, in that one man can inseminate many females, but women, on the average, can gestate only one child every two years during their relatively brief period of fertility. The surplus males, those over the number required to maintain viable population levels, can be assigned to the dangerous, high casualty "perimeter" tasks on which physical security and survival are based. "When it comes to slaughter, you do not send your daughter" is one of our most predictable human rules; and there are very good reasons for it. By the same token, the sex on whom the population level ultimately depends is less expendable; thus, women are generally assigned to secure areas, there to supply the formative experiences that give rise to emotional security in children.

This special role of the father, to be close from a distance, reveals itself early after the infant's birth. Thus, basing her argument on cross-cultural research, Niles Newton (1973) asserts that mothers are central in the experience of the infant—whether a boy or a girl—and that fathers play an auxiliary, supportive post-natal function. Newton argues that coitus, birth, and lactation—the three major expressions of female sexuality—are also strikingly vulnerable, prone to shut down in the face of outer threat. In order to reach their reproductive goal, these maternal activities all require external buffering and protection, most often provided by men. Newton cites ethnographic descriptions of young mothers in South Africa, the Middle East, and China, all pointing to a standard pattern of maternal engrossment with the infant, in an intense bond that can persist through the first years of the child's life. At all these sites, the infant sleeps next to the mother, is nursed at the first sign of restlessness, and nursing takes precedence over any potentially competing activity.

The mother can devote herself almost exclusively to nurturing the child because she herself is being nurtured, "mothered," by her husband. The father's task is to maintain a protected zone, one in which his gratified and secure spouse can bring about the mother-child enmeshment that is so necessary to the infant's early emotional development. The father may not be on the physical periphery of his community, but he is, at this point, on the emotional periphery of his family, relatively excluded from the intense mother-infant link. At this juncture, the father connects to the mother-infant dyad through intermediaries: He tends to identify, vicariously, with the mothering that his child receives from his wife—and with the "mothering" that his wife receives from him.

Achieving Distance Via the Father

At the outset of life, this mother-child merger—a continuation in psychological terms of the intrauterine umbilical link—is necessary for the infant's future development, away from the mother. Assured of a stable home base, the infant can begin to explore his world and to provoke change in it. Thus, human development proceeds by paradox, in a dialectical fashion: The almost exclusive mother-child bonding that is so crucial in the first year of life prepares for the period of early autonomy, during which the child practices psychological and physical separation from the mother. During this pivotal exploratory period, the linear arrangement of the family—father tends the mother, mother tends kids—begins to break down and the father, because he is different from the mother, and because—in his own way—he also nurtures, becomes a psychological "object," a presence in the emotional life of the child. The linear arrangement gives way to the family triangle: Daughters fall in love with their daddies and sons—even while they revere him—take the father as a kind of rival for the mother's affection. In either case, in step with the child's development, the father's role in the family has taken on a new and special meaning: As an alternate, less proximal figure of strength and provision, he is a magnet, a way-station on the child's road outward to the world, and away from an unboundaried union with the mother. The father is still primarily responsible for providing physical security, but at this point—even under conditions of affluence and assured supplies—he can become a vital agent in the child's emotional life. If the father can maintain a distinctive presence, then at this time of early mother-child separation, he will support the maturation of daughters as well as sons.

On the whole, sons have the more pressing need to separate psychologically from the mother. Daughters are much more likely than sons to follow—at least for some significant period—the mother's domestic destiny; the daughter can continue as the mother's daughter without significantly prejudicing her future adult role, as a mother in her own right. But sons are pointed towards a different fate, towards a life on some version of the perimeter, beyond the edge of the mother's domestic world. From here on, we will track their journeys.

Unlike daughters, boys start out as creatures of the domestic world, as sons of their mothers; but early on, they must diminish their ties to her and prepare for the extra-domestic paternal role, in large part among men. At some point, the son has to redefine himself, from being the son of his mother to being the son of his father. This crucial redefinition can only come about if the father is strong in his own right, and different from the mother.

Sons of physically or psychologically absent fathers do separate from the mother in the social sense: They find wives; but because they have not separated in the psychological sense, they bring the maternal transference with them into the marriage, and turn their spouse into another "mom." This special arrangement can work, but only as long as the supply of maternal surrogates lasts. These mother's sons are put at risk in the post-parental years, at the time when their older wives—having raised their kids, having paid their species dues—begin to defect from the mothering way. They still share the husband's bed, they still get the meals out; but their feelings towards their husbands have changed—they are still willing to be the wife, but not the husband's mother. The older wife has imposed, on the husband, a separation from the maternal figure that he himself has never encountered, expected, or initiated. This belated separation from "mom" can precipitate the much-debated "mid-life crisis" in vulnerable men: In order to hold the wife's attention, in order to keep her in a nurturing mode, predisposed men can develop significant somatic symptoms. Their symptoms also bring them to the attention of clinic personnel, internists, and nurses; and nurses (female ones) can be, for such men, the final mother figures of the life cycle.

In short, failures of early separation can—under ideal circumstances—be compensated for a long time; but they eventually declare themselves, sometimes so late in life that the original deficit can no longer be traced to its origins.

But in the normal course of development, the son who has closed out the necessary rivalry with his father, and conceded that he is the Boss, does conserve love and respect for him. He can go on to learn from his father, and from other authoritative figures: uncles, older brothers, teachers, coaches. This is the so-called "latency period"—the time when the child, no longer distracted by powerful appetites or fears, can devote himself to the rapid acquisition of new learning, new skills. The school becomes a world in its own right, alternate to the family.

The Fathers and the Rites of Passage

However, this is the calm before the storm. The onset of puberty shakes up the psychological status quo: the personality is subject to tectonic shocks as the body moves toward sexual maturity and adult physical powers. There is no mind-body dichotomy in human psychology, and the expanding, surgent body sends shock waves through the whole psychological system. Boys are suddenly thrust into adult bodies, even as their emotional life regresses to a primitive form. The Oedipal struggle with the father may be revived, but now in a more dangerous form: The pubertal boy's challenge to the father is now more than the grandiose delusion of a physical and mental midget; now it is backed up by a body that can be more powerful than the father's.

In effect, the growing boy's commitment to an extra-domestic destiny on the perimeter is put at risk by the tectonic shocks of puberty: He is prone to fight the father, to reject the father's way, to turn again toward the mother, and her way.

This pubertal transition is universal; and most viable cultures have developed fairly predictable ways to ensure that the biological transition to puberty does not lead to social crisis, in the face of aggravated adolescent rebellion. Particularly in traditional societies, the whole age-grade of male elders is mobilized to back up the father's threatened authority, to help the boy complete the separation from the mother, and to turn him back towards the perimeter, and towards the ways of men.

The biological father helps the son achieve the first vital separation, from the mother; the collective fathers are required to bring about the second great separation: From the family as a whole, and even from the physical precincts of the home community. Now, the pubertal son deals not only with his own father, but with his father's colleagues, the elders and fathers of his community—and ultimately, through them, with the ancestral fathers of his people. The collective fathers arrange an ordeal, a *rite de passage*, through which the pubertal son is consecrated to these various forms of paternity. The *rite de passage* takes as many forms as there are distinct cultures; it can range from penile subincision with cowry shells as practiced by Papuan natives, to the Bar Mitzvah ceremonial of orthodox Jews. But in all cases, the young candidates are exposed to a trial, usually under the attentive, critical gaze of the assembled fathers, who watch for signs of weakness. Whiting and Child (1953) found that the severity of the ordeal varied, across cultures, with the length of the breast-feeding period. The ritual is a passage away from the mother: Since late weaning implies a strong maternal bond, a stringent ordeal is required to break it. By the same token, if the boy is too visibly frightened or tearful, then he has not passed the test. He has cried for his mother, he still belongs to her world, and he has not been reborn—as a father's son and junior colleague— into the company of men. But if the lad endures with some grace and fortitude, then he has begun to make it as a man: he is one of the "twice born," reborn as a son of the collective fathers, and as an age-grade brother of the initiates who have endured with him. Success in the passage ritual demonstrates that the young man has the fortitude necessary for assignments beyond the boundaries of the community. But besides testing his fitness, the *rite de passage* provides the initiate with "brothers": The age class of young men who are bonded to him through the ritual, and who represent the piece of the community that will go with him on his journeys beyond its borders.

But even more important, the ritual begins the attachment to some totemic sponsor, whose supernatural powers—his "medicine" or his mana—will also provide the initiate with luck and protection on the road. In other words, the *rite de passage* extends the idea of paternity, beyond the biological father, into the collectivity of community elders, and beyond them to the ultimate fathers: the spiritualized ancestors, and the mythic fathers of the people and their world.

Typically, a culture is founded on an origin myth: A story of how the people, at some time of trial and supreme danger were sponsored, rescued, and rendered special by the intervention of unordinary—usually supernatural—beings. The typical puberty ritual recapitulates this drama: Like his people in the origin myth, the candidate is in a liminal condition, a state of emergency, and if he survives the ordeal, it is because he too—like his people in the founding myth—has found favor with a totemic sponsor. As a young child, he became for a time the son of his father; now, as a youth, he becomes—*via* the ritual—the protégé of some favoring deity. The earlier, post-Oedipal alliance with the biological father endowed the son with some sense of inner resource, allowing him to separate from the mother. This later affiliation, with the spiritual fathers, gives the son the courage that he needs to separate, physically, from the community as a whole—from the mothers again, and from the biological fathers as well. More importantly, it refreshes his sense of inner resource—the conviction of having captured some of the totemic "father's" substance—that will help him to become, with confidence, a father in his own right.

Knowing that he can leave the home and the community, knowing that he can live off his own psychic substance, the son can look towards mating, marriage, and fatherhood for himself. Like his father before him, he can court a woman, he can attempt the frightening but exciting voyage into her body, and—secure in his manhood—he can return to the domestic world, the world of the mothers, not as a needy child, but as a mate, and as a providing father.

Erik Erikson once remarked that deprivation *per se* is not psychologically destructive; it is only deprivation without meaning, without redeeming significance, that is psychologically destructive. Human cultures, whatever particular forms they might take, have a great and universal function: to provide the routine sacrifices of human parenthood with high significance and dignity. Without culture—as we can see all around us—children are at risk, and too often from their own resentful parents. But when the young man has been linked—through his father and through the rituals managed by the elders—to some part of the myth on which his culture is founded, then he too can become an adequate father. Rather than seeming to intrude on his freedom, the state of fatherhood will grant him a special dignity, an identity, precisely because of the sacrifices that this condition demands.

The World Without Fathers

I have briefly outlined the developmental stages and the universal practices whereby fathers turn sons into fathers. But what happens when—as in our American case—this transmission belt of the father's substance into the sons breaks down?

There appear to be three major consequences; and, some minor qualifications aside, none of them are good: Poorly fathered sons are less likely to separate from their mothers; young men become so vulnerable to women that they end by avoiding them; and young men inseminate women but avoid fatherhood. Thus, in everincreasing numbers, young men stay home with their mothers, but they do not—

by becoming fathers in their own right—help daughters to become mothers in their turn.

The deconstruction of fatherhood in our own society can lead to abortive, often destructive attempts to achieve separation from the mother, and to gain, without fathers, the sense of inner resource usually provided by adequate parental figures. Thus, when sons cannot achieve psychological distance from the mother, they will either cling to her and her surrogates, or they will amplify, anxiously, their physical and social distance from her. They may become vagrants, and swell the ranks of the homeless; through delinquency, they may shock and provoke the mother to the point where she drives them out of the home; or they might find impersonal replacements for the mothers, in the form of addicting substances.

Thus, booze and drugs can provide, at least temporarily, the sense of inner resource that makes it possible for sons to separate from the mother. When there is no strong father to aid the son in this developmental task, then he will too often turn to the kinds of substances which—temporarily at least—fill him with the sense of strength and goodness. In our addictive society, drugs substitute for fathers to bring about separations from the mother.

Men who have not separated psychologically from their mothers find it hard to enter into intimate relations with women. Intimacy always carries the risk of losing the intimate other, the unique other who cannot be replaced. Better to look for good feelings in impersonal substances—booze, and drugs—that cannot be used up, that can always be replaced. Drinkers call the empty bottle a "dead soldier," but—unlike the mother, unlike the girl friend—the bottle will never really leave or die; the bottle always comes back, gleaming in its unchanging uniform, ready to serve and die again. It is not the bottle or the syringe that finally dies, but the user.

Young men have recently discovered another, more drastic means for achieving social distance from their mothers, while at the same time avoiding fatherhood: The homosexual community. Again, like bottles or vials, homosexual sex tends to be impersonal and its objects tend to be replaceable. In the gay community, as with other forms of addiction, one finds pleasure without risking intimacy and the possibility of loss. At the same time, distance has been gained from the mothers: The homosexual world is a world of men that excludes—even mocks and caricatures—the "breeders," the dangerous mothers.

Finally, in the absence of reliable fathers and elders, young men try to create their own puberty ritual and administer to each other their own initiations. In the parental society, the tests of manhood are administered by the male elders and are in the service of lawfulness, order, and male productivity. But when the tests are conducted by unsupervised gangs of adolescent males, the passage is not into responsible manhood, but too often into the world of the criminal. Instead of curbing anti-social rebellion, the puberty rites of teen-age gangs too often augment it.

The Ultimate Fathers and the Final Passage

We have seen that the biological father sponsors the separation from the mother, within the family. Later, teachers sponsor some separation from the family, though still within the larger community. And the massed fathers of the community underwrite the physical separations from the whole community—the separations that are essential to the male role on some vital perimeter.

Finally, fatherly beings, spiritual and supernatural in nature, stationed beyond the pragmatic community, are necessary to endorse the final passage of the male life cycle, from vigorous manhood to old age, and finally from life into death. In the traditional community, senior post-parental men can achieve great status, not because of their physical strength and ferocity, but, paradoxically, because of their relative mildness. Typically, they, rather than young men, are the interlocutors between the community and its gods. There exists a generational rule of some universality that compensates the traditional aged for their losses of physical power, by the acquisition of supernatural power.

Simmons (1945) reports many examples of the older man's awesome tabu powers, the most striking coming from the Hottentot of Africa, where the old men initiate young men, who have passed their early life among women, into manhood. The climax of the rite comes when the old man urinates on the candidate, who receives the urine with joy, rubbing it vigorously into his skin. His old sponsor then tells the candidate that he will increase and multiply and that his beard will soon grow. Clearly, in this case, even the urine of the old man has heroic power, the *mana* of the patriarchal phallus through which it passed. In the most concrete sense, it "marinates" the young man with the powers of the old man, thus bringing the lad in his turn to manhood. Here we see, unequivocally, the strong face of aging, the face that is hidden from us in our own secular, contragerontic society.

In sum, whether by virtue of their special weakness or their special strength, the elders are elected. While young men live on the physical perimeter of the community, to contain and harvest the forces of ordinary nature, the old men retreat physically to the interior, domestic zone. Having established a secure home base, they then move out to the spiritual perimeter, there to fend off the bad power and to harvest the good power of the gods. As in most developmental sequences, the seeming withdrawal is the precondition for a later advance—an imaginative leap outward, to the supernaturals.

Thus endowed by the ultimate fathers, older men can, with few regrets, give up the potencies of youth. They can even endure, with some courage, the final separation, from life. As they accomplish these final transitions, senior men become the social "fathers" that young men need, as they face, in their turn, their own life tasks, their own entry into fatherhood.

References

1. Gutmann, D. L. "Good outcomes and pathological consequences of post-parental androgyny." (Unpublished manuscript) Dept. of Psychiatry, Northwestern University Medical School.
2. Kardiner, A., and Linton, R. (1945). *The psychological frontiers of society*. New York: Columbia University Press.
3. Levy-Bruhl, L. (1928). *The "soul" of the primitive*. London: Allen and Unwin.
4. Newton, N. (1973). "Psycho-social aspects of the mother/father/child unit." Paper presented at meetings of the Swedish Nutrition Foundation, Uppsala.
5. Simmons, L. W. (1945). *The role of the aged in primitive society*. New Haven: Yale University Press.
6. Whiting, J. W., and Child, I. (1953). *Child training and personality: A cross-cultural study*. New Haven: Yale University Press.

12 Psychological Development and Pathology in Later Adulthood

This final piece represents a kind of culmination: In it, the developmental processes that we have been tracking are mapped onto the clinical phenomena of later life, and in a final burst of grandiosity I turn the tragedy of a literary giant—Ernest Hemingway—into an illustration of my theory. But I am only the messenger and not the bad news. There is a developmental process afoot in the postparental years, and even unordinary individuals are not exempt from its powers. Much as in adolescence, the new psychic forces released by the postparental transition can be pathogenic for certain vulnerable individuals. While most older men and women accommodate to their new appetites and even come to enjoy them, a minority of predisposed individuals do respond to their own potentials for gain as though they were losses, as though they were toxic. Despite his genius—or perhaps because of it—Ernest Hemingway was clearly one of these vulnerable ones.

But this is not People *magazine, and Hemingway is not included for his star quality. I use him to show the ubiquity of the developmental forces and the kind of diagnostic clarity that can be gained if we take them into account. Hemingway's tragedy goes beyond his suicide; it includes his psychiatric treatment, which bordered on malpractice.*

Hemingway's psychiatrists were clearly overawed by their celebrity patient, and he conned them from the beginning. So far as I can determine, his doctors stuck to drug and electroshock therapy and took no account of the powerful and, in his case, toxic forces released by Hemingway's postparental transition. Raised by his mother to be her daughter and his sister's twin, "Papa" Hemingway always needed a convoy of honorary "daughters" to hold and externalize for him this dangerous but seductive identity. His later years were relatively barren of "daughters," and so he was left alone to face the horror—the bad presence within himself. My hunch is that he did not need eminent Mayo Clinic psychiatrists; a medical "daughter"—an adoring but no-nonsense female resident in psychiatry—might have become his counter-player, might have lifted his depression, and might have prevented his suicide.

But before treatment comes understanding, and understanding rests on hard-won knowledge. I hope that my work—despite its pretensions and prolixity—has added something to the necessary fund of clinical knowledge.

The Sources of Late Adult Development

In our generally sentimental psychology, almost any change in behavior or attitude that does not involve frank psychosis is likely to be eulogized, vaguely, as "growth," as the outcome of a developmental process. In this imprecise modern view, "self-actualization" is the goal of any developmental sequence, and progress in these terms can be tracked on the "life-satisfaction" scale. But a sterner doctrine recognizes that true development has, by definition, a genetic basis; as a product of human evolution, it will have goals and consequences that go beyond individual satisfaction.

In short, development entails more than superficial shifts in attitudes or interests; it involves tectonic changes at the deepest strata of personality, revisions that change basic appetites as well as the ways in which we think about appetites and their objects. Such powers, prepotent though not necessarily conscious, can bring about new psychological structures: new executive capacities of the personality on the one hand or late-onset pathology on the other, depending on the settings—both intrapersonal and interpersonal—in which these forces are expressed.

From this dynamic perspective, we will review the linkages between development and pathogenesis in later life, with particular reference to the inner changes that are set in train by the postparental transitions of late adulthood. A model of late-onset pathology will be presented, along with biographical material from a great artist who was a clear casualty of later life transitions, and a prime exemplar of the model presented here—the writer Ernest Hemingway.

The Stressful Passage Toward Androgyny

My studies of older men and women in various cultures have led to this conclusion: late development and late-onset pathology are often fueled by the same forces. They are driven by energies, released in men and women, in the course of the postparental transition toward androgyny. This tendency of older individuals to become androgynous, to acquire appetites, attitudes, and even behaviors characteristic of the opposite sex—for example, the *contrasexual* transition—was first clinically identified by Carl Jung (1933) and was first studied empirically in non-clinical and non-Western populations by this author (Gutmann 1964, 1987).

Regarding androgyny, it appears that (save for neurotic individuals) bisexuality does not become a significant problem, does not take on crisis proportions, until normal men and women stand down or demobilize from the "emergency" phase of parenthood. The gender distinctions, which emerge most sharply when young parents enter what I have termed the "chronic emergency of parenthood," get blurred as the last children are launched, usually in the parents' middle years. Thus, when maturing children demonstrate that they can assume major responsibility for supplying their own physical and emotional security, the stringent requirements of parenthood are relaxed. Fathers and mothers can then reclaim the strivings and capacities that conflicted with the parental assignment and therefore had been either repressed or lived out vicariously, through the spouse.

Postparental men appropriate qualities of nurturance and tenderness that were once relatively alien within themselves, and only tolerable in their dependents— their wives or children. By the same token, postparental women adopt some of the ascendant, competitive qualities that their husbands are relinquishing. As each postparental spouse becomes as the other used to be, the couple moves toward the normal androgyny of later life.

Given its linkage to the generic requirements of parenthood, the so-called contrasexual transition is, like paternity and maternity themselves, a seemingly universal event. As such, it usually precedes a developmental advance. Indeed, after some period of psychic dislocation, most men and women do accommodate to the changes in themselves and in their spouses. They gradually craft the energies liberated by the postparental reversal into new executive capacities of the personality. They do not at the same time lose their gender identities as men or women: instead, they revise their self-conception to include the new powers that accompany the midlife transformation. The result, for most men and women, is an expanded sense of self rather than a loss of self-continuity. The contrasexual upheavals of the postparental period have brought about new constancies, in the form of new structures, new ego capacities for knowing and enjoying: psychological development has taken place.

Androgyny and Pathology: A Model

Our clinical studies (conducted under the auspices of the Older Adult Program at Northwestern University Medical School) show that significant numbers of men and women do become casualties of this same contrasexual reversal. Like the minority of adolescents who become disturbed following puberty, these seniors become casualties of their "allergic" reaction to their own surgent energies. In the course of working with patients in their late fifties and early to middle sixties, we have identified some predisposing characteristics. These render certain patients particularly vulnerable to their own contrasexual potentials, to the point where they convert a normal, universal transition into a pathogenic stressor.

Despite his informal study methods, Jung accurately described the pathological as well as the healthy outcomes of later life androgyny. He noted that the resulting "sharpness of mind" of the wife as well as the unexpected "softness" of the husband could lead to marital troubles for the couple and to neurotic difficulties for individuals who experience such untoward changes in themselves.

When we investigate the developmental histories as well as the clinical pictures presented by older men (aged fifty-five to sixty-five), those hospitalized for the first time with acute psychiatric illness, we find ample evidence to support Jung's original insight. We will first consider the presenting symptoms, and then the deeper pathogenic issues—the personality characteristics and formative experiences that render these men particularly vulnerable to late-onset disorders.

Taken by themselves, we find that the presenting symptoms do not tell us very much about the causes of these late-blooming disorders. The symptom pictures range across the whole DSM-III and include severe alcoholism, diffuse anxiety states, significant and often suicidal depressions, and paranoid psychosis (in which the patient believes that other men are accusing him of being gay or effeminate). Nevertheless, although the symptoms may vary they are in all cases severe, and their strength sharply contrasts with the precipitating circumstances, which for the most part are relatively undramatic. In many patients it is difficult to find a clear precipitant, and those that can be identified do not involve some disastrous loss of the sort predicted by conventional, depletion-centered geropsychiatry. Rarely do we find major losses in health, work, social relationships, or finances severe enough to account for the flagrant symptoms.

Though the victims of late-onset disorders are generally located within a relatively narrow age band, they are widely dispersed across the entire social, economic, and ethnic spectrum. These disorders afflict cab drivers and executives with equal impartiality. Despite their wide-ranging symptoms and social backgrounds, these men strikingly resemble each other in the more personal sense. They tend to be intelligent; and despite some problems with success, they are driven to achieve and to feel shame when they fail. These ascendant qualities appear early in life. As boys, these patients sought out and excelled in the rougher, more dangerous sports. In their young manhood, most of these patients were in the armed services, usually as volunteers rather than draftees. They went to war as they had once gone to the playing fields: pressing to the forefront of the battle, they typically became paratroopers, submariners, or combat infantrymen.

The factors that truly characterize these late-onset patients are connected to their formative rather than their adult experience—particularly, their early experience of their mothers, in their families of orientation. All these men also report much the same kind of mother—destructively dominant. This picture of the witch-mother is not a product of clinical inference. These men state quite bluntly that the mother was a dragon, and that the father was her prey, her meat. In some cases, the mother freely disparaged the father; in other cases she attacked him physically as well as verbally; and in a few instances, the mother openly cuckolded the father by bringing her lovers (in some cases, her customers) into the marriage bed, without bothering to disguise her peccadilloes from the husband or even from her son, the future patient.

But where the father was openly debased, the son was often elevated by the mother, to the point where he was sometimes equated with the mother's idealized parent, his own maternal grandfather. In the patient's experience, the mother put the hopes and expectations that had been disappointed by the husband into her son; he became, in effect, the grandfather's true heir—the son that she had dreamt of having by her own father.

Despite this maternal favoritism, the sons usually split their feelings, reserving fear and grudging respect for the mother, and sympathy, even love, for the father. In a reversal of the usual triangular family drama, the son wanted to protect the father, to be *his* St. George against the dragon, but without knowing how to accomplish that feat. However, being Oedipal victors, these men also knew that they had conspired with the mother to bring about the father's defeat; and that they had drawn pleasure from it. Their Oedipal victory was tainted; deep down, these men knew that the father's stolen power would ultimately turn against them. Thus, they bore through life the guilty conviction that they were doomed to share the father's fate.

But despite their distrust of her, these men inherit strong ego ideals from their mothers; and they are driven as much by shame as by guilt. While they cannot whole-heartedly accept their own victory, neither can they accept the prospect of defeat. Thus, their identification with the defeated father is counter-acted by an equally strong need to deny their linkage to such a shameful, victimized man. Guilt pushed them toward the father; shame wrenched them away from him.

However, *both* guilt and shame combined to lever these patients away from the mother. Lacking a potent (Oedipal) father to interpose between themselves and the possessive, seductive mother, these men were always in danger of remaining in the shameful "Mama's Boy" position. By the same token, guilt made them fear (and covertly seek) the father's fate at the hands of a castrating woman; and the mother has already shown her fitness for the executioner's assignment. The combination of guilt, fear, and shame drove these patients to distance themselves from the mother in all major spheres: physical, social, and if possible, psychological. Both avoidances, of the father as well as of the mother, were managed through the same kind of bold action. By seeking danger in a "man's world," these men rejected with one inclusive stroke the Oedipal trophy, the title of "Mama's Boy," and the equation with a castrated father. They showed the courage that was unavailable to the father and the nonconformity that would shock, even alienate the mother.

Because they cannot achieve secure psychological separation from the mother, these men compensate by amplifying their physical and social differences. Physical separation is gained outside the domestic orbit, in the man's world of male allies, mentors, hunters, athletes, and soldiers. Social distance is gained *via* the kinds of rebellious and delinquent behavior that violate the mother's rigid rules and standards. In effect, they force the mother to push them away, and thus bring about the social distance that they cannot achieve on their own.

Furthermore, as these men gain sexual maturity, they finally achieve a tolerable degree of psychological distance from the mother, usually through their attachments to women who are completely unlike her: demure, soft-spoken, dependent, even adoring. Through such sexual liaisons these men distance themselves from the mother in at least two ways. The submissive wife is herself distant from the mother's character; and in addition, through this so obviously feminine creature, these inwardly divided men can distance themselves from their own feared passivity. The dependent mate becomes the outward metaphor of their own "feminine" qualities, now decisively excised from the self and relocated externally in the wife. In effect, these men conserve the mother's strength for themselves, but they eject her "softer," feminine aspect into the psychosocial ecology or *niche* conveniently provided by the wife. In the family of procreation the wife assumes the passive role that was played out by the father vis-à-vis the mother in the family of orientation. The wife then becomes the linchpin, the guarantor of the husband's delicate psychological balance. Through her he can demonstrate his unlikeness to the father as well as his own distance from internal and external mothers.

As long as these men can retain this life arrangement—the psychological niche provided by their wives—they do not become patients, and they do well in the crucial realms of work and even love. Intelligent, if somewhat driven (perhaps Type A) men, they advance in a variety of careers, and they tend to become responsible husbands and fathers. These seemingly strong protectors of weak people do well as long as they can rely on dependent women and children to remove from them the stigmatized figments of their androgynous nature: the woman, the "Mama's Boy," the castrated father.

But children grow up, take over the responsibility for their own security, and become less dependent. And, as we have seen, after the launching period, postparental development levers even a submissive wife out of the closet to assume a more independent, sometimes a more competitive and domineering stance toward her husband. This liberation happens precisely during the period when surgent postparental tides are pushing the husband in the opposite direction: toward the weakened position of passive mastery, toward the position that the father had held in the family of orientation. In short, the wife rejects a passive stance precisely at that time when the husband acutely needs an external repository for that same stance. In effect, the ascendant wife abandons the passive position and in so doing gives back to the husband the hidden aspect of his own sexuality: she forces him to confront his own masculine/feminine bi-modality. In addition, the midlife pacification of the man and the corresponding activation of the wife have a specific and catastrophic meaning for these men. In their eyes, the traumatic situation of childhood has been reconvened: The middle-aged husband is turning into his own weakened father, and the middle-aged wife is turning into a *simulacra* of the castrating mother. Thus, for many at-risk men, we find that their current domestic life with a strengthened wife is for them the *reprise* of a traumatic past and a threat to their established lifeways and defenses. Their protection against any repetition of their father's traumatic history is being weakened: the long-avoided (but also long-awaited) Sword of Damocles is about to fall.

The afflicted men react to their changed external circumstances and to their internal crisis in ways that reflect their life situation as well as their various temperaments. Wealthy men, who can afford multiple alimonies, may stave off neurotic symptoms for a while, by divorcing the aging wife and by replacing her with a young, fresh, and still adoring "father's daughter"; they find a new external vessel for the suspect feminine side of their own bi-modality.

Less affluent men, or men whose religion does not allow divorce, may try to change their wife's responses rather than get rid of her, particularly if the spouse herself feels guilty about her nascent aggression. The wife, whose guilt is reciprocal to her husband's shame, may damage herself in a last-ditch attempt to preserve her husband in the psychological sense. In order to keep the husband whole, the wife may develop a midlife depression or become a psychosomatic cripple. Thus, some women that we have studied will stay in the closet and take on for themselves what would otherwise be the husband's depression. Through this sacrifice, the wife performs a late act of nurturance toward the husband; she satisfies his unconscious requirement, of a needy, damaged wife. In those cases, the wife rather than the husband is the one likely to end up as a patient.

However, the men we see clinically are precisely those who cannot change external matters—in this case, the wife—in their favor. Lacking wives who will not surrender their own newfound ascendancy, these men have exchanged outer harmony for internal conflict. They sometimes express their inner, troubling sense of sexual bi-modality through psychosomatic disease. They bring some damaged organ—a metaphor both of the wife and of the damaged, needy aspect of themselves—for medical treatment. The organ, rather than themselves, takes on the status of patient. Others turn to alcoholism, a state that permits them to live out both sides, active and passive, of their own bi-modality; in the course of the same drinking bout, one can be first a hero and then a helpless baby. Others, in shamed revulsion against their own passive aspect, become depressed, sometimes to the point where they might launch a suicidal attack against this despised, alienated part of themselves. And some avoid unconscious awareness of their inner split by projecting that awareness in the form of paranoid sensitivity: Other men, they claim, are accusing them of being effete or homosexual.

Androgyny and Pathology: The Case of Ernest Hemingway

Before discussing Ernest Hemingway as a classic exemplar of the at-risk type of man, I make the usual (and decent) disclaimer. By tracing out the precursors and manifestations of Hemingway's late-onset disorders, I do not claim to account for all aspects of his complex personality, or of his literary genius. In this discussion, we limit ourselves to tracing the threads of his major preoccupation with the tragic dilemmas of manhood. We will look at the influences that underpin these concerns, as well as the ways that the aging Hemingway struggled to preserve the sense of uncorrupted masculinity. Hemingway's genius made him unique, but it did not save him from the common human fate, when in the later years his sense of manhood was fatally compromised.

As his final doom took shape, Ernest Hemingway ran the whole gamut of behaviors and symptoms—from serial divorce, to paranoia, to suicide. Hemingway had four wives, and he got rid of three of them at the point when they either lost the bloom of youth or stood up to him. Mary Hemingway, the last wife, may have preserved her marriage at the cost of chronic disability; she kept herself in a state of continuous damage through various self-inflicted accidents.

Symptomatically, Hemingway, always a heavy drinker, became increasingly alcoholic to the point where his writing and even his thinking were often affected. In addition, Hemingway suffered from hypochondriasis, as well as hypertension and other psychosomatic disorders; he finally lapsed into frank paranoia and the suicidal depression that ended his life at age sixty-one.

Hemingway's later writing (as well as his later behavior) reflected the themes that we have been tracking in the population of older male patients. Thus, Hemingway's novel *The Garden of Eden* (1986), a work that he began at age forty-five and worked on until his final years, is a story of a wife who becomes explicitly masculine and who attempts to destroy her husband's manhood.

Hemingway is also of particular interest because, like the majority of men in the late-onset population, his psychopathology was not prompted by objectively catastrophic circumstances. As he sank toward his final psychotic depression, Hemingway was wealthy, revered, married to an attractive and considerate wife, and not lethally ill in the physical sense. In order to understand his illness (and in order to locate the true precipitants), we have to look at the predisposing character and the roots of that character in Hemingway's early experience.

Hemingway's developmental history aptly fits our model. Grace Hemingway was a classic example of the pathogenic mother that we have already identified in the accounts of less gifted men. Trained as an operatic singer, she never accepted her domestic fate. Her children were raised by nannies; Hemingway's father, although a doctor, was responsible for the cooking; and Grace made it quite clear that she had given up a great artistic career for a man who was not worthy of her sacrifice. Apparently she was disappointed in Dr. Hemingway's ability to provide, and she may have disparaged his sexual abilities as well. As a teenager, Hemingway saw his father angrily evict from their home a woman suspected of being Grace Hemingway's lesbian lover. In these domestic wars, Hemingway clearly sided with his father.

Though disparaged within the home where he was deferential toward his imperious wife, Hemingway's father came into his own in the outdoors. As a doctor he commanded the respect of neighbors (including Michigan Indians) whom he treated; and he was an accomplished hunter and fisherman who taught those skills to Ernest. The young Hemingway seemed to have learned from his father that manhood was always at risk within the domestic world of women, but that it could be preserved and even enhanced outside the home in tests of courage, in conflict with physical nature and with other men. In the world of combat or raw nature, men could be defeated and even killed; but as long as they lived by the tragic code, their manhood was never really at risk. But the trophies of war or of the hunt would not survive the transition into the home. Hemingway angrily recalled how his mother, while moving the household, deliberately burned Dr. Hemingway's prized collection of nature specimens.

His mother gave Ernest compelling reasons to sympathize with his father; they were both targets of the mother's castrating drives. Thus, while Grace regarded Ernest (the first son) as a replacement for her own idealized father and dubbed him her "precious boy," she also dressed him as a girl for the first three years of his life. Grace claimed that, of her six children, Ernest was most like her, and this sense of twinship seemingly overrode the gender differences between mother and son. Thus, as reported by Kenneth Lynn (1987), Grace dressed Ernest, longer than was customary for that era, in pink gingham gowns with white Battenberg lace hoods, fluffy, frilly dresses, black patent-leather shoes, high stockings, and picture hats with flowers on them. He was also coifed in the manner of a girl-child of that time, with long, carefully bobbed hair. Grace Hemingway titled a picture of Ernest in this get-up (taken before his second birthday) as "A Summer Girl." Finally, Grace enacted her sense of oneness with her son through the oldest child, her daughter: Marcelline and Ernest were treated like twins of the same sex—sometimes as two boys, sometimes as two girls, but always paired. (Like Ernest and their mutual father, Marcelline eventually committed suicide.)

However, Ernest was temperamentally a dynamo, and he tugged strongly against the golden cord. At age three, he announced, "I ain't afraid of nothing!" and in his first-grade school compositions he already displays his lifelong interest in the outdoors, in competitive sports, and in hunting. Clearly, he was gaining some precocious distance from the mother by identifying with the "sportsman" aspect of the father—the aspect that evaded Grace Hemingway's control and disparagement.

As Ernest grew up, he compensated for the lack of psychological distance by putting maximum *physical* distance, as soon as he could, between himself and his mother. He went to war in his father's way, as a medic, enlisting in the ambulance corps of the Italian army, and suffered grave leg wounds. Hospitalized, Ernest fell in love with his nurse, an older woman named Agnes Von Kurowski. This choice was par for the course: until his later years most of Hemingway's lovers and wives were older than himself. Returning home from the war (and jilted by Agnes), Ernest again lost the necessary physical distance from his mother. But he quickly interposed social distance in its place, and became towards her a sullen, provocative, and disappointing adolescent.

After his job as a reporter, Hemingway made an early marriage to his first wife, Hadley (again, an older woman) and moved with her to Paris. There he began his full-time career as an author and began to turn out the bold, realistic, and hard-edged writing that would be his signature. Predictably, his writing offended—as it was meant to—both his parents, but particularly his mother. Interestingly, Ernest ignored the father's criticism of his raunchy prose but expressed great bitterness about his mother's critique, and accused her of being disloyal to him. The social distance between mother and son was now entrenched. Ernest never forgave his mother, avoided her company, and in 1928 blamed her for his father's suicide by gunshot. In his later years, Ernest referred to his mother only as "that bitch," and claimed that she would be more dangerous dead than most women would be alive. General "Buck" Lanham, his wartime buddy, observed that Hemingway hated his mother more than any man he ever knew. Ernest did not attend her funeral.

During the Paris years Hemingway had established physical, social, and—*via* his wife, Hadley—psychological distance from his mother. But when Hadley herself became a mother, and became matronly in bearing, Hemingway enacted the typical pattern: He left Hadley for a new love, the adoring, obsequious (and again older) Pauline. Ernest had once more relied on a passive and dependent woman to gain psychological distance from the maternal person. But Pauline in her turn became a mother; and Hemingway subsequently kept his distance from *her* through frequent fishing trips on the *Pilar,* as well as some intense and protracted love affairs. One lover was Martha Gellhorn, a correspondent whom Ernest met and courted during the Spanish Civil War. He subsequently divorced Pauline and married Martha in 1939.

For the first time, Ernest had taken a wife who was younger than himself. Although she was young, Martha was also spirited; unlike his more adoring and biddable wives Hadley and Pauline, Martha was, like Hemingway, an accomplished writer and an adventurous reporter. True, during the Spanish war, Martha had been for a brief honeymoon period the ideal Hemingway woman. Ernest knew Spain, and he knew war; and Martha was content to be the admiring young companion of "Papa" Hemingway.

But after the honeymoon, in Cuba, Martha quickly tired of the housekeeper and sex-kitten role that Ernest assigned her, and she became disenchanted with Hemingway's self-indulgent and alcoholic lifeways. Against Hemingway's bitter opposition, she took off to pursue her trade in the European theater of war. It has been said that Martha Gellhorn was the first woman, besides his mother, to stand up to Ernest, and he reacted predictably. Becoming sullen and depressed, he played, aboard the *Pilar,* at submarine- and spy-chasing around the coasts of Cuba. Back from a real war front, Martha saw through these self-dramatizing games and accused Hemingway of sitting out the war against fascism, while good men died to defend his freedom and comforts.

Finally shamed into action, Ernest became a war correspondent for *Colliers,* the same magazine that employed his wife. Hemingway was now openly competitive with Martha. He mocked her assignments and writing and never forgave her for going ashore on D-Day while he stayed offshore on a landing craft. Again, Hemingway handled the deterioration of his third marriage in typical fashion. In wartime London, while still married to Martha, he started an affair with Mary Walsh, the woman who would become his fourth wife.

Mary was in Ernest's comfortable mode: obedient, self-effacing, appreciative, and rather masochistic. Even though he had found a replacement for Martha, there is solid evidence that Hemingway never really recovered from his first rejection— and a scornful one at that—by a wife. Ernest's shame was compounded by his continuing attachment. Although he ridiculed Martha publicly, he continued to carry a torch for her. Even after his marriage to Mary, Ernest kept Martha's portrait in his living room, and she appears in barely disguised form as the hero's lost love in a post-humously published book, *Islands in the Stream* (1970).

In losing Martha, Hemingway lost more than a desirable woman; by her rejection he appears to have lost an essential fulcrum of his psyche. Bear in mind that this insult from an independent woman came when Ernest was forty-five years old. He was at the stage when most men, having launched their children, begin to feel stirrings from the occulted, passive side of their nature. This is the age when men with Ernest's background need a dependent wife to hold and externalize for them the dangerous internal burden. In Hemingway's case, the woman who should have been the adoring one, the repository of his softer side, had refused that assignment. She had seen through his macho posturing, she had disparaged his manhood, and, instead of holding his *anima* in escrow for him, she had returned it to him.

Hemingway's separation from his dangerous but seductive feminine identifications depended on a strong union with a needful woman; by splitting the couple, Martha had in effect handed back to Ernest the dangerous side of his nature. Once separated from Martha, Ernest was no longer separated from his feminine side, and he may have come to the shocked recognition that these dangerous qualities were part of himself and not of the woman "out there." Martha had left Papa alone with his own bad presences.

The foregoing comments on Hemingway's inner life are of course musings and speculations. But Hemingway did in fact begin to write *The Garden of Eden,* his long (and until recently unpublished) novel on the dangers and temptations of explicit androgyny, about a month after the divorce with Martha became final. In this novel Hemingway tries to make art out of the occult concerns of men in his life stage, particularly those with his early background and psychic constitution. *The Garden of Eden* is the story of a brief and strange marriage between two beautiful young people, Catherine and David. Their union starts as an idyllic honeymoon in southern France but ends disastrously, owing to Catherine's explicit desire to be a man and to turn David into her androgynous twin. At first a typical Hemingway woman, Catherine starts out as an adoring, passionate lover, but she soon reveals her secret wish to be manly in all possible ways: to wear her hair short, to wear men's clothes, and to take the male role in sex. Additionally, Catherine requires that David take up complementary roles: he should play sexual games in which the roles in intercourse are reversed. In addition, she requires that David cut and dye his hair in her fashion, that he acquire her deep shade of tan, and that he wear matching clothes. Moving more drastically toward masculine sexuality, Catherine brings in a very attractive young woman, Marita, to be her own lesbian lover.

Marita is the passive, hyper-feminine member of the lesbian pair, and David—like Hemingway, a war veteran and a writer—in effect saves himself through her, by seducing and converting the complaisant lesbian to passionate heterosexuality.

But before she leaves the sexually reconstituted couple, the now psychotic Catherine strikes a final blow against David's manhood. She burns her husband's treasured manuscript, the record of his boyhood adventures on safari with his father.

This last vignette tells us who Catherine really is: a condensation of Grace and Marcelline Hemingway, the two imperious older women of Ernest's childhood. Thus the fictional Catherine acts toward David as the mother had acted toward both Ernest and his father, and as the sister had acted toward her little brother. She dresses a man like a woman, she coifs his hair like a woman, she twins him with a woman, and she burns the manuscript about the male hunt, the life away from women. Catherine burns David's book about the hunt in the same manner that his mother burned the father's relics from the hunt. The witch-mother and the witch-sister returned at that point in the life cycle when most men, writers or illiterates, begin to face those demons within themselves. In our research, we find equivalent "Catherine" fantasies making their first appearance in projective test protocols of middle-aged men.

In Hemingway's case, the bad dreams did not stay within the unconscious; after Martha left him, the dream of the castrating mother became the stuff of his fiction, that hidden part of his *oeuvre*, which remained for a long time unpublished. In that occulted body of his work, Hemingway used his genius to confront the ogre, to explore and come to terms with his own emerging sexual bi-modality. Although this effort at self-therapy through art may have delayed his breakdown, it did not finally prevent it. The myth of castrated androgyny was not finally containable within the fictional world. In the remaining fifteen years of his life, the fantasy of destruction by a fierce woman was taken over and enacted by Hemingway himself, as he moved into alcoholism, "accidental" injuries, paranoia, depression, and the shotgun blast to the head, which mimicked his father's suicide and terminated his own life. Hemingway was his own prey in his own last hunt.

In summary, Hemingway used *Eden* to explore and master the sexual duality that is uncovered as part of development in later life. But his courageous attempt at self-discovery failed; Hemingway had finally to kill himself in order to kill off the twin-mother that he found growing within him. In the minds of some men, death restores the mother to them; but in Ernest's troubled mind, death was the final escape, the only trustworthy separation from the "feminine," from the "Mother" emerging within "Papa" Hemingway.

References

Gutmann, D. L. (1964). An exploration of ego configurations in middle and later life. In B. Neugarten (Ed.), *Personality and later life* (pp. 114–148). New York: Atherton.

Gutmann, D. L. (1987). *Reclaimed powers: Towards a new psychology of men and women in later life*. New York: Basic Books.

Jung, C. G. (1933). *Modern man in search of a soul*. New York: Harcourt, Brace and World.

Lynn, K. (1987). *Hemingway*. New York: Simon & Schuster.

About the Book and Author

Chronicling the evolution of David Gutmann's cross-cultural, empirical studies on which his developmental theories of aging are based, this volume reveals how descriptions of the developmental sequences (as they show themselves in older men and women) lead to identification of the psychological forces that drive these processes across the years.

This book of new and previously published work first reports on the research that buttressed the more hopeful view of aging as a period of growth and then sets forth the broad, unifying ideas that came out of the empirical work. These concepts include the theory of the "Parental Imperative"—the engine of human development in early and later adulthood; observations on the "gentling" of the older man and the increased assertiveness of the older woman; essays about the unique qualities of aging leaders and the special role of the aged as representatives of the community to its gods; and ideas about the evolutionary basis of the third age—aging as a human adaptation, a legitimate life stage, rather than the grim prelude to death.

The last group of selections focuses on the clinical perspective, applying developmental insights to the psychological disorders of later life, ultimately leading to a more hopeful view of these conditions as well as more effective approaches to their treatment. Each section contains original commentary placing the material in the context of current research.

This text is for gerontologists, for all students of human development, and for all thoughtful readers who are concerned with the great themes of the human life-cycle—including their own.

David Gutmann is the director of the Older Adult Program, Division of Psychology, Department of Psychiatry and Behavioral Sciences at Northwestern University Medical School and professor in the School of Education at Northwestern University. He is the author of *Reclaimed Powers: Men and Women in Later Life*.

Index

Active coping, 52–53(n8), 61

Active Mastery

among American men, 1, 2, 99

and Desert Scene TAT card, 21, 22, 23, 25

dreams, 41

among Druze, 69, 74, 97–98, 128–129

as a factor of age, 2

features of, 4–5

and Heterosexual Conflict TAT card, 17, 18, 20

among Mayan, 128, 129

and memory, 26

among Navajo men, 26, 33(n6), 33–34(n9), 34(n10), 128–129

and Rope Climber TAT card, 12, 13–14

among survivors, 128–129

and young men, 1, 2, 26, 69, 74, 97, 98, 113

See also Active Mastery stories, features of; Active Mastery subtypes

Active Mastery stories, features of, 11

Active Mastery subtypes

coping, 21

productive-autonomous, 5, 12, 17

Promethean-competitive, 5, 12, 17

realism, 22

Aggression

and Active Mastery, 5, 6

concern with among American men, 20

and the extended family, 117(n1)

interpretation of, 91

men as exporters of, 89, 92, 117 (n1)

and passive mastery, 6

phasing out of, 121–122

rejection of among youth, 131

in relation to the superego, 161

See also Aggression in women

Aggression in women

channeling of, 87–88, 89, 92, 117(n1), 124

reclaiming of, 78, 94, 113, 179

Aging, normal psychology of, 121–124

Alcohol use

among Druze, 50

and Ernest Hemingway, 230, 235

among homosexuals, 159

during later life, 230

among Maya Indians, 170(n13)

among Navajo men, 42–43, 49–50

and orality, 37, 50

passivity and disease, 49–50

and power, 159

as substitute father, 220

Alienation

described, 141

role of the superego in, 155, 158, 161

and selfhood, 155, 162

among youths, 142, 165–166

Alinsky, Saul, 139 (n9)

Allah 52(n5), 64, 74, 76, 203, 206

Allocentric self

definition of, 167–168(n2)

development of, 152–155

and the superego, 155–158, 161

Ambivalence, 191–192

Androgyny

as a condition of late adult development, x, xii, xiii, 74, 78, 79, 94, 95, 102, 112–113, 124, 148, 178, 179

among counter-culture youth, xii, 133–134

among elder Druze, 74, 113

and Ernest Hemingway, 230–235

among lower primates, 178

at mid-life, 124

and pathology, 224–230

and supernatural power, 181

Animism

death of, 152, 153–154

in traditional societies, 142, 144–145, 149

See also Autocentric mind

Anthropology, 186

and oral eroticism, 18
Self
  development of, 152–155, 158
  sense of, 142, 154, 160, 192–193, 225
  See also Allocentric self; Autocentric
    mind; Self-continuity
Self-continuity, 192, 198, 199
Sensuality, 123, 126, 132–133
Separation
  from parental figures, 216, 217, 218,
    219–221, 229
Sexual development, 103
Sexuality, 33(nn 7, 8)
Shamanism, 147–148, 158
Simmons, L.W. 38, 51–52(n4), 76, 194,
  221
Social bonding, 192
Socialization, 86
Social sciences
  on collectivism, 110
  methodology, 56
  as "other directed," 109–110
Social status, 129, 197–199
Society
  hunter and gatherer, 175
  marginal-subsistence, 85–86
  transition from folk to urban, 154
Society, Preliterate Agriculturalist. *See* Traditional Communities; Traditional Society
Somaticism, 217
Sorcerer, 151, 157, 158, 160, 165–166,
  169(n9), 169(n10)
Splitting, 191–192
Students, 142. *See also* Counter-culture
  youth
Suffering, 147–148
Suicide, 230
Superego
  and aggression, 161
  and alcoholics, 159
  death of, 166, 167
  old men function as, 182, 183
  as power bringer, 155–158
  and psychopathology, 158–161
  reconciliation with, 170(n12)
  role of, 155–158

and self-esteem, 158
Survivors, 173–174
  and active coping, 52–53(n8)
  and active mastery, 128–130
  characteristics of, 44, 128–130
  Druze, 52–53(n8)
  and magical mastery, 130
  Navajo, 34(n11), 44, 138(n3)
  social prestige of, 129
Syntonic Orality Scores, 39, 41, 42
  and chi-square, 43
  and health status, 44–45, 46–47

Taboo
  homosexuality, 159
  incest, 177–178, 179, 180, 182
  parricide, 176–177
  violation of, 151
Tabu power, 145, 149, 150, 151, 191, 195,
  196, 201, 203, 221
Tahitians, 81
Thematic Apperception Test (TAT), 4, 127
  accuracy of, 3
  administration of, 2
  and American women, 100
  analysis, 11, 25
  and disengagement theory, 76
  and orality, 29–30, 37, 39, 41–42
  parenting stage and ego development,
    91, 97, 98, 99, 100
  and passivity, 44, 72, 74, 76
  See also Desert Scene TAT card, Fam-
    ily/Farm TAT card, Heterosexual
    Conflict TAT card, Rope Climber
    TAT card, Thematic Apperception
    Test cards
Thematic Apperception Test cards, 138(n2)
  administration of, 2, 45
  description of, 10
  difficulty with, 10
  and other measures, 7
  See also Desert Scene TAT card; Family/
    Farm TAT card, Heterosexual Conflict
    TAT card, Rope Climber TAT card
Totem and Taboo, 176
Totemic power, 75, 146, 165, 173, 176,
  180, 181, 201, 218, 219